Routledge Revivals

Latin Historians

First published in 1966, *Latin Historians* gives an account of some of the most important Latin historians. There are chapters on Caesar, Sallust, Livy and Ammianus Marcellinus, together with an account of earlier historians, and on Polybius, the Greek who had much influence on the Roman World. Bede, the earliest of the great Christian historians in England, is also discussed. This book will be of interest to students of history, literature and classical studies.

Latin Historians

Edited by T. A. Dorey

Routledge
Taylor & Francis Group

First published in 1966
By Routledge & Kegan Paul Ltd.

This edition first published in 2023 by Routledge
4 Park Square, Milton Park, Abingdon, Oxon, OX14 4RN
and by Routledge
605 Third Avenue, New York, NY 10017

Routledge is an imprint of the Taylor & Francis Group, an informa business

Publisher's Note
The publisher has gone to great lengths to ensure the quality of this reprint but points out that some imperfections in the original copies may be apparent.

Disclaimer
The publisher has made every effort to trace copyright holders and welcomes correspondence from those they have been unable to contact.

A Library of Congress record exists under LCCN: 67089251

ISBN: 978-1-032-60820-4 (hbk)
ISBN: 978-1-003-46066-4 (ebk)
ISBN: 978-1-032-60831-0 (pbk)

Book DOI 10.4324/9781003460664

LATIN HISTORIANS

Chapters by

E. A. Thompson F. W. Walbank
T. A. Dorey P. G. Walsh
J. Campbell G. M. Paul
E. Badian

Edited by
T. A. DOREY

ROUTLEDGE & KEGAN PAUL
London

First published 1966
by Routledge *&* *Kegan Paul Ltd*
Broadway House, 68-74 *Carter Lane*
*London, E.C.*4
Reprinted 1968

Printed in Great Britain
by T. & A. Constable Ltd
Hopetoun Street, Edinburgh

SBN 7100 1293 4

To

A. H. McDONALD

a great scholar and historian

Contents

Introduction

IT has been said that the most impelling motive for a writer is a burning desire to know himself. This is often true of a writer of history, with the qualification that a historian will desire to know himself not as an individual in isolation but in relation to the society of which he is a member. His insight will be social rather than psychological. Polybius, for example, saw himself involved, though in some respects unwillingly, in a city-state that grew into a world power. Livy saw himself as part of this same state when it had achieved its growth and begun to fall away; but emotionally he identified himself with Rome's greatness rather than with her decline. Sallust looked upon Roman society in rapid decay, to which he himself had made some small contribution. Tacitus gazed back in masochistic gloom along the trough of corruption and crime into which Rome had fallen. Caesar saw himself as the general of a nation arrayed for war; he could not see how to lead that nation when organized for peace. Bede, writing in another age, saw his country as part of a society directed by God.

There were two other motives that affected the classical historians. First, an objective one, the desire to provide a record for posterity, a feeling that a duty existed and that the writer had qualifications—opportunity for research and capacity for self-expression—that were necessary for carrying out the task. Livy was a supreme example of the working of this motive, though all historians must have been influenced by it to a greater or lesser degree. The second motive was more subjective. The writing of history was regarded at Rome as a suitable adjunct to an active career in public life. It seems in many cases, Roman and Greek, to have been adopted as a suitable 'second-best' to a frustrated public career. Thucydides was an Athenian general and Polybius had been Hipparch of the Achaean League when they were exiled. Both belonged to prominent political families and could have advanced to greater heights. But in both cases exile and the blasting of a political career gave time, opportunity, and an incentive for their great historical works. Sallust turned to history to win the 'gloria' in the world of literature which had been snatched from his grasp in the world of politics. Tacitus, it is possible, may have found that political success brought little satisfaction under a political system that he despised, and turned away from politics as earlier he seems to have turned away from oratory.[1]

Latin and Greek historians had little influence on historiography until after the Renaissance, and even then it was comparatively slight, though they were widely read and had great influence on the actions and ideas of men engaged in public life. The first decade of Livy had a very great effect on 'The Prince' of Machiavelli, but it was not until the nineteenth century that Livy's influence was felt to any wide extent, notably on Taine and on Macaulay, who carried on the Livian tradition of representing historical characters as 'good' and 'bad' according to their political allegiances.

On the historians of the Middle Ages the classical Latin historians had little effect. There are echoes of Sallust in William of Poitiers, and in the Prologue of Henry of Huntingdon's *Historia Anglorum* (quorum mors et vita sempiterno dotanda est silentio. Cf. Sallust, *Catiline* II, 8: eorum ego vitam mortemque iuxta aestumo, quoniam de utraque siletur), while Livy was known, probably indirectly, to William of Malmesbury, but the most familiar histories were those of the late imperial writers and the epitomators, men like Aurelius Victor, Justinus, and Eutropius. A writer of considerable influence was Suetonius, particularly on Einhard's *Life of Charlemagne*. It was the poets, however, that were read and quoted, Virgil, from whom William of Poitiers took his theme of a hero '*pietate insignis et armis*', Horace, Lucan, Juvenal, the *Thebaid* of Statius, Persius, Ovid, and the *Latin Iliad*.

The main purpose expressed by the medieval historians was the preservation of a record of notable events for the benefit of posterity. Emphasis is placed on the transmission of edifying examples of human conduct. Eadmer, in the Preface to his *Historia Novorum*, says: 'videor mihi videre magnum quid posteris praestitisse, qui suis gesta temporibus, futurorum utilitati studentes, litterarum memoriae tradidere'—'I feel sure that a great service is done to posterity by those who, in their eagerness to serve the future, have put on record the events of their own times'. William of Newburgh says in the Proemium to his *Historia*

Rerum Anglicarum: 'nostris autem temporibus tanta et tam memorabilia contigerunt ut modernorum negligentia culpanda merito censeatur, si litterarum monumentis ad memoriam sempiternam mandata non fuerint—'such great and notable deeds have happened in our times that there would be good cause for censuring the men of today for neglect if those deeds were not comitted to writing, and so put on record for ever', while in his letter of dedication he makes reference to 'studium rerum memorabilium ad notitiam cautelamque posterorum conscribendarum'—'the desire to record notable events for the enlightenment and edification of future generations'. So, too, William of Malmesbury, in the Preface to the *Historia Novella*: 'quid porro iucundius quam fortium facta virorum monimentis tradere litterarum, quorum exemplo ceteri exuant ignaviam, et ad defendendam armentur patriam?'—'What is more pleasant than to put on record the deeds of brave men, as an example to others to shake off sloth and take up arms in the defence of their country?' It was, in fact, the moral lesson provided by history that was usually stressed. Matthew Paris, in the Preface to his *Historia Anglorum*, talks about the need to preserve a record of events—'memoria'—'ut perversorum devitentur gressus, bonorum quorum gesta describimus vestigia sequamur—'that we may shun the footsteps of the wicked and follow in the tracks of the good, whose deeds we describe', while Gervase of Canterbury says that history provides 'gloriosa et imitanda exempla', and that in a historical account 'bene vivendi repperiuntur exampla'—'examples of virtuous living are found'. Henry of Huntingdon, also, sees in history an easy means of encountering examples of human vices and virtues, though it is interesting to note that the first historical work to which Henry refers is that of Homer—'Homerica historia'.

Some writers, however, realized that there were other things to be aimed at by the historian than the provision of moral teaching. William of Malmesbury had a high standard of veracity. He warned his readers in the Preface to *Gesta Regum*: 'me nihil de retroactis praeter cohaerentiam annorum pro vero pacisci; fides dictorum penes auctores erit; quicquid vero de recentioribus aetatibus apposui, vel ipse vidi vel a viris fide dignis audivi'—'about the distant past I can vouch for nothing except a consistent chronology; my sources must be their own guarantors; but whatever I have set down concerning more recent times, I have either been an eye-witness or heard of it from a reliable informant' (cf. also *Historia Novella*, sec. 514). William showed considerable discrimination in the evaluation of his sources, as did William of Newburgh, who rejected Geoffrey of Monmouth in favour of Bede and Gildas.

In all this there are little indications of classical influence, except for the insistence on the importance of preserving 'memoria' (and the value of 'exempla'), which may go back to Cicero. There does, however, occur one clear trace of Ciceronian influence. Gervase of Canterbury, writing at the end of the twelfth century, has an interesting passage in the Prologue to the main part of his Chronicle (Rolls, p. 87):

> Historici autem et cronici secundum aliquid una est intentio et materia, sed diversus tractandi modus est et forma varia. Utriusque una est intentio, quia uterque veritati intendit. Forma tractandi varia, quia historicus diffuse et eleganter incedit, cronicus vero simpliciter graditur et breviter. 'Proicit' historicus 'ampullas et sesquipedalia verba'; cronicus vero 'silvestrem musam tenui meditatur avena'. Sedet historicus 'inter magniloquos et grandia verba serentes', at cronicus sub pauperis Amiclae pausat tugurio ne sit pugna pro paupere tecto. Proprium est historici veritati intendere, audientes vel legentes dulci sermone et eleganti demulcere, actus, mores vitamque ipsius quam describit veraciter edocere, nihilque comprehendere nisi quod historiae de ratione videtur competere. Cronicus autem annos Incarnationis Domini annorumque menses computat et kalendas, actus etiam regum et principum quae in ipsis eveniunt breviter edocet, eventus etiam, portenta vel miracula commemorat.

This passage has considerable similarities, both in ideas and, to some extent, in language, with *De Oratore* II, 51-64, where Cicero draws a distinction between the early annalists and the later rhetorical historians, the *narratores* and the *exornatores rerum*, in a manner that has a basic resemblance to Gervase's distinction between chroniclers and historians. In this passage Cicero also stresses the fundamental importance of veracity in all types of historical composition, as does Gervase, and certain phrases in this passage—*actus*, *postea eventus*, and *de cuiusque vita atque natura*—are also echoed. The *De Oratore* was widely read in the Middle Ages: in particular, John of Salisbury possessed a copy, and the '*Polycraticus*', which was written when John was at Canterbury, shortly before Gervase started his *Chronicle*, was partly influenced by it.[2] It is likely that the *De Oratore* had a considerable effect on medieval historiography.

This volume contains chapters on Early Historians, Polybius, Caesar, Sallust, Livy, Ammianus Marcellinus, and Bede. A later volume will be devoted to Tacitus, and it is hoped subsequently to attempt a more exhaustive treatment of the historians of the Middle Ages.

NOTES

[1] R. Syme, *Tacitus* (Oxford, 1958), p. 111. 'The *Dialogus* advertises and justifies a proud renunciation of oratory.'

[2] Cf. M. L. Clarke in *Cicero* (Routledge and Kegan Paul, 1964), p. 88. C. C. J. Webb, *Notes on books bequeathed by John of Salisbury*, Medieval and Renaissance Studies I, 1941, p. 128 f.

I

*The Early Historians**

E. BADIAN

IN Rome, as in Greece, written history is a late development. Some of the raw materials had probably been there for centuries: treaties and (probably) valid laws were carefully preserved; noble families prided themselves on their ancestors and kept some record of their achievements, and the *pontifices* appear to have recorded events of religious importance. Polybius, in the middle of the second century B.C., saw a treaty that claimed to be 350 years old and was (whatever its true date) written in archaic and difficult Latin; and Cicero, in his youth, still saw what claimed to be the venerable treaty of Spurius Cassius with the Latins—again, at least without patent absurdity.[1] That family records, in a state in which high office conferred nobility, went back a long way is self-evident. In the second century they were kept with great care, and the first of the Scipionic epitaphs show that even public record extended further back; nor was there later any really violent disagreement over the outline of the history of the early Republic, such as might have been expected if the facts alleged had been arbitrary invention.[2] Cicero was to complain that funeral eulogies had falsified history[3]; but probably none were preserved in writing until the third century B.C. and few as early as that; and the harm they did was perhaps less serious than that done by literary historians. As for the pontifical *annales*, Cato was to scoff at their interest in famine and eclipses (fr. 77). But at least they recorded the names of consuls and mentioned triumphs, and perhaps they gave much more extensive (though often trivial) information,[4] connecting omens with the events they portended and offerings with the occasion for gratitude; and even eclipses later turned out to be useful for establishing a chronology.[5] In fact, however, the compilation of the pontifical annals in the form in which they were later published can only have begun after the Gallic fire and perhaps even later[6]: the early part of these records should be regarded as an attempt at historical investigation (we do not know by whom) rather than as documentary evidence available to historians, and there may have been some rewriting in the second century (see, e.g., Gellius iv.5: a Hesiodic verse translated in Book XI).

In the third century the *Annales Maximi* (as they were later called, after the *Pontifex Maximus* in charge of them)[7] provided a current record of sorts; yet they inspired no literary historian for generations. The war with Pyrrhus and the First Punic War firmly established contacts between Rome and the Hellenistic world and provided what might seem suitable subject-matter for history. Yet no one accepted the challenge until the man and the occasion came together.

I. GRAECI ANNALES

Q. Fabius Pictor[8] came of rather an unusual family. The Fabii were of the highest Patrician nobility, among the leaders of the state in peace and war as far back as anyone could remember. Yet in 304 B.C. a Fabius took it into his head to paint the walls of a newly dedicated temple; and if this could be forgiven as an act of piety, what could not was the fact that he actually took such pride in this unaristocratic achievement that he signed the work with his name.[9] It was thus that he received his *cognomen*, at first no doubt derogatory; and he is not known to have held office. This was the man from whom the first Roman historian was descended. It is not fanciful to suppose that he owed his urge to artistic self-expression to his ancestor. However, our Q. Fabius Pictor served his country in war, politics and religion, as was expected of him, though he did not reach any great distinction, except possibly in the religious sphere. He must have been known for an interest in Hellenic culture: after the disaster of Cannae (216 B.C.) he was chosen to consult the Delphic oracle about the future.

His chosen task of writing a Roman history in Greek was not only unprecedented: it was ambitious, not to say presumptuous, as a literary attempt. Not only was Greek historiography a highly developed literary form, which no foreigner might lightly attempt; but Greek historians had actually written about Rome—best-known of them Timaeus of Tauromenium, with whose work Fabius was, of course, familiar.[10] We have no idea of Fabius' stylistic achievement. But his history, although Cicero calls it *Graeci annales*,[11] was by its very nature far removed from the pontifical annals. He dealt at length with the earliest period (which Greek antiquarians had studied), more briefly with what followed, expanding his scale as he approached his own time, until the work became a detailed account with (at the latest) the First Punic War. The very scheme helps to show that Fabius was consciously putting himself in the tradition of Greek historical writing.[12] He must have given the consuls of each year, at least in the detailed history; but he certainly used Olympiad dating, in the new Greek manner of establishing an internationally acceptable chronology (fr. 6). Polybius, who used him as one of his main sources in his account of the First Punic War, may well have found the difficult synchronization already accomplished. The fragments, few as they are, also show him in the tradition of Hellenistic historiography: the moralizing anecdote; the enlivening autobiographical touch; the description of pageants; the concern with morality and its historical influence (frr. 15, 27; 24; 16; 20, 25, 27)—these, no doubt, were not uncongenial to the Roman noble and priest; but they are far removed from primitive chronicle such as the priestly annals.

It is more difficult to form a clear idea of Fabius' purpose, especially as we do not know precisely when he wrote: his aim might well be very different before 202 and after.[13] His choice of Greek as a medium has suggested to many that he wrote for a Greek audience, trying to explain Roman history and institutions to it rather as Polybius was to do.[14] Though up to a point this must be correct, it should not be thought the whole explanation. We must not forget that the Latin language was not yet fitted for literary prose (even literary poetry had only just begun), and there was no tradition that could even be adapted for the purpose.[15] On the other hand, Fabius' work fits into a series of 'barbarian' (including Egyptian and Babylonian) historical works written in Greek;[16] and there is no doubt that Fabius' peers, educated Roman senators, will have been able to read him. It is chiefly for them that he intended such family lore as the proud tale (fr. 18) of an act of high-spirited insubordination by an early Fabius. Again, it has been pointed out that one attested Fabian interpretation—the assignment of responsibility for the outbreak of the Hannibalic War to the Barcids rather than to the Carthaginian state—might best be understood as addressed to Carthage![17] Fabius wrote for the educated world—Greek, Roman and barbarian.

But more can be said, without positive rashness. When could this interpretation of the cause of the War have been written, for both Romans and Carthaginians, if it was to have any point? Soon after 218 B.C., when a Fabius had just replied to the intransigence of the Punic Senate by shaking out war from the folds of his toga? Surely not. Possibly towards the end of the War, when the vanquished might be persuaded to turn against their unsuccessful leader and the victors—as was the policy of Q. Fabius Maximus in the last years of his life—to be moderate in success. More probably still, after the end of the War, with Hannibal ruling Carthage and the Romans—and many noble Carthaginians—uneasy spectators. Then it might appear that Hannibal had carried out what Hasdrubal was supposed to have intended: to achieve monarchic power at home. Thus it seems impossible to assume that Fabius wrote on the causes of the War soon after its outbreak, and very likely that he did not do so until after its end.

This brings us back to his purpose in addressing the Greeks. Once we abandon—as we surely must—an early date, around the time of his mission to Delphi, we are again inevitably led to the period after the War: for during the War itself the Senate took no political interest in Greece. Involved, against its will, in a war with Philip V, it persuaded the Aetolian League to bear the brunt of it, and after the collapse of its ally made an inglorious peace in 205. Nor did Rome make any effort to gain or even maintain the friendship of the Greeks. Only after Hannibal's defeat was intervention in the East decided on, and a new policy emerged slowly during the next few years, its spokesman T. Quinctius Flamininus.[18] It is in this context that we must see a Senator's attempt to explain Roman institutions and policies to the Greeks.

A third line of approach converges with these two. In his account of the First Punic War in Book I Polybius combines—sometimes rather unskilfully, as he was still learning his profession—a Roman and a Carthaginian source. He mentions the histories of Fabius and of the Sicilian Greek Philinus as those considered the best and praises the authors for their honourable character, though he accuses them of unintentional distortion because of their partisanship for Rome and Carthage respectively. Hence it is rightly held that these two, rather than others unnamed and unknown, were his main sources which he critically followed.[19] Once this is recognized, it is clear that the account of the debate on whether to help Messana must be based on Fabius.[20] In this account, the Senate and People disagree, the Senate refusing to ratify the aid (which must lead to war) and the People, led by demagogues, voting it in the end. As it happens, there was one and only one other occasion on which Senate and People disagreed on an issue of war and peace: the debate (in 201) on the second war against Philip V;[21] though this time the roles were reversed, and this time the People allowed itself to be persuaded. Again, it seems likely that Fabius' account of the first of these events is not unconnected with his experience of the second.

The wisdom of the Senate, as against the blindness of the People and its demagogues, seems to be the burden of Fabius' message to his Roman readers. It would not be unwelcome at a time when the Senate, strengthened by its successes in war, had reached the apex of its power and was preparing to defend that power against insubordinate members of its own ranks. It is surely an inescapable conclusion that it is ultimately to Fabius—relative of Q. Fabius Maximus, as Plutarch (*Fabius* 18, 3) reminds us—that we owe the stress, in the surviving tradition, on the great Delayer's wisdom and strength, against the folly and incompetence of his opponents. And this wisdom is throughout shown as exercised on behalf, and with the support, of the Senate. Our last dated extract from Fabius Pictor (fr. 26) deals with the battle of Trasimene; but it is reasonable to suppose that his history covered the years of his relative's greatest glory and that it then stopped (probably owing to the author's death): the end of the War is dominated by Scipio, and Fabius Maximus sometimes cuts a miserable figure.[22]

Nor must we overlook the moral warning in Fabius' message: this Hellenized Roman senator was interested in the relation of morality to history, and he was to pass on this interest to the whole line of his successors. When he mentions the strict moral code ruling in Rome both in private life and in public (frr. 27-8), he clearly connected this, as others were to do later, with Rome's rise to greatness; and, like his successors, he may have already looked back to a Golden Age, from which standards had now declined (fr. 20).

Didactic in his message to Romans and perhaps even to Carthaginians, he was no less so in his message to the Greek world: as we can disengage it from the first two books of Polybius,[23] it is one of Roman strength, perseverance, moderation and good faith. Rome may lose battles, but will win wars; the Senate will not enter wars lightly or unjustly, but will show patience even under provocation; but where its *fides* is engaged, it will take strong action in the end. This is not to accuse Fabius of deliberate distortion, any more than Polybius did[24]: it is very likely that the third-century senator saw Roman history in those terms, just as he wanted foreigners to see it. It was Fabius who informed the Greeks of the vast forces at Rome's disposal, to which even the dreaded Gauls ultimately presented no problem; it was Fabius who tried to explain to them the Roman concept of *clientela*, to which, as Flamininus' policy of 'freedom' enmeshed them, they would have done well to attend.[25]

In his attempt to explain Rome to the Greeks he failed: that was to prove impossible for another two generations. For the moment, none of them took much notice of another barbarian writing about his country in undistinguished prose. But professional historians, Greek and Roman, were to come back to Fabius. He had created a kind of writing that was to be followed down to Tacitus and beyond: history as a serious enquiry into the past, but one morally and politically committed—a fit subject for the leisure hours of a senator. We shall see that, on the whole, serious senatorial history remained different from its inferior imitations.[26]

Fabius' example was soon followed.[27] L. Cincius Alimentus, a contemporary who had been praetor and a prisoner of Hannibal,[28] also wrote a history in Greek, clearly using that of Fabius. But we have only about half a dozen fragments, and he is a very shadowy figure: it was Fabius who was regarded as the father of Roman history. C. Acilius and A. Postumius Albinus[29] produced Roman histories in Greek about the middle of the second century. Both were senators: Acilius was a man of philosophical inclinations, who acted as interpreter to the famous 'embassy of philosophers' from Athens (155 B.C.); Postumius rose to the consulship (151) and headed the commission for the settlement of Greece after 146. He too had literary interests: Polybius, who disliked him, tells us that he exaggerated them to everyone's disgust. He is best known for his apology, in his preface, for any errors there might be in his Greek: Cato asked him who had forced him to write at all! The question deserves reflection: Cato may have implied that he could have written in Latin. By then, Cato had made it possible. In fact, someone (perhaps the author) did translate the work into Latin; but this did not help it to survive. Acilius, by an extraordinary chance, is the only Republican historian the publication date of whose work is known (141).[30] We do not know much else about it. He seems to have carried phil-Hellenism to excess, reviving the myth that Rome was a Greek colony (fr. 1); and—probably following Cato—he seems to have shown an interest in the origins of Italian cities.[31] His main recorded contribution is the tale of the interview between Scipio and Hannibal (fr. 3); it justifies us in doubting whether the loss of his work is calamitous.[32]

2. CATO AND THE CREATION OF LATIN HISTORY

The serious work of Fabius thus appeared to be already degenerating into trivial Hellenistic romance in the hands of his *epigoni*. But by then Roman historical writing had been transformed by the *Origines* of M. Porcius Cato.[33] It cannot be quite certain that Cato was the first to attempt a Roman history in the vernacular.[34] But a personality like his could not touch any subject without profound effects. Not surprisingly, Cato's history is the first of which we have numerous fragments, many quoted *verbatim*—enough to enable us to grasp the shape and style of the work.

It falls into two (or perhaps three) parts:[35] the first three books, true to its name, deal with the origins and earliest history of Rome (I) and of the cities of Italy (II and III). This part seems to have been written earlier, Book I probably some time before the rest. Book IV has a new preface, indicating later publication: it contained the First Punic War and went down at least to 216; Book V narrated the main part of the Hannibalic War and went down at least to 167. The last two books (VI and VII) seem again to mark a new departure: the scale expanded considerably, and they took the story down to a few months before Cato's death (149). In these books he included some of his own speeches—as he had already begun to do in Book V, but now clearly at much greater length. Rejecting the triviality of pontifical annals (fr. 77), he also rejected their chronology: he arranged his material by subject-matter (*capitulatim*), at least up to his own age. Nepos also tells us that he refused to mention the names of military leaders, and this is confirmed by the elder Pliny[36] and by the fragments, which always use terms like 'consul' and 'dictator'. This applies not only—as some explanations assume—to Rome, but also to her enemies; not, however, to great men in the non-military sphere.

Cato's work, though written in Latin, is as clearly in the Greek tradition as that of Fabius: we have noted his rejection of the Roman *annales*. Hellenistic influence appears in the very title (probably meant to translate the Greek *ktiseis*: like the latter, it is interpreted to include a certain amount of early history, after the actual foundation). It is no less clear in the broad manner of presentation, apparently surpassing even that of Fabius. Cato is interested in geography, plant and animal ecology (as a student of agricultural science would inevitably be), but particularly in human life, customs and character.[37] According to Nepos, he liked *admiranda*, but his interest was not scientific. The charge is probably true; but how many Greeks, from Herodotus to Timaeus, had done better? It might be said, with some truth, that this Hellenistic model was simply the only one to follow. But Cato's Hellenism was of a more positive kind. It is clear that he was interested in political theory and had read some of the classics in the subject; perhaps he had talked to Polybius about it.[38] He speaks of the 'mixed constitution' of Carthage,[39] and he may have compared the Roman constitution (moulded by history) with those of Greek lawgivers like Lycurgus (thought up by one man), much as Polybius does.[40] Moreover, he goes out of his way to link the best of Greece with Rome: he thinks the Aborigines (a legendary tribe said to have inhabited Latium and its vicinity) of Achaean origin, and he derives Roman austerity from Lycurgan Sparta *via* the Sabines.[41] It is clear that Cato's anti-Hellenism, if it was ever more than a useful political platform,[42] rejected only what was degenerate in contemporary Greece.

Cato's chief aims, like those of Fabius, were didactic and political. This appears at once in his initial statement that men must give an account of their leisure-time no less than of their time of (public) activity—a sentiment that he appears to have got from Xenophon.[43] History is thus connected with what was the proper sphere of action of a senator. Cato's general commendation of history (fr. 3) does not survive; but it must have pointed out its use to the statesman—probably (in view of their agreement on political theory) rather on Polybian lines. It is worth mentioning that a good source says that he wrote his history for the education of his elder son.[44]

History as a senator's leisure-time activity had other problems and purposes besides the training of future senators. There was, as we have seen, the continuing challenge of Rome's relations with the Greeks—a challenge no longer political, but more than ever cultural. Fabius had responded nobly: writing in Greek, he gave Greeks an account of Rome as a city in the Greek sphere and a eulogy of Roman character and principles. Cato wrote in Latin, for upper-class Romans and Italians: Latin was now a developing literary language, and the Greeks no longer counted. What he was concerned to show was that Italian cities had a venerable antiquity worth studying; that Greeks and Italians were related by blood, and that Rome had incorporated what was most widely admired in Greece (the Spartan way of life, in particular) and developed a mixed constitution superior to that of Sparta. Cato's message is addressed to his countrymen: they had nothing to be ashamed of, no need for a cultural inferiority complex, such as many of them were showing, much to his chagrin: modern Greece was not worth imitating. Polybius, whose estimate of his contemporaries was not unlike Cato's, might have agreed.

But towards the end of his life Cato found still another use for history, and one that was to bear much fruit. Still putting into practice his view that it was a suitable leisure-time activity for a man in public life, he consistently used it to carry on his political struggles: history could become polemic and apologia. Inserting his speeches, he advertised and recorded his sagacity and flayed his enemies. This is the beginning of the tradition of political autobiography and of *ex parte* contemporary history—a tradition that was to find many followers in the next few generations, some of them deliberately going back to Cato as a model.

There is another idea for which Cato must bear responsibility. We have seen that it was an important part of his purpose to show that Rome could challenge comparison with what was best among the Greeks. However, Rome had no great epic poetry. (We know that Cato did not think very highly of Ennius.) How could Roman heroes be compared with Greek, if they lacked the sacred bard?

Cato found the answer. He reported that in days long past it had been the custom to sing the praises of great men at banquets—a custom that had unfortunately lapsed.[45] One would like to think that Cato had evidence for this custom, of which he had no personal experience; but it is difficult. In any case, the story had a long and happy life. Repeated and refined in antiquity,[46] it was taken up in modern times and, under the aegis of Niebuhr (and against the protests of Mommsen), produced not only the *Lays of Ancient Rome*, but a theory of the origin of Roman historiography that was quite unknown to any ancient writer and that still occasionally haunts romantic scholars.[47]

Cato made Latin history a living fact. Affected *epigoni* could still write in Greek, incurring ridicule or neglect; but they could have no influence on the future. Politically, the Greeks no longer counted; the Latin language was both progressing and spreading; the choice of Fabius could not reasonably be made again. The task of interpreting Roman history to the subject Greeks—for their own benefit, not for Rome's—could be left to a reliable Greek: Polybius, in his way, is the continuator of an important aspect of Fabius' work. But the history that mattered was now written by Romans for Romans.

Yet Latin, though it knew oratory of a sort and was fast becoming a medium for poetry, could not, when Cato began, provide a model for narrative prose. Cato, drawing on native resources and Greek models, set out to fill the gap.[48] We have few long *verbatim* quotations; but we can see the rich variety of his sources. Weighty and dignified language, as in fr. 63 ('in maximum decus atque in excelsissimam claritudinem sublimauit'—the last word is from Ennius) or part of fr. 83 ('gloriam atque gratiam praecipuam claritudinis [again!] inclutissimae [an epic and tragic word] decorauere monumentis'), stands beside plain every-day speech, as in fr. 57 ('ubi hordeum demessuit, idem in montibus serit, ubi hordeum idem iterum metit'—it could come from the *De agri cultura*!) or, in a famous example of blunt speech, fr. 86 (Maharbal's advice to Hannibal—a passage that will occupy us later). Sentence structure is rudimentary and monotonous, subordination slight, especially in narrative; e.g. (fr. 83, on a heroic officer) 'eum sustulere isque conualuit saepeque postilla operam rei p. fortem atque strenuam [notice the change to 'atque' in the solemn formula] perhibuit illoque facto . . . exercitum ceterum seruauit'. In the speeches, particularly, effect is obtained by pleonastic synonyms and the use of vigorous words (including inceptives—this was to find many imitators) and phrases, as well as the simple artifices of assonance and alliteration. Thus in the great speech on the Rhodians (fr. 95a): 'Scio solere plerisque hominibus rebus secundis atque prolixis atque prosperis animum excellere atque superbiam atque ferociam augescere atque crescere' (and notice later 'transuorsum trudere').

Cicero was to group Cato together with Piso and Fannius as being 'meagre' (*exiles*), though he grants them vigour (*leg.* I, 6): they know of no ornament except brevity (*de or.* II, 53). Aware of the hard-won progress of artistic Latin prose in his generation, he was totally insensitive to what preceded. Cato's style, in addition to its sententious *breuitas*, is rich and varied—incredibly so for a first attempt—even though it lacks subtlety. Such as it was, it became a model in a new *genre*, and Cicero's protests were to prove unavailing.

Cato's *auctoritas* precluded immediate further development.[49] But one step was soon taken. In all the early annalists (as far as we can see) the earliest history (for which there were Greek authorities) and contemporary events (for which they could call on their experience and that of their elders) are told at greater length than what intervenes. Cato had taken this tendency to its extreme. Between the third and the fourth book, his work almost broke in half. Two paths could be pursued if this was to be avoided: the easier one, that of filling out the neck of the hour-glass, was taken first. It took many further stimuli to lead men of different temperament to the other solution: that of boldly breaking off the past. Unfortunately we cannot follow this interesting process accurately, as we do not know precise dates of publication. But the outlines can perhaps be traced.

3. THE EXPANSION OF THE PAST

Cn. Gellius and L. Calpurnius Frugi were contemporaries. They both followed the only kind of historical writing they knew and went back to the origins of the city—and beyond. Gellius,[50] especially if the book numbers quoted for him can be trusted,[51] set himself the task of filling in what had hitherto existed only in outline. Book I apparently did not even reach the founding of

Rome, but was filled with what might be called cultural anthropology; Book III only completed the regal period. An event of 389 (?), which Cassius Hemina had treated in Book II, appears in Gellius' Book XV (fr. 25). The last book cited is XCVII. Admittedly, the number of books is a rough guide. But it is worth while comparing Gellius' work with the eighty books of the *Annales Maximi*, of which the fourth had not yet dealt with Romulus (*or. gent. Rom.* 17 f). Gellius cannot have started his work after their publication; but he clearly had access to them and, perhaps for the first time, chose to transmit the information they contained. This must surely be the basis of his expanded account, whatever other sources (e.g. family archives) he consulted. It is probably the voluminous Gellius who introduced into the writing of annals those details of portents and similar matter that Cato had scoffed at and that was to become a characteristic ingredient. However, it is difficult to avoid the conclusion that there was simply not as much information to be had as Gellius produced. He must have used to the full the freedom that Hellenistic historians allowed themselves of inventing the verisimilar to eke out the meagre truth. We have seen an example in the case of Acilius (p. 7, above): Gellius clearly transferred the custom into Latin. History was becoming entertainment.[52]

Gellius was not very successful: in his chosen task he was superseded by men who could do that kind of thing better. Cicero vaguely knew of him (since he was a senator); the elder Pliny and his namesake A. Gellius read him; possibly Dionysius found him congenial; but—with one significant exception (see p. 22, below)—no other historian is known to have used him. Only late scholiasts, for their own purposes, dipped into that bulky work.

More important was the work of L. Calpurnius Piso, who was consul in a crucial year (133 B.C.). Whenever the work appeared, it is clear that it begins to show the influence of the Gracchan troubles, though it is not yet pervaded by them. Piso, originally perhaps not opposed to moderate reform,[53] was one of the many whom Ti. Gracchus had finally alienated. There is no evidence that his history reached Gracchan times;[54] but his attitude is made clear in his account of the demagogue Sp. Maelius and perhaps in his hostile presentation of the low-born aedile Cn. Flavius.[55]

But in spite of this political element, he is not to be classed among the Gracchan historians. True to his name 'Frugi', which even C. Gracchus had to admit he deserved, he is mainly interested (as many of his predecessors had to some extent been) in virtue and vice, and hence in the past. His portrait gallery of heroes and villains starts with Romulus and Tarpeia—both models of virtue—and includes a freedman who knew his station and filled it well (fr. 33). He gives the exact date (154 B.C.—the occasion was marked by the growth of a fig-tree to replace a palm-tree on the altar of Jupiter) when Roman virtue began to decline (fr. 38): the young generation—as Polybius had recently remarked of an earlier time (xxxi, 25)—was hopelessly depraved (fr. 40). This seems to have been his chief comment on the age of revolution in which he lived. Piso's style is simple and unadorned, banishing striking words and phrases, perhaps in conscious opposition to Cato and return to the *annales* that Cato rejected. As in Cato, there is little structure. Cicero, this time, cannot be blamed for calling him *exilis*.[56] More important: Piso seems, at the least, to have taken little trouble to get his facts right; and he clearly was not above deliberate distortion or even invention where it suited his purpose: as in Gellius (though for worthier reasons), the line between improving fact and improving fiction was not clearly marked.[57] It is possible that his *auctoritas* helped to make such practices acceptable later; though they are perhaps inseparable from a tradition in which moral or political purpose takes precedence over truth.

4. THE GRACCHAN HISTORIANS

Great events, in a free and literate society, will produce historians (though not necessarily great ones): the impact will compel reaction—interpretation of the present, perhaps also reconsideration of the past. All the more so where history is the responsible statesman's leisure-time pursuit, with a recognized political background and function. After all that had gone before, the age of the Gracchi was bound to produce a new outlook and new activity in this field; and the events of the next century kept it in being.

C. Gracchus had much to do with producing the new type of writing, with a propagandist biography of his brother, dedicated to his friend M. Pomponius.[58] We have only two citations, but one of them vital—the revelation on the journey to Spain; this makes it clear that much more in Plutarch—particularly the fragments of Tiberius' speeches—will ultimately come from this work. It must therefore not be underrated as a friendly source for the life and aims of Tiberius Gracchus. Much of what we know of the latter—including some very dubious items, which Gaius made part of his own programme[59]—will go back to it. That the work will have been influenced by Greek models—such as Polybius' *Philopoemen*, which Gaius must have known—is obvious; but it was Cato who had shown Romans the possibilities of partisan history. Gaius was the first to follow the new path.

He was not to have his own way for long: the Optimate tradition was ultimately to go a long way towards overpowering his version. Its first representative was C. Fannius, the man who had gained the consulship of 122 as a friend of C. Gracchus and then turned decisively against him.[60] As a member of the Scipionic circle, he had literary interests; but there is no doubt that, like Cato, he carried his political activity into his history. At the beginning of his work, he apparently defended his change of party by explaining that men grow wiser with age (fr. 1); and he included a speech by Metellus Macedonicus against Tiberius Gracchus, of which (perhaps *via* Posidonius) we have traces in Plutarch.[61] His friend Aemilianus he compared to Socrates, clearly in refutation of attacks on his character (fr. 7). This sufficiently shows his attitude and aims. All the datable fragments deal with his own lifetime: we have no reason for doubting that he went back to the origins of Rome, but perhaps only in the few perfunctory sentences that were to become traditional vestiges. Cato's work had made *historia* (in the later strict sense of contemporary history) possible; Fannius was the first to make it a fact.[62]

His style is again not differentiated by Cicero from that of other early historians. We cannot say much about it, except that he seems to be the first historian who deliberately uses an archaic manner, to achieve *dignitas* and perhaps to evoke Cato. In fact, he carried it to exaggerated lengths.[63] His influence, however, is undoubted. This first account by their victorious enemies is probably the basis of the hostile tradition on the Gracchi. Fannius was a close friend of Panaetius, and the latter's pupil Posidonius will have known him and cannot have failed to use his work. Posidonius' history, however, in turn contributed a great deal to later works, particularly those of Diodorus and Plutarch. P.

Rutilius Rufus, a younger member of the same circle, may be presumed to have shared and reproduced his friend's views on the events of his age; perhaps it was Fannius' example that inspired him, when he had the leisure, to write history himself. In the crucial year 133 Rutilius was not in Rome; there can be no doubt that Fannius furnished him with an interpretation. Fannius' work was known to Cicero; Brutus made an epitome of it; and Sallust, generous in appreciation of historians with whom he disagreed, attributed truthfulness to Fannius as his chief quality.[64]

At about the time when Fannius was writing, Roman historiography was shattered by the publication (by P. Mucius Sacevola, consul 133 and *Pontifex Maximus*) of the *Annales Maximi*, in eighty books, from the foundation of the city or (in fact) long before. There can be no doubt that these records, whenever compiled, had always been accessible to the senators who wrote history: in fact, they could hardly have written otherwise. But it is very likely (see, e.g., Cato's remark) that none of them, for a long time, showed much interest in some of the things they recorded. Gellius clearly did; and it is tempting to bring their publication into connection with the interest he had recently shown. In any case, the effect was enormous. This authoritative account was now available to the educated public: a basic framework would henceforth have to be respected. Moreover, the writing of annals was now made possible to men of less exalted rank, and less attractive to their betters. For a long time, there are (so far as we know) no annals, from the foundation of the city, written by senators. Such men now concentrated (as Fannius had probably already done) on the events of their lifetime, which still gave them the opportunity of privileged access to sources of information, or on specialized research. Two exceptions only prove the rule: as we shall see, C. Licinius Macer and L. Aelius Tubero thought they had fresh documentary evidence, Macer perhaps also a fresh point of view. But, on the whole, traditional *annales* now became, long before Livy, a pursuit carried on in the study and based on other men's books: there was no longer any need to consult archives, or to know about war and politics.

Specialized research need not be confined to one's own lifetime, as the author of the *Catiline* was to rediscover. Not long after C. Gracchus' death, L. Coelius Antipater (who had known Gracchus) decided to write the history of the Hannibalic War. He was well fitted for the task.[65] Brother of a senator of at least aedilician rank, and learned in literature, rhetoric and law, he was the teacher and friend of the great orator L. Crassus. He announced as his aims both accuracy and a more careful style than his predecessors (fr. 2); and though Cicero has a pleasant task railing at his pretensions, he admits that Coelius' work was epoch-making.[66]

As his main sources he clearly chose Fabius and Silenus—perhaps also those of Polybius[67]—for the early part of the war; though he read widely (he certainly knew Cato)[68] and will have been familiar with most of what had been written. His accuracy is evident even to us: he gives the length of the Alps as 1,000 (Roman) miles, that of Hannibal's route to Italy as 1,200—both good estimates. That Hannibal crossed the Alps by the Little St Bernard is still perhaps the most likely solution of that difficult puzzle.[69] That Q. Fabius Maximus was—against all precedent, in an emergency—*elected* Dictator in 217 is not as unlikely as critics from Livy to Mommsen have thought it.[70] His detailed account of Hannibal's circuitous march on Rome in 211 (fr. 28) fits in with what Polybius gives us, against those who excogitated a lightning dash. Where opinions differed, he took trouble: he consulted various sources (including documents) and made up his mind (fr. 29). Unfortunately his love of truth was impaired by his rhetorical training, which made him seek pathetic effect. He is fond of portents and divine interventions (such as Hannibal's vision of the 'devastation of Italy')[71]; he stresses sacrilege and its consequences[72]; and he is not above dramatizing, where the truth could not be recovered and the details did not seem to matter. Thus an uneventful sea-crossing might be enlivened by a storm—provided there were no losses (fr. 40); or a vaguely exaggerating, but not numerically false, statement might be made about the size of an army.[73] In this, he was simply following tradition, and not its worst excesses. If he repeated travellers' tales (fr. 56), he deserves no more blame than Herodotus, Caesar or Tacitus; if he included imaginary speeches, no more than almost any ancient historian. The fact that he did not write *ab urbe condita* shows how he felt about the truth of ancient legends; but he would use myth to adorn a digression, in the accepted manner.[74]

It is obvious that, although his standards were not ours, Coelius belongs to the class of serious historians, with his care for accuracy and his readiness to consult anti-Roman sources. But it was chiefly in style that Cicero saw his importance. Unable to appreciate Cato, Cicero finds in Coelius a consciousness of style and a rhetorical background that he can understand, though not admire. The man who thought that transpositions of words were sometimes 'necessary'[75]; who applied rhetorical and even poetical rhythm and cadence to the extent of actually using verses in prose, not to mention quite Ciceronian prose rhythms[76]—this man was on a different level from those who merely used archaism to achieve solemnity. Though in this very tradition Coelius was an important link: he did not depart from what had become the custom of the *genre*.[77] That this was not, as Cicero seems to have thought, a sign of immaturity, is made clear by Cicero's own judgment on the man and by the fragments: the attempt to apply the rules of the new rhetoric to the traditional style was deliberate, if not entirely successful. As it turned out, his way of rhythmed prose was not to be that of the great historians; but, with all his faults, he is the only real stylist between Cato and Sisenna.[78]

Luckily, an example survives that epitomizes a chapter in the development of Latin prose. Maharbal's advice to Hannibal after Cannae had been couched by Cato in plain, blunt language, such as might have been used at the time (fr. 86): 'Mitte mecum Romam equitatum: diequinti in Capitolio tibi cena cocta erit.' Coelius did not object to the plain words, and he liked 'diequinti' (by now an archaism); but he expands and introduces structure and rhetorical rhythm (fr. 25): 'Si uis mihi equitatum dare et ipse cum cetero exercitu me sequi, diequinti Romae in Capitolium curabo tibi cena sit cocta.' It was left to Livy (xxii, 51, 2) to vary the structure, improve the rhetoric, give up the rhythm and remove the *humilia* and *inusitata uerba*: 'Die quinto, inquit, uictor in Capitolio epulaberis. Sequere: cum equite, ut prius uenisse quam uenturum sciant, praecedam.' We should like to know how the famous 'Vincere scis' appeared in Coelius.

Sempronius Asellio[79] did not care so much about style: Cicero puts him, with 'Clodius',[80] among those who did not keep up Coelius' standards. But he was one whom the Gracchan troubles had forced to think about their craft. Moreover, he had read Polybius and must have known him: he was a military tribune at Numantia, with other men known to be connected with Scipio Aemilianus.[81] He decided to write serious and rationalist history, on the Polybian model: in a Polybian introduction he distinguished his own work that showed causes and connections from mere *annales* listing portents and cataloguing facts.[82] Naturally, he wrote a history of his own time, perhaps starting where Polybius had left off and going on (we do not know how far) for at least 14 books.[83] But his lack of style condemned him to remain unread: no one before A. Gellius quotes him, and if historians used him, we have no means of knowing it. Nor can we assess the quality of his performance.[84]

5. THE LATER ANNALISTS

It will be convenient, henceforth, to separate traditional annals —for the moment socially degraded—from the various forms of contemporary history. Annalists are now lesser names: a Vennonius, a Q. Claudius Quadrigarius, a Valerius Antias.

Vennonius is a mere name to us, though Cicero and Dionysius knew him.[85] Claudius, on the other hand, is to us more substantial than any other of Livy's predecessors.[86] He is cited in the extant and was used in the lost books of Livy. His style was praised by Fronto, with the result that A. Gellius has left us numerous extracts. His *praenomen* and *cognomen* between them make it clear that he is not a Patrician Claudius. He may have come from northern Italy, with the topography of which he seems to be specially familiar[87]; and he shows no undue partiality towards his great namesakes. (They are not well treated in our tradition.) Starting (perhaps) with a translation of the Greek work of Acilius, he went on to launch out on his own.[88] We have no reason to think that he treated the earliest history (except perhaps in a conventional introduction). Our first fragments deal with the battle of the Allia, and Book I probably went down to the Samnite Wars. The treatment then broadens: the Pyrrhic and probably the First Punic War were in III, Cannae in V (the Hannibalic War perhaps ended in VII), the younger Tiberius Gracchus' Spanish treaty (137 B.C.) in IX. XVIII contained the siege of Grumentum (90), XIX Marius' return and the siege of Piraeus (87), XXI perhaps the revolt of Lepidus. The last book cited is XXIII: perhaps there were twenty-four, the work going down to about 70.

It will be seen that the scale depended entirely on how much there was to interest the author: the Hannibalic War probably had a book for every six years; but then three or four books cover everything down to the Gracchi. (From this alone it is clear that the author did not discover Polybius.) If his lifetime is told in greater detail,[89] this was because it contained plenty of war, foreign and civil, that provided scope for his art. It was not because he had anything original to say. His station ensured that he was always a secondary source, using his betters. Nor can we see any social or factional bias or even serious moral purpose. On the other hand, there is no love of truth and enquiry: his patriotism is brazen, but conventional, calculated to please the reader rather than to elevate; and facts are freely distorted or invented. Thus the famous story of the Senate's warning to Pyrrhus, when one of his aides proposed to murder him, was found by both Claudius and Valerius Antias in some predecessor. Claudius adds the actual letter sent by the consuls and the fact that Pyrrhus was so grateful that he returned all Roman prisoners fully dressed (frr. 40-1). His figures for enemy losses surpass even those of Valerius in impudent ineptitude.[90] It may be regarded as certain that Claudius and Valerius (two of Livy's main sources) are responsible, in elaboration of what had been done by their predecessors, for the presentation of all Roman wars as just and all Roman dealings as honourable (even where the reverse is clear to us) that marks so much of Livy[91]: to him this attitude was congenial, unlike that of Polybius, whom he respected far more, but whose facts he sometimes found uncomfortable.[92] Where earlier annalists, for serious moral and political reasons, had prepared the way, the entertainers followed without scruple, converting history into romance.

Entertainment is clearly the chief purpose. The poignant anecdote (copied from Hellenistic writers even by the earliest Roman historians) here runs riot; the vicissitudes of battle, described by one who had probably never raised a sword or shield, are his stock-in-trade. Again, Livy found it congenial. Claudius' lack of interest in politics and personalities is phenomenal: he is not even cited for the trials of the Scipios (the *cause célèbre* of early second-century politics); and though modern scholars have tried to conjecture how he dealt with them, the very scale of his work at that point makes it clear that he in fact showed little interest. He had deliberately avoided the Struggle of the Orders, and the few specimens we have of his account of Marius and Sulla (there are none on the earlier seditions) are confined to conventional mutual abuse. The difference between Cato and Claudius is that between the political class and mere entertainers.[93]

His style received high praise from late critics—not altogether unjustly.[94] He has little that is original, but fits well into the tradition. There is the display of *inusitata uerba*, new and archaic, technical, poetic and vulgar. Gellius notes *sanctitudo* and *frunisci* as archaisms, *multi mortales* as poetic.[95] Others can be added. Claudius likes going back to an old use of a word, e.g. *concessus*, *delectare* (frr. 10, 41); and he coins freely by analogy, which was fashionable at the time, e.g. *cantabundus*, *cumprime*, *congermanascere*. There are inceptive and frequentative verbs, adverbs in *-im* and *-iter* and adjectives in *-bilis*, often in odd senses.[96] Technical and vulgar words are quoted, one of the latter in a real tour de force—a hendecasyllable about the grunting of pigs.[97] Similar devices (archaism, poeticism, analogism) appear in accidence and syntax, often interchangeably with normal forms (for we must remember that Claudius was a contemporary of Cicero).[98] It would be unjust to conclude to blind affectation: these features had become traditional in the *genre*, though Claudius certainly shows signs of inadequate skill and polish in his use of them. Yet he is far from naive or indiscriminate: the two stories of single combat (frr. 10b and 12) show all the enhancements of solemnity; but these are conspicuously absent in the plain dignity of the consuls' letter to Pyrrhus (fr. 41). The story of Q. Fabius Maximus' meeting with his son (fr. 57) uses archaic, but not new or poetical, features, relying for its effect mainly on the simple structure that Cicero thought *exilis*. This style, indeed, is characteristic of swift-moving narrative:[99] on this the purple patches are deliberately grafted. From Coelius, Claudius takes over a care for word order, rhythm and cadence, though he applies it with his usual lack of finesse and tact.[100]

It will be clear from this brief survey that our Claudius is not likely to be the 'Clodius' in Cicero's list of those who lapsed from Coelius' standards.[101] With all his prejudices, Cicero could hardly have charged him with *languor*. This has some bearing on Valerius Antias as well: Valerius is omitted in Cicero's list, and it can be held that his work had therefore not yet been published by 52 B.C., the date of the *De legibus*. This conclusion is inescapable, if Claudius is in fact included; but it becomes improbable, if he is also omitted. In that case it is far more likely that both these writers were not deemed worthy of inclusion, perhaps for social rather than for literary reasons.[102]

Valerius Antias, among those whom we can judge, marks the nadir of historiography.[103] Livy, who used him extensively, calls him credulous and impudent in his lies[104]; Fronto contrasts him with Claudius as writing *inuenuste*. Even if the isolated reference to Book XCVII be scaled down, his work was probably longer than any of his predecessors': Books LXXIV and LXXV are reliably cited. For at least some stretches, his treatment was broader than Livy's. His approach was quite unhistorical: he fully observed the Isocratean canons of (in fact) plausibly detailed mendacity.[105] This had long been a commonplace among less conscientious historians, for ornament and entertainment: Polybius had put Timaeus in the stocks for it and defended himself in advance against similar charges.[106] The tradition of Roman historiography made plausible lying easy: its true content was to some extent based on archival material, written in simple and archaic style and clamouring for imitation. It is not likely that the senatorial historians (with the possible exception of the voluminous Gellius) had indulged in large-scale forgery of public documents. Treaties might be invented, which the Carthaginians could be said to have broken,[107] and family pride might stretch a point on ancient 'facts'. Claudius, as we have seen, had no scruples about inventing 'documents', and with Valerius the invention of 'archival material' seems to have reached new heights.[108] Unfortunately he achieved his effect: breadth of treatment and plausibility recommended him to many who knew no better or who did not care, from Livy to Silius Italicus and (probably) Plutarch. It has been the unenviable task of scholars to separate the substratum from his additions; and for the early part of Roman history the task is almost hopeless. His disregard for facts is clear from his handling of the trials of the Scipios, in what should have been the full light of history,[109] his effrontery from his invention of an ancestor for himself, whom he slipped into an officer post under two Valerii in the Hannibalic War.[110] No wonder Silius (who extensively uses this technique) was impressed; but he did not claim to be writing history. Moreover, having attached himself to the Patrician Valerii, Antias tried to cast reflected glory on himself by exaggerating their achievements, particularly in the Struggle of the Orders, which made good topical reading in his day.

Lacking any serious purpose, Valerius did not make up for his defects by style and presentation. Not many quoted fragments survive; but Fronto's comment is borne out by the picture (much improved by a great artist) that we get in Livy. And a fad for (sometimes artificial) reduplicated verb forms is almost the only tribute this voluminous author pays to the tradition of historical style.[111] We can imagine the work, alternating 'archival' passages, true or false, with speeches and plain narrative in smooth, nondescript flow.

Before we come to Livy, however, there was to be another infusion of more serious matter. C. Licinius Macer, a last-minute Sullan who had soon tired of the new establishment,[112] found an unused source for early history in the archives of the temple of Juno Moneta—a series of books written on linen, which contained at least a list of senior magistrates. Unfortunately we have hardly any information on these books, which differed from the accepted tradition at various points. They obviously existed, since they were critically used by a later writer.[113] Whether these authors really believed the linen to be several centuries old, or how the documents came to be where Macer found them, the scant relics do not tell us. But he certainly considered them to have some authority. This is surely why he, after about two generations, was the first senator to write annals *ab urbe condita*.[114] He was a proud aristocrat (he named his son—Calvus—after one of the fourth-century Licinii), and it is perhaps significant that he used his last senatorial predecessor Gellius, rather than Claudius and Valerius, whose early books must surely have been available.[115] Being also a *popularis*, he interpreted the Struggle of the Orders in contemporary terms, painting (it seems) a great portrait of C. Licinius Stolo and insisting on the importance of the Licinian Rogations in restoring *concordia* and settled government. Unfortunately little is directly known about his work—not even its scale, except that it reached at least Book XVI.[116] Macer died prematurely in 66: he may not have got much further.[117]

No more is known about Aelius Tubero, who followed Macer in his use of the linen books, though with less confidence.[118] He will be Cicero's friend L. Tubero, who certainly wrote history;[119] though his son Quintus has been suggested. Perhaps he, after Macer's death, decided to take up his new source. Little can be said about the scale and nature of his work.[120] Modern efforts to reconstruct it have sometimes exceeded all bounds of legitimate conjecture. Tubero clearly followed his predecessors, perhaps added to them, e.g. in the account of Regulus' torture (fr. 9); and he certainly spread himself on *admiranda*, such as the snake that Regulus killed by means of heavy artillery (fr. 8). His style, to judge by very slight evidence, is undistinguished and traditional. We need hardly regret the loss of Livy's last predecessor.

6. AUTOBIOGRAPHY AND CONTEMPORARY HISTORY

Having followed the annalists to where Livy was to supersede them, we may turn to a more rewarding subject. We have seen that various influences in the late second century B.C. had created new forms of historical expression, chief of them contemporary history as written by Fannius and Sempronius. Contemporary history written by prominent politicians merges into political autobiography. Cato and Fannius had approached the latter, but incorporated it in a work of wider scope. It took a ruthlessly ambitious and socially impregnable man to write openly *de uita sua*. This was M. Aemilius Scaurus, chief senator for twenty-five years and perhaps the most powerful man of his generation.[121] Like Cato, he had throughout his life been involved in feuds and lawsuits; and like Cato—or even more so—he was interested in literature.[122] It was probably late in the first decade of the first century that he wrote his apologia, in three books. Little is known about the work, which even a generation later was ignored by the reading public.[123] Nevertheless, the *auctoritas* of the writer must have made it influential in its day. It is clear that Scaurus intended the work to take its place in the tradition of historical writing: enough specimens survive to establish the style he chose.[124] The fragments tell us only of Scaurus' modest beginnings and of the discipline he enforced in his army. But other Scaurus anecdotes may safely be assigned to the work, e.g. his prominence in the suppression of Saturninus, his treatment of an unworthy son, perhaps his proud reply to his accuser Q. Varius.[125] His biography in the *De viris illustribus* must be ultimately based on his own work.[126] We should like to know whether, like Cato, he included his speeches; but we cannot be certain.

Of far greater importance was the work of P. Rutilius Rufus, the Roman Socrates.[127] Rutilius was a Stoic, had been a member of the Scipionic circle, a friend of the Metelli and (with them) later an enemy of Marius, who finally secured his exile on a trumped-up charge in 92.[128] In exile—perhaps stimulated by the work of Scaurus—he took to the writing of history.[129] Two works are cited, *Historiae* and *De uita sua*; their relationship cannot be deduced, and they may even be identical (the former being in Greek): the events before his lifetime (frr. 2 and 3) may easily come from digressions, especially as each fragment is based on Polybius.[130] Book I of the autobiography mentioned the election to the consulship of Q. Pompeius (for 141), perhaps the first political event he chose to record as typical of the decline in standards: it was disliked by Scipio Aemilianus, and Pompeius long remained an enemy of Rutilius' friend Metellus Macedonicus. Though these men became politically reconciled, Rutilius was not one to forget old feuds, once they could be displayed without doing political harm: he attacked the first consul of the Pompeii almost as bitterly as the second (Pompey's father, 'a thorough rascal'), one of his enemies.[131] 'Tristis et seuerus' by temperament, he used his work for an uninhibited indulgence in old feuds.[132] Marius too was fiercely denounced, as was his friend and colleague of 100 B.C., L. Valerius Flaccus, and probably Apicius, who had prosecuted Rutilius in 92;[133] and even Plutarch, who admired Rutilius, doubted if he could be believed when he spoke of an enemy.

This truth-loving, censorious and embittered man may well be responsible for much of our tradition on his lifetime. His work (the early part of it perhaps based on that of his friend Fannius) seems to have been used by Posidonius (another friend), and Plutarch knew it, either through him or even directly. Sallust clearly used it. The importance of Rutilius as (with Marius) Q. Metellus' chief legate in Numidia will go back to his account; so, basically, will Sallust's admiring portrayal of Metellus himself, which often puzzles the modern reader. The description of Q. Scaevola's just administration of Asia in Diodorus (Rutilius was exiled for his share in it), as well as some of the accounts of his own subsequent trial, may be added. Sallust's puzzlingly hostile account of M. Scaurus—absurd on its own facts—may well be due to his old *inimicus*: they had prosecuted each other in 116, and Rutilius, though politically reconciled, never forgave. Rutilius was an obvious source for Sallust to read—much more so than a Greek philosopher (Posidonius) not even domiciled in Rome.

The portrait of Marius, where unfavourable, will also come from this source, as—directly or indirectly—it does in Plutarch. Rutilius' censorious moralism would be highly congenial to Sallust. The hatred of Pompey that appears in his *Histories*[134] will owe something to Rutilius' condemnation of that family of villainous intriguers and demagogues. No work, in this section, is a more grievous loss than the apologia of P. Rutilius Rufus.

Various minor works of this period need not detain us.[135] But two great men now call for treatment: L. Cornelius Sulla and L. Cornelius Sisenna. Between them, they are largely responsible for our tradition on one crucial decade of Roman history.[136]

Sulla[137] probably started on his memoirs before the Social War: he could hardly have completed the work of 22 books after his retirement. We cannot tell the starting-point. Presumably he traced his family back to its beginnings. It is only in Book II that he reached the first Sulla (P. Sulla, *c.* 250). Book X had already got past the battle of Chaeronea (86). Book XXII ended with the prediction of his own approaching death. Plutarch refers to the work as *Hypomnemata*, Latin authors usually as *Res gestae*: he probably pretended to regard it (as Caesar did his *Commentaries*) as raw material for history, not as history proper. Perhaps he intended his friend L. Lucullus to write the history based on it (see fr. 1). Gellius, who knew the work, quotes no instance of peculiar speech from it (in fact, he cites it for *correct* Latin) and the grammarians only one.[138] It is clear that we can look to Caesar's work for an indication of the style of Sulla's (who was also a highly educated man): a style distinguished by purity and simplicity and (unlike that of Scaurus) right outside the learned historical tradition. Plutarch, Appian and Livy are indebted to this work for subject-matter and interpretation, Caesar for form and style. As political apologia, the new *genre* was to prove highly effective.

Lucullus did not carry out the task entrusted to him; but, in a sense, it was at once done by a young historian destined for fame: L. Cornelius Sisenna.[139] A Patrician senator, moving in the highest circles, he decided to write the history of the Social and Civil Wars in the brilliant manner of Clitarchus.[140] He seems to have stayed in Rome in the eighties, and his account of Sulla's Eastern war was no doubt firmly based on Sulla's books: Sallust, who admired Sisenna, was to censure him for partiality to Sulla.[141] On events in Italy he could speak from experience, presenting the case of those who had joined Sulla late, but just in time.[142] An Epicurean and a master of words, Sisenna developed a recherché style—made up of historical tradition, analogist theory and individual sensitivity—which he used, to the general amusement, even in the law-courts.[143] His historical work was a treasure-house of *inusitata uerba* that invited grammarians to preserve nearly 150 excerpts (most of them short). Adverbs in *-im* (with which his predecessors had experimented) were known to be his favourites: we have a dozen unusual ones, including *praefestinatim* and *saltuatim* (see frr. 126, 137). This ruthless analogism appears throughout. Thus he favoured *mediterreus* (cf. *terreus*) for *mediterraneus* and *false* for *falso*.[144] 'Historical' archaisms are common, e.g. *congenuclare* (fr. 33—cf. Coelius, fr. 44), *indulgitas* (fr. 46—cf. Coelius, fr. 48); so are dignified words in *-tudo*[145] and masses of military technical terms. Accidence and syntax also show the traditional oddities, touched by analogy.[146] New coinages can be freely combined with venerable archaisms and poetic diction, the whole linked with alliteration and sound-painting, to produce startling effects such as Latin prose was not to achieve again for centuries.[147]

But, though much concerned with style, Sisenna also thought about the historian's craft: he rejects excessive adherence to chronology for grouping by subject-matter, to aid comprehension.[148] As a philosopher, he discusses the age-old question of whether the gods care for men or live in an Epicurean heaven;[149] and in other digressions he seems to have dealt, in the traditional manner, with geography and myth:[150] this was implied in a Clitarchean form.

His work at once became the standard account of its subject. Cicero reluctantly admitted that it had merits; Varro gave Sisenna's name to a dialogue on history.[151] Sallust expressed admiration and refrained from a major rewriting of the period: his *Histories* seem to start where Sisenna left off. But in manner and style Sisenna was a unique phenomenon: Sallust was to react violently, going back to Cato.

7. EPILOGUE

Not much need be said on the age of Cicero. Undistinguished work proliferated, but nothing stands out except Caesar's *Commentaries* (at once appreciated)[152] and the work of the antiquarians, notably Atticus and Varro. Atticus' *Liber annalis* and genealogical researches were a major achievement, probably the basis of the Capitoline Fasti. Varro devoted several works to history and genealogy. But, apart from settling the date of the foundation of Rome (753 B.C.) and the lists of senior magistrates, it is not clear how much influence these works had on the later tradition.[153] We know very little about them, except for small points cited by encyclopaedists and grammarians.

By the end of the Ciceronian age, Roman historiography is fully developed: from antiquarian studies, through traditional annals, to contemporary history and political autobiography and pamphleteering, the forms and traditions have been established. Perhaps, as Cicero thought, no master had yet appeared.[154] But Cicero objected to the main line of the tradition as such, and we cannot take his word even for that. In any case, a master, when he appeared, would find everything ready for him.

NOTES

* The early Roman historians have been extensively studied in Germany and Italy. Unfortunately there is no comprehensive treatment in English. It is hoped that this essay may stimulate further interest. The best short discussion (with wide bibliography) will be found in A. H. McDonald's article on 'The Roman Historians' in *Fifty Years of Classical Scholarship* (ed. Platnauer, 1954). On individual historians, see McDonald's short articles (with bibliography) in the *Oxford Classical Dictionary* (1949). For a general survey in German (now a little out of date), see Schanz[4]-Hosius, *Römische Literaturgeschichte* (1927), 168 f. There is much of value in H. Bardon, *La littérature latine inconnue*, vol. 1 (1952). A. D. Leeman, *Orationis Ratio* (1963), chapters 3 and 7, now provides an elementary introduction for students, with special attention to style; unfortunately the author, while he (inevitably, for his purpose) presents didactic facts and ignores problems, has failed to give any bibliographical information whatsoever for those who might be interested in more serious study.

Of older works, K. W. Nitzsch, *Die römische Annalistik* (1843), is still useful in parts. In the last generation, the most interesting work has been done by M. Gelzer and A. Klotz. Some of this is cited in the notes, below. Klotz's most important study, *Livius und seine Vorgänger*, published in Germany during the war and therefore practically unobtainable in this country, has just been reprinted (1964). Many of his conclusions, in his patient and ingenious attempts to trace material in Livy and other authors (especially Dionysius) back to individual annalists, claim more precision than can in fact ever be attained and have not found much acceptance. Gelzer, whose articles on the subject have just been collected in the third volume of his *Kleine Schriften*

(1964), while occasionally guilty of the same error, has opened up an entirely new understanding of these writers and their aims and methods.

There has been no serious and comprehensive study of the historical style (Leeman, *op. cit.*, now provides a beginning). The fragments are few and their nature might seem to discourage it. But the excellent survey of Claudius in Zimmerer's dissertation (cited n. 86, below) shows what can be done. There are brief, but masterly, general comments in W. Kroll, *Glotta* 22 (1934), 1 f, and a useful chapter in Kuntz, *Die Sprache des Tacitus* (1962).

The fragments themselves are collected in H. Peter, *Historicorum Romanorum Reliquiae*, vol. 1^2 (1914), with full discussion (in Latin). They will be cited from this edition. Peter's discussion of the individual authors is always worth consulting, but will not (in general) be referred to here.

With few exceptions, concerning small points, I have not been able to take into account work that became accessible after the early part of 1964. This, unfortunately, includes Ogilvie's *Commentary* (see n. 103), the Introduction to which is the most valuable recent contribution in English on the subject as a whole. I should like to thank Mr Ogilvie for looking at the proofs of this article.

[1] Polybius III, 22 (first treaty with Carthage); Cic. *Balb.* 53. On the pontifical records, see Westrup, *Kgl. Danske Vid. Selsk., Hist.-fil. Medd.* 16, 3 (1929).

[2] It is the large measure of agreement (even though each prominent family had its axe to grind) and the large number of names unknown in the later Republic that call for comment. (See the Index to Broughton, *Magistrates of the Roman Republic* (1951-2).)

[3] For these eulogies see Pol. VI, 53, 4 f.

[4] For conjecture on their contents see Crake, *CP* 35 (1940), 375 f. Cf. Fraccaro, *JRS* 47 (1957), 60 f; Balsdon, *CQ*, N.S. 3 (1953), 162. Cato's ridicule (cf. Sempronius Asellio, frr. 2-2A) must not be understood as completely defining their actual content in his day or earlier. Bömer, *SO* 29 (1952), 34 f, and *Historia* 2 (1953-4), 189 f, tries to reinstate them as a proper official chronicle; but he minimizes the achievement of Fabius in going beyond them (see below).

[5] Cic. *rep.* I, 25, quoting Ennius based on the *Annales.*

[6] Any earlier records were almost certainly lost in the fire of Rome (LIVY VI,1). Gelzer, *Hermes* 69 (1934), 50 f [= *Kleine Schriften* 3 (1964), 98], as corrected by Crake, *loc. cit.* (n. 4). See Westrup, *op. cit.* (n. 1).

[7] Paulus, s.v. 'annales maximi'; Macr. *sat.* III, 2, 17. Since the Romans were perfectly capable of realizing that this was not the *prima facie* meaning of the phrase, there is no reason to doubt this interpretation.

[8] Münzer, *RE*, s.v. 'Fabius', no. 126. Cf. Hanell, 'Zur Problematik der älteren röm. Geschichtsschreibung', *Entretiens* (Fondation Hardt) 4 (1956), 147 f (with useful discussion after); Momigliano, 'Linee per una valutazione di Fabio Pittore', *AAL*, s. 8, 15 (1960), 310 f (the most important recent study).

[9] See Valerius Maximus' comment (VIII, 14, 6): 'sordido studio deditum ingenium'.

[10] Momigliano, *op. cit.* (n. 8). On Timaeus see T. S. Brown, *Timaeus of Tauromenium* (1958). Cf. Walsh, *Livy* (1961), ch. 2.

[11] Cic. *div.* I, 43.

[12] Bömer (*opp. citt.*, n. 4) has rightly reclaimed Fabius as an annalist, against Gelzer (see n. 14 below), who makes him practically a Hellenistic historian. But Bömer closes his eyes to the Hellenistic influences that are implicit in the very choice of language and can be clearly discerned in the treatment. Gelzer restated and revised his opinion in *Hermes* 82 (1954), 342 f [=*Kl. Schr.* 3 (1964), 104 f].

[13] Momigliano, *op. cit.*, emphatically makes this point, refusing to decide.

[14] This view (Niebuhr's) has been persuasively argued by Gelzer, *op. cit.* (n. 6); *Hermes* 68 (1933), 129 f [=*Kl. Schr.* 3 (1964), 51 f]—implying a time after 201.

[15] Rightly Peter, LXXV f; Hanell, *op. cit.* (n. 8), 171 f. The *Annales Maximi* cannot be called literary; and it would take a good deal to persuade us that Appius' speech of 280 B.C., which Cicero read (*Brut.* 55-61) and which had no consequences for nearly a century, was genuine in the form in which Cicero saw it. It took a man of outstanding genius to create Latin prose, twenty years after Fabius started.

[16] Schanz^4-Hosius, *Röm. Literaturgeschichte* (1927), 170 f; Momigliano in Hanell, *op. cit.* (n. 8), 172 f. Bömer (*opp. citt.*) denies this and, rather unreasonably, wishes to exclude the author's considering a Greek audience.

[17] Momigliano, *op. cit.* (n. 8), 317. Cf. fr. 25. Momigliano rightly warns against exaggerated conjecture; but it would be exaggerated caution to confine oneself wholly to the attested fragments, refusing even to follow up their implications.

[18] See my *Foreign Clientelae* (1958), 55 f.

[19] Pol. I, 14. This is quite certain for Fabius (more so than for Philinus): there were no other reputable Roman accounts of the War in existence when Polybius wrote (*c.* 160). Cincius Alimentus, the only other name that could be suggested, was distrusted by Livy, never mentioned by Polybius and read by few others. The odd principle that the main source of a surviving work is never the one mentioned by the author has done a great deal of harm in source investigation.

[20] Pol. I, 10 f. The basic facts must be from Fabius, and they imply the interpretation. The society in which Polybius lived and wrote was not very different from that of Fabius, and Polybius would find him congenial.

[21] See McDonald and Walbank, *JRS* 27 (1937), 180 f.

[22] For this interpretation see Dorey, *Orpheus* 2 (1955), 55 f; Hanell, *op. cit.* (n. 8), 178. But the grossness of Fabius' distortion must not be exaggerated: Polybius' judgment, and what we have of the fragments, would hardly suggest that he was given to it. The vilification, e.g. of C. Varro, can hardly be contemporary: he became an elder statesman in his own day, was given a command in Etruria, sent on important embassies and appointed to head a colonial commission (Broughton, *op. cit.* (n. 2), 1, 296, 313, 325). The bias, once there, would be seized upon and exaggerated by those who cared above all for a dramatic story.

[23] See Gelzer, *Hermes* 68 (1933), 129 f [=*Kl. Schr.* 3 (1964), 51 f]—too positive in many details of attribution, but incontrovertible in its general thesis, despite Bömer's objections (*opp. citt.*, n. 4).

[24] The view that, e.g., Fabius committed the infantile falsification of moving the attack on Saguntum from 219 to 218, in order to gloss over the Senate's inaction, is absurd: it is clear that this was attempted by a later generation, and one that did not care about truth.

[25] The 'army list', reproduced in Polybius II, 24 f, is Fabian (cf. Mommsen, *Röm. Forschungen* 2, 382 f). For *fides*, see the instructive account of the punishment of the mutineers at Rhegium (Pol. I, 7), for *clientela* (a very un-Greek concept, taken from the source and left quite undeveloped by the Greek author), see the account of the outbreak of the Second Illyrian War (Pol. II, 16 f—cf. my comments, *PBSR* 20 (1952), 86 = *Studies in Greek and Roman History* (1964), 15 f).

[26] It was only in the first century B.C. that a freedman dared to write *historia* (Suet. *rhet.* 27)—It should perhaps be mentioned that the *Ineditum Vaticanum* is not to be assigned to Fabius, as its first editor thought. (See Wendling, *Hermes* 28 (1893), 335 f.)

[27] We have some references to Latin annals by a Fabius Pictor (Peter, 112 f), but cannot be certain of their date or their connection with the Greek work. The simplest view is that they are a translation of the latter, done some time in the second century (see Hanell, *op. cit.* (n. 8), 171 f; Momigliano, *op. cit.* (n. 8), 318). It is difficult to assign them to a different author (thus Peter, Münzer, *opp. citt.*), since no source makes any attempt to distinguish.

[28] Münzer and Cichorius, *RE*, s.v. 'Cincius', no. 5.

[29] Klebs, *RE*, s.v. 'Acilius', no. 4; Münzer, *RE*, s.v. 'Postumius', no. 31, rightly warning against accepting Polybius' denigration of a man he disliked at its face value. But what little we know of the work does not suggest outstanding merit.

[30] Livy, *per.* LIII.

[31] To judge by his remarks on Rhegium (fr. 2, with Peter's note: the theory was not original).

[32] Greek annals could be written even much later: the praetorian Aufidius found this activity the comfort of his old age (Cic. *Tusc.* V, 112), and dilettanti attempted it even in the first century. But nobody cared very much.

[33] Gelzer and Helm, *RE*, s.v. 'Porcius', no. 9; particularly coll. 156 f (Helm). On Cato as a man and as a politician, see Kienast, *Cato der Zensor* (1954).

[34] His polemic against the trivialities of the pontifical records (fr. 77) has been misinterpreted to imply that he was not; but Cicero apparently thought that he was. If there were any predecessors, we do not know it: Hemina was a contemporary and probably did not publish before (at any rate) Cato's first book (see below).

[35] Two in Nepos, *Cato* 3. But the first book may have been written separately, much earlier.

[36] Pliny, *n.h.* VIII, 11. (Pliny adds that Cato named a brave elephant.) This practice may be characteristic of early annalists (Bömer, *SO* 29 (1952), 39, n. 4).

[37] See frr. 32; 33; 34 (the famous characterization of the Gauls); 35; 39; 52 (wild mountain goats); 78 (Punic *mapalia*), 93 (the Spanish mines); 61 (Arpinate law); 111-14 (Roman laws and customs); and many others.

[38] See Kienast, *op. cit.* (n. 33), 111 f, 114 f.

[39] Fr. 80; he may have called it *politia.*

[40] Cic. *rep.* II, 2 f—'probably after the *Origines*' (Kienast).

[41] Frr. 6, 50-51 (though either Dionysius or Servius has misunderstood him in detail).

[42] See Kienast, *op. cit.* (n. 33), 101 f.

[43] Cic. *planc.* 66 (often cited later). Cf. Xen. *conv.* 1.

[44] Plutarch, *Cato Maior* 20. The best explanation is that Book I (the early history of Rome—self-contained and most suitable for Cato's purpose) was written first, for this purpose, in the 180s and the rest added later. Book II apparently was written after the outbreak of the war with Perseus, but probably not long after its end (fr. 49).

[45] Cic. *Tusc.* IV, 3 (cf. *Brut.* 75).

[46] See Peter, 93. Varro improved on Cato by bringing in 'pueri modesti' to sing the songs (one wonders how he gained the information); Valerius Maximus has old men as performers, for the benefit of the young—and adds the illuminating reflection that it was better than any sort of Greek education. (Perhaps this point should also be considered in connection with Cato.)

[47] On the 'ballad theory' see Fraccaro, *JRS* 47 (1957), 59 f, and Momigliano, *ibid.*, 104 f, 109 f. Both are sensibly sceptical.

[48] There is no full treatment of Cato's style, in spite of its importance; and this is not the place to attempt it. For some brief remarks, particularly about Greek models, see Skard, *Sallust and seine Vorgänger* (1953), 75 f, and comments in Kroll, *Glotta* 22 (1934), 1 f.

[49] On L. Cassius Hemina (the *praenomen* is given in fr. 25, though Peter, oddly, calls him 'L.' in the Introduction and 'C.' in the text), *uetustissimus auctor annalium* (fr. 37; cf. 26), see Cichorius, *RE*, s.v. 'Cassius', no. 47. His *History* (we know nothing about its form or length) must have been published over a long period, at least some of it before the last part of Cato's. The title of his Book IV (fr. 31: 'Bellum Punicum Posterior') shows that it was written before 149; fr. 39 mentions an event of 146. Pliny cites him four times (three of them on Numa); there is no firm evidence that anyone earlier read him, and though it is likely that some historians did, he clearly had no extensive influence. For some other obscure historians, see Peter, CLXXIV f, 112 f.

[50] Münzer, *RE*, s.v. 'Gellius', no. 4. Two Cn. Gellii appear to be known about the right time: one whom Cato opposed in a private suit (Gell. XIV, 2, 21) and one who was *monetalis* about 134 (Sydenham). If the date given for the latter is correct, they may be father and son. The historian, at any rate, is likely to be identical with the former. The emendation that inserts him in Cic. *leg.* I, 6, is not acceptable.

[51] High book numbers must, in general, be suspect. Münzer, in an important early article (*Hermes* 32 (1897), 469 f), showed the absurdities that arise if we accept all the ones quoted. He suggests that scholiasts, to display vast reading, would cheerfully falsify a number. But Gellius' work is long enough at the best.

[52] Of his style not enough survives to enable us to judge: he seems to be mostly quoted for an affectation of dative/ablative forms in *-abus* (e.g. *puellabus, paucabus*), and for oddities like *regerum* (< *rex?*) and *lapiderum* (< *lapis*).

It is an interesting question, which might well occur at this point, to what extent he and his successors turned to epic (Naevius and Ennius) for some of their subject-matter. Stylistic borrowing, for *poeticus color* in appropriate scenes, is certain. Dependence for subject-matter is likely, particularly for the early 'history', but has not been convincingly traced in any historian. For attempts, see, e.g., Aly, *Livius und Ennius* (1936), with fanciful absurdities (e.g. p. 35); Strzelecki, *RFIC*, s. 3, 91 (1963), 440 f (proving only that there were variant versions of early 'history', up to the founding of Rome, and that some historians follow a version that Naevius can also be shown to have followed).

[53] Earl, *Athenaeum*, N.S. 38 (1960), 291 f. But by the time of C. Gracchus (*pace* Earl) it is clear that he had changed his mind.

[54] The last datable reference is to 146 (fr. 39).

[55] Frr. 24, 27. Latte, 'Der Historiker L. Calpurnius Piso', *SDAW* 1960, 7, concentrates on the Flavius fragment, but reads far too much into it. However, his highly critical remarks on the work in general are not entirely unjust.

[56] Cic. *Br.* 106; cf. *de or.* II, 51 f; *leg.* I, 6.

[57] Latte, *op. cit.* (n. 55). Whether Livy used Piso directly we cannot tell. But it is very likely that he did not.

[58] Peter (CLXXIX) shows that the two extracts come from one biographical work.

[59] One might pick out, in Plutarch, Tiberius' moderation in offering payment for land held illegally (9, 2—a Gracchan source misunderstood); the vicious attacks on Scipio Nasica, with insinuations about his motives (13, 3); Tiberius' speech in his own defence (15); and perhaps some of the projected 'other laws' (16). Since Plutarch did use the pamphlet, the hypothesis is not unsupported. Other authors may also show traces—e.g. Appian's 'pan-Italic source' (it is certain that Gaius, but not Tiberius, was interested in the Italians) and the author of the rhetorical showpiece on Ti. Gracchus' death (*ad Her.* IV, 68 f).

[60] Münzer, *Hermes* 55 (1920), 427 f: the identity can now be regarded as certain.

[61] Fr. 5 (see Peter's note). He also gave Tiberius credit for an early military exploit in which he himself shared (fr. 4).

[62] This strict sense of *historia* (Gell. V, 18) is a later development. Fannius' work was probably called *Annales*. The new approach was just developing.

[63] E.g. fr. 2 (the infinitive *biber!*).

[64] See fr. 9 (on the text, see Bailey, *Towards a Text of Cicero 'Ad Atticum'* (1959), 55 f). For Sallust, see Maurenbrecher's note on *hist.* I, 4. Cf. Sallust's comment on Sisenna (*Jug.* 95, 2).

[65] Gensel, *RE*, s.v. 'Coelius', no. 7. It is still sometimes stated, on the strength of his *cognomen*, that he was of freedman stock; but this is as absurd as to assert the same thing of (e.g.) the Marcii Philippi. Cichorius (*Unters. zu Lucilius* (1908), 5) suggested that the historian might be a brother of the aedilician C. Coelius C. f. who appears on the *SC de agro Pergameno* (129 B.C.). A senior officer called Antipater appears in the next generation (App. *b.c.* I, 91).

[66] Passages collected by Peter, CCXII. Bömer (*Historia* 2 (1953-4), 208, rightly stresses his importance.

[67] See Walbank, *Commentary on Polybius*, 1 (1957), 27 f, 316.

[68] See p. 10 (above) on Maharbal's offer to Hannibal.

[69] Fr. 14 (with Peter's note). Cf. Walbank, *JRS* 46 (1956), 44 (not accepting it himself); Walsh, *Livy*, 155.

[70] See Broughton, *op. cit.* (n. 2) 1, 243 and 245, n. 2.

[71] Fr. 11. (Cf. Livy XXI, 22, 5 f, with splendidly mysterious atmosphere and polite disbelief.)

[72] Fr. 20 (Flaminius before Trasimene—perhaps from Fabius: Q. Fabius Maximus thought this Flaminius' chief fault: Livy XXII, 9, 7). The story is similar to that of P. Claudius Pulcher and the sacred chickens and Coelius may have made up the details from this model. Cf. also frr. 28, 34.

[73] Fr. 39. Livy (a shrewd critic when he cared) noticed the difference between positive misstatement and rhetoric.

[74] Frr. 35 (Tarentum), 52 (Capua).

[75] Fr. 1. For a notorious example, see fr. 24B.

[76] *Ibid.* (hexameter), frr. 5 (trochaic tetrameter), 23 (init.: four cretics). Livy, *praef.* 1, and Tac. *ann.* I, 1, show that this affectation acquired a conventional place. For prose cadences that Cicero ought to have approved or tolerated, see frr. 2, 8, 12, 24, 25, 36, 44 (first colon), 45 (both cola), 47 (first colon)—a yield well above random figures. For carefully sustained prose rhythm, see frr. 44, 57. Kroll, *op. cit.* (n. 48), 11, oddly cites fr. 44 as 'schwerfällig'; but the changes of subject and tense are conscious art, not primitive inexperience.

[77] E.g. deponents in a passive sense or with active forms (frr. 45, 62); passive participle used actively (fr. 32); odd features of accidence (frr. 2, 3 (cf. 4), 37) and construction (frr. 7, 12); solemn and unusual words or unusual uses of common words (frr. 5 (*bellosus*)—cf. 36 (*morbosus*); 9; 16; 25 (*diequinti*—from Cato); 30 (*dubitatim*)—cf. 57 (*pedetemtim*); 43 (*paucies*); 44 (*congenuclat*); 47). In this Coelius was to be followed as he had followed others. Scaurus uses *poteratur,* no doubt deliberately (fr. 4), Claudius *pedetemtim* (fr. 92); Sisenna was to multiply such words.

[78] It is not quite clear what Fronto meant (*ad Ver.* I, 1, 2) by contrasting his *singula uerba* with Cato's *multiiuga uerba*. On *multiiugus*, see Gell. XI, 16, 4: it ought to mean compound words, as used by (e.g.) Ennius. But Cato does not seem to affect them.

[79] Klotz, *RE*, s.v. 'Sempronius', no. 16; Till, *WJA* 4 (1949-50), 330 f. He may well be one of the numerous Sempronii recorded (without *cognomen*) in magistracies.

[80] Cic. *leg.* I, 6. On whether 'Clodius' can be Claudius Quadrigarius, see p. 20 (above). That Sempronius did follow in the stylistic tradition of the *genre* is clear from the few fragments (frr. 10, 13, 14: words in *-osus, -ose* and *-im*).

[81] Broughton, *op. cit.* (n. 2), 1, 491 f.

[82] He also stressed his didactic purpose (frr. 1-2A). He probably had the *Annales Maximi* in mind, but also (no doubt) men like Gellius, who followed them. This (so far as we know) is the first time that rationalism appears in

Roman historiography, with its priestly associations. But we cannot be sure about Fannius. The text of fr. 2 is corrupt (see Till, *op. cit.* (n. 79), for discussion) and the sense is not as clear as we might wish.

[83] An isolated citation from Book XL is not to be believed (cf. n. 51, above).

[84] He seems to have gone beyond literary sources (fr. 8, from a *laudatio*).

[85] On Vennonius, see Gundel, *RE*, s.v., no. 1. Peter has him out of order. A single citation in *or. gent. Rom.* 20, 1.

[86] See Zimmerer, *Der Annalist Qu.* [sic] *Claudius Quadrigarius* (1937).

[87] Zimmerer, *op. cit.* 73 f.

[88] Livy once refers to a translation and once says that Claudius 'followed' Acilius (frr. 57A, 64A). I have given what seems to me the most likely solution, particularly in view of the brief treatment of the earliest period in Claudius' own work. The matter, of course, is highly uncertain.

[89] Fr. 76 (a Metellus returns to his house after a speech) is assigned by Peter to 99 B.C. (Metellus Numidicus' return from exile). But as it comes from Book XIII, this is impossible. Claudius could not have filled up four books with events between 99 and the Social War (Grumentum is in XVIII)—a period to which Livy allots two. The reference may be to the trial of the same Metellus, at which the jurors refused to look at his account-books (Cic. *Balb.* 11 *et al.*), perhaps 107 B.C. See the famous incident from the trials of the Scipios (Gell. IV, 18, 3 f), on which Claudius apparently modelled his story.

[90] E.g. 32,000 enemy dead at Cynoscephalae (fr. 62—Polybius gives 8,000); 34,200 pounds of silver per year imposed on Philip in 196, plus 2,000 to be paid immediately (fr. 63—Valerius has 4,000 per year for ten years); 40,000 Gauls killed in two battles by Manlius in Galatia (fr. 66—Valerius has one battle and 10,000 dead, and Livy rightly doubts even this figure).

[91] See (most conveniently) Walsh, *Livy*, 133 f. This tendency begins with Fabius, but is greatly exaggerated by the late annalists.

[92] Walsh, *Livy*, 151 f.

[93] M. I. Henderson (*JRS* 47 (1957), 83 f) makes Claudius an expounder of *popularis* theory, misinterpreting his Fabius fragment (fr. 57). The point of the story (quite possibly taken from Fabius Pictor) is simply that the *imperium*, which goes with public office, ought to be superior even to *pietas* towards a father. That the proconsul is inferior to the consul is taken for granted and was almost certainly true: the lictors hesitate 'quod pater erat'. Mrs Henderson also includes Sisenna among those spreading *popularis* propaganda and claims that no one will dispute this.

[94] It is very usefully analysed by Zimmerer, *op. cit.* (n. 86), 88 f. Fronto said that he wrote *lepide* and Gellius is profuse in admiration.

[95] Frr. 2, 23, 76. *Mortales* and words in *-tudo* are characteristic of elevated historical style. On the historical vocabulary (especially new coinages), see Kroll, *op. cit.* (n. 48), 5 f.

[96] Frr. 7, 12 (*immaniter*), 37, 41 (*inimiciter*), 48, 50, 88, 92, 93. Even Livy was to produce *perniciebilis* (xxvii, 23, 6—surely the correct form for MSS *perniciabilis*, unless Livy was being too Patavine).

[97] Gellius cites *copiari* (fr. 24) as technical, *arboretum* (fr. 29) as *ignobilius*. Note fr. 77 'grundibat grauiter pecus suillum'.

[98] The alternatives show both deliberation and lack of skill (cf. Gellius' comment, fr. 30). See Zimmerer, *loc. cit.* (n. 94). Note striking phrases like 'grandia ingrediens' (fr. 12).

[99] Cf. fr. 81 (second half). There is much of this in the two single combats. On the style of these two episodes, see the analysis by McDonald, *JRS* 47 (1957), 158, 167.

[100] For occasional poetic rhythm, see n. 97 (above). For word order, note fr. 85 (ending 'defendebant facillime funditore'); fr. 81 ('ut Archelai turrim unam quam ille interposuit ligneam incenderet'); fr. 58 ('quin castra relinquerent atque cederent hosti'). In each case, cadence seems to be a consideration.

[101] Cic. *leg.* I, 6 (see p. 16, above).

[102] As for their time: Velleius appears to mention them as *aequales* of Sisenna, together with P. Rutilius Rufus (II, 9, 6). Since Rutilius was a consular candidate in 116 and Sisenna praetor in 78, the statement clearly cannot be pressed. But a publication date after 52 for both Claudius and Valerius, though it cannot be wholly rejected, is perhaps rather unlikely. On the mysterious 'Clodius', see Peter, CCXXXVIII f and 178. He was perhaps a senator.

[103] See Volkmann, *RE*, s.v. 'Valerius', no. 98. He may have come from Antium (the name makes it possible, but not necessary): the importance of that city as the chief Volscian power is stressed (overstressed, one might feel) in the early books of Livy. Ogilvie, *A Commentary on Livy Books* 1-5 (1965), 14 f, shows his interest in municipal men.

[104] One can understand the irritation of that *candidissimus* of men from a passage like XXVI, 49, where Silenus (i.e. probably Coelius, careful—as usual—about facts and figures) mentioned the loss of 60 *scorpiones* by the Carthaginians. Valerius raised the figure to 6,000 large and 13,000 small ones: 'adeo nullus mentiendi modus est.' But on occasion he was surpassed by Claudius (see n. 90, above). For the additional charge of credulity, see XXXIX, 43, 1. Sometimes, indeed, Livy, who did not read many sources, is unjust: thus the statement attacked XL, 29, 8 (fr. 9) as a plausible lie by Valerius apparently comes from Cassius Hemina (fr. 37) *via* Piso (fr. 11).

[105] See Gelzer, *Hermes* 70 (1935), 271 f [=*Kl. Schr.* 3 (1964), 222 f]; *Gnomon* 18 (1942), 223 [=*Kl. Schr.* 3 (1964), 272 f]; Ogilvie, *op. cit.* (n. 103, above), 14.

[106] Pol. XII, 5 f; cf. III, 33, 17 f.

[107] Cato set out six such breaches down to 219 (fr. 84). Polybius (III, 21, 9 f) only knew six treaties altogether, including two early ones which Cato may not have known; and some of them the Carthaginians would certainly not be described as having broken.

[108] See Fraccaro, *Opuscula* 1 (1956), 410 f, citing Cic. *Brut.* 42 for the kind of theory that Antias and his like followed: not negligence, but deliberate invention. Cf. *ibid.*, 263-415, ending with the (ironical) hope that the instance is not typical of Valerius. On the 'archival material', see Gelzer's arguments against Klotz, who accepts most of it (*Gnomon*, *cit.* n. 105, above). Since some of it is certainly forged, all of it must be suspect. See, e.g., the Senate's decree ordering the destruction of the 'books of Numa' (fr. 15): the story had been told before, but Valerius is the first to quote the 'document'!

[109] See Fraccaro, *op. cit.* (last note).

[110] On the prefect L. Valerius Antias, see Volkmann, *RE*, s.v. 'Valerius', no. 99. No other Valerius Antias (except for the annalist) is known; and the 'prefect', once smuggled in, is quietly dropped before the end of the story. (See Broughton, *op. cit.* (n. 2), 1, 258, n. 9.) On the whole incident, involving a trio of Valerii, see Petzold's comment (*Die Eröffnung des 2. röm.—maked. Krieges* (1940), 50, n. 16): he thinks it cannot be meant seriously; yet scholars like Münzer and Volkmann have been taken in. Petzold's book (very hard to obtain) is a useful study of late annalistic method.

[111] Arnobius: fr. 6 (as can be seen, closely following the text). Verb forms: frr. 57, 60, 62 (*descendidit*!). One or two other archaisms are quoted, including the neuter *prior* (fr. 16), which also appears in Claudius (frr. 73-4). Perhaps bearable in Cassius Hemina's day (fr. 31), it must surely have been quite intolerable by the time of Cicero.

[112] See Münzer, *RE*, s.v. 'Licinius', no. 112, Ogilvie, *op. cit.* (n. 103), 7 f—he had no personal grievance since he must have been quaestor in 78 or 77, and his *cursus* is normal.

[113] On Tubero's use of the *libri lintei*, see p. 22, above.

[114] On the *libri lintei*, see Ogilvie, *JRS* 48 (1958), 40 f, suggesting a second-century compilation. Yet several difficulties remain: for what purpose could they have been compiled and by whom, since nobody found them? And why, in an age full of historical activity, *did* nobody find them?

[115] Dionysius three times cites Gellius together with Macer and three times alone; but it is possible that he—like most historians—did not read Gellius, but knew him only from citation in Macer. The use of Gellius by Macer must be significant, in any case.

[116] That Pyrrhus was treated in Book II is utterly incredible, in view of what we can safely conjecture about Macer's work. We cannot tell what the figure ought to be.

[117] On Macer's attitude and interests, see Ogilvie, *op. cit.* (n. 103), 8 f, probably overstressing his inventive activity, but right on his interpretation. Nothing is known about his style.

[118] Cf. fr. 6. On Tubero, see Peter, CCCLXVI f (opting for Quintus). Thus also Ogilvie, *op. cit.*, 16; cf. 571 (on Livy IV, 23, 1).

[119] Cic. *Q. fr.* I, 1, 10. Thus most recent scholars. On Suetonius' mention of Quintus, see next note. Peter is probably right in rejecting the possibility that both wrote annals: Dionysius, who was attached to the family, would have distinguished them.

[120] Suetonius cites biographical details about Caesar from a Q. Tubero (frr. 10A, 11): perhaps he wrote a biography of Caesar. In fr. 6, 'atque' should probably be read.

[121] On his life and career, see G. Bloch, *M. Aemilius Scaurus* (1909). On him and the next few men, historical as well as literary works should be consulted, e.g. Scullard, *From the Gracchi to Nero*[2] (1963), with further bibliography. Some of them are discussed in *Historia* 6 (1957), 318 f [now in my *Studies* (n. 25, above), 34 f]. On Scaurus, Cicero makes the famous remark: 'cuius . . . nutu prope terrarum orbis regebatur' (*Font.* 24).

[122] He paid the highest price recorded down to Pliny's day for a literary

slave (*n. h.* VII, 123); this was Daphnis (Suet. *rhet.* 6), who later passed to Q. Catulus and was freed by him. It may be assumed that Daphnis helped Scaurus with his literary work.

[123] Cic. *Brut.* 112. It was dedicated to a L. Fufidius, whom Cicero mentions (*Brut.* 113).

[124] The very few fragments show *-ere* for *-erunt*, the passive of *possum* (cf. Coelius, fr. 7; Claudius, frr. 33, 47), and adverbs in *-im*—clearly a deliberate claim to be writing history.

[125] Val. Max. III, 2, 18; V, 8, 4; Asconius 22 Cl. Valerius' source had read Scaurus (fr. 1), and the scholar Asconius may be presumed to have done so.

[126] It contains two of these anecdotes and alludes to the third. If the Varius story was in Scaurus' work (as is likely: it is not found in Cicero, the only probable alternative), the last book was published just before or even after Scaurus' death.

[127] See Münzer, *RE*, s.v. 'Rutilius', no. 34. Cf. (with caution) Hendrickson, *CP* 28 (1933), 153 f.

[128] On Rutilius and the circle of the Metelli see *Historia* (*cit.* n. 121).

[129] Oros. V, 17, 13, tells us that he lived at Smyrna.

[130] The explanation of *nundinae* (really of *trinundinum*) in fr. 1 clearly belongs to a political issue, perhaps the *lex Caecilia Didia* of 98.

[131] Theophanes of Mitylene tried to repay him posthumously for this hostility towards his patron's family; but nobody believed his blatant lie (fr. 5).

[132] The characterization of his temperament is Cicero's (*Brut.* 113).

[133] Apicius: Posidonius *ap.* Athen. IV, 66, 168d-e: probably from Rutilius. Marius and Flaccus: Plut. Marius 28 (=fr. 4).

[134] Syme, *Sallust* (1964), 201 f, 212.

[135] Q. Lutatius Catulus, a man devoted to literature, celebrated his achievements against the Germans, which were being overshadowed by those of Marius; but no one read the book a generation later. L. Lucullus in his youth wrote a history of the Social War in Greek as the result of a wager; it attained some fame—so much so that Sulla (fr. 1) apparently thought Lucullus would become a historian. A corresponding epic in Latin (by Q. Hortensius—Vell. II, 16, 3) was also produced. On these works and Sisenna's, see *Athenæum* 1964, 429 f. Catulus' book on his exploits may have been used by Sulla; if so, it has entered our tradition *via* Plutarch in the anti-Marian version. But Sulla fought in the war himself and clearly wrote his own account, critical of Catulus (see Plut. *Sulla* 3).

[136] For an attempt to trace their influence, especially on Livy's account of the eighties, see *JRS* 52 (1962), 48 f [=my *Studies* (n. 25 above), 208 f].

[137] See Peter, CCLXX f.

[138] Gellius I, 12, 16; an invariable future infinitive in *-urum* is the only oddity quoted (fr. 20).

[139] Peter, CCCXXXIV f; cf. my works cited in nn. 135 and 136.

[140] He seems to have included some early legends, but perhaps not all in Book I (thus Peter): they would make good subject-matter for digressions, such as this kind of history demanded. Book I already mentioned Aesernia (fr. 6): there could not be much early history. The number of books is unknown: XXIII is quoted, but seems too high.

[141] *Jug.* 95, 2.

[142] See *opp. citt.* (nn. 135-136, above).

[143] Cic. *Brut.* 259 f ('quasi emendator sermonis usitati'—no doubt chiefly referring to his analogism).

[144] Frr. 141, 143. With the latter Sallust, himself not an analogist, disagreed (*Jug.* 1, 1, init.)—emphatically and perhaps not unintentionally: such things were known and taken seriously among educated men.

[145] Frr. 49, 98 (cf. Cato, frr. 63, 83; Asellio, fr. 5). Sisenna may have coined *crebritudo.*

[146] E.g. frr. 10, 17, 119 (*senati*: perhaps to be read in fr. 136); 48, 128, 142; 42, 135.

[147] See especially fr. 104 (the beginning of a storm at sea): 'Subito mare persubhorrescere caecosque fluctus in se prouoluere leniter occepit.' For simpler poetic colouring, see fr. 130 ('caelum caligine stat').

[148] Fr. 127: he will not write *uellicatim aut saltuatim.* But this, of course, does not mean rejection of annalistic method *in toto.*

[149] Fr. 123. Perhaps Tacitus was thinking of this when he wrote *ann.* VI, 22, 2: Tacitus knew Sisenna's work (cf. *hist.* III, 51).

[150] See n. 140, above.

[151] See *op. cit.* (n. 136).

[152] See Cic. *Brut.* 262—hardly entirely disingenuous.

[153] These works are discussed in Peter's second volume (1906).

[154] Cic. *leg.* I, 6.

II
Polybius

F. W. WALBANK

THE Romans produced no historians until the third century B.C. Earlier, like most peoples, they had of course some sort of written records of their own past—a chronicle kept by the priests, the traditions of religious associations and aristocratic families, including funeral orations pronounced over famous men, some official lists such as the details of the census and the holders of magistracies, together with public documents like calendars, laws and the texts of treaties.[1] But for the writing of history, as the Greeks had known it from the time of Hecataeus and Herodotus in the fifth century, Rome had to wait until the time of the Punic Wars. The long struggle between Rome and Carthage was watched with interest and apprehension by the whole Greek world, and it was largely a desire to present the Roman case in the most favourable light that led to the appearance of Roman histories from the pens of Q. Fabius Pictor and L. Cincius Alimentus, whose main purpose, as senators, was to familiarize Greek readers with the Roman past and with the sound principles underlying the Roman state and its policies. These men and their second century successors, C. Acilius and A. Postumius Albinus, wrote in Greek; and although their works contained such jejune and parochial items as the details of the corn supply, the filling of magistracies and the expiation of prodigies, topics which interested the Roman nobility,[2] their primary purpose was to further Roman policy in the Greek world.[3]

How far they were successful is not easy to ascertain. Undoubtedly Rome had been a subject of interest to the Greeks at least since the defeat of Pyrrhus of Epirus in 275 and the extension of Roman power to include the Greek cities of southern Italy. But it was perhaps not always easy to take very seriously writers like Postumius Albinus, who admitted to writing indifferent Greek[4]; and it was probably to Greek authors such as Hieronymus of Cardia[5] and especially Timaeus of Tauromenium[6] that the Greeks turned for their knowledge of the new power in the west. But these authors touched on Rome only incidentally, and with the rapid spread of Roman influence into Illyria, then Greece and finally Asia Minor, and the successive defeats of Philip V and Perseus of Macedonia and of Antiochus III of Syria, it became important to the peoples and especially the statesmen of Greece to acquire a proper understanding of the power which now dominated the Hellenistic world. It is in this context that we have to consider the work of Polybius, the historian of Rome's rise to world dominion. He was a Greek statesman who knew his own countrymen well and who, by force of circumstances, came to know the Romans too. Fabius had written a reputable history, but one perhaps too obviously designed to eulogize the Roman cause—'like a man in love,' Polybius remarks,[7] 'he will have it that the Romans are always wise and brave'. Polybius too is a supporter of the Roman cause, but from a more objective position, as indeed the details of his life would lead one to expect.

I

We know a good deal about this, much of it from his own pen, for he is not like Thucydides a reticent and impersonal writer. He was born towards the end of the third century at Megalopolis in Arcadia of a distinguished family.[8] Lycortas, his father, was a leading statesman of the Achaean Confederation, which covered a large part of the Peloponnese, and Polybius looked like following in his footsteps. From an early age he showed a keen interest in politics and warfare; he was the author of a textbook on *Tactics*[9] and the inventor of an improved system of fire-signalling[10] and his passion for this kind of thing comes out in many digressions in the *Histories*. Like any upper-class Greek boy of the time he had the usual education in literature with a smattering of philosophy, and his work contains literary reminiscences and, especially in his account of the Roman constitution (see below, pp. 55-56), he shows a knowledge of what we should call political philosophy; indeed he twice uses the word 'unphilosophical' as a form of insult.[11] Nevertheless, it is not unfair to suggest that his acquaintance with both philosophy and literature was rather superficial and largely at second hand.

In 182 Philopoemen, the greatest man in Achaea, met his death as a prisoner of war in the hands of the Messenians, and Lycortas' son was chosen to carry his ashes at the funeral.[12] This incident may have inspired him to write his life of the hero in three books.[13] This has not survived, though Plutarch used it as a source for his own *Life of Philopoemen*. Gradually Polybius' importance grew. In 170/69, when the Romans were involved in the Third Macedonian War, he held the post of Cavalry Commander, the second most important office in Achaea, and in this role he was obliged to conduct some delicate negotiations with the Roman authorities, who were proving both irritable and hypersensitive. The more extreme pro-Roman parties in the Greek states had their ear, and after Perseus' defeat at Pydna the Achaean Callicrates furnished them with a list of 1,000 leading Achaeans, whose loyalty towards Rome might be called in question. These men, who included Polybius, were forthwith deported to Italy, and once there they were detained without a hearing and without redress. The majority were relegated to detention in the country towns of Italy, where many died as the years went by.[14] But Polybius was fortunate. A stroke of luck won him the friendship of P. Scipio Aemilianus, the son of L. Aemilius Paullus, the victor in the battle of Pydna, and through his influence Polybius was allowed to stay in the capital and later, apparently, to accompany the young Roman outside Italy. In his *Histories* Polybius tells us[15] of journeys which he made in pursuit of his studies through Africa, Spain, Gaul and in the ocean beyond. The visit to Spain will belong to 151/0, when he accompanied Scipio on a military mission, which took him on to North Africa to meet the king of Numidia, the aged Masinissa[16]; and it was probably on the same occasion that Polybius crossed the Alps in Hannibal's footsteps 'to learn for myself and see'.[17]

Meanwhile friends of the exiles continued to agitate for their return, and in 150 on the eve of the third Roman war with Carthage these efforts bore fruit, when the influential Cato at last somewhat ungraciously withdrew his opposition.[18] The Greeks now went home; but since Scipio was put in command of the Roman army, Polybius on his invitation very soon returned from

Achaea to join him and perhaps advise on siege problems. It will have been in 146, immediately after the fall of Carthage, which he witnessed in Scipio's company,[19] that Polybius made his much-vaunted voyage on the outer ocean, sailing some way down the African coast, and then northward up that of Portugal. Perhaps he was glad not to be in Achaea at that moment, for thanks to the intransigent policy of a new generation of radical politicians, whom he thoroughly detested, Achaea was at war with Rome. Polybius would certainly have been embarrassed to watch Corinth being sacked by the Roman legions. But once the war was over, he devoted himself to mitigating the harshness of the settlement and appeasing the anger of the victors. His services were recognized throughout Achaea.[20] Statues were erected in his honour at Megalopolis, Tegea, Pallantium, Cleitor, Mantinea and Lycosura. The inscription on the last of these is typical; it asserted, says Pausanias,[21] that 'Greece would never have foundered, had she obeyed Polybius in all things, and having come to grief, she found succour in him alone'. That at Megalopolis recorded that[22], 'he had roamed over all the earth and sea, had been the ally of the Romans, and had quenched their wrath against Greece'; and from Cleitor we possess a *stele* which represents him dressed as a soldier, with his right arm raised in a gesture of prayer, and idealized as a hero of Arcadia.[23]

Of his later years we know less. He visited Alexandria and Sardes,[24] but the dates are uncertain; indeed the visit to Sardes may belong to his youth. His friendship with Scipio was maintained and he may, like the poet Lucilius,[25] have formed a member of his staff in 133, when he commanded the Roman army besieging Numantia in Spain—though the fact that Polybius wrote a monograph on the Numantine war[26] is not in itself evidence of this. He certainly outlived Scipio, who died in 129; and a reference in the *Histories* to the Via Domitia in southern Gaul[27] suggests that he lived at least until the laying down of that road in 118. According to one source[28] he died at the age of eighty-two after a fall from his horse—a fitting end for a man who, like his friend Scipio, had enjoyed riding and hunting from his early youth.[29]

II

Such briefly was Polybius' life and background; and his *Histories* grew directly out of his personal experience. Like Thucydides he is a man dedicated to a purpose. Confronted with a situation which he believed to be without parallel in history—the rise of a single power to become mistress of virtually the whole civilized world in the space of fifty-three years—and placed in a position of exceptional advantage for understanding it, he considered it to be his duty to enlighten his fellow-Greeks (and anyone else who cared to read his book) on the significance of those fateful events. When he first envisaged becoming a historian we do not know. It has been argued[30] that he had already drafted a history of Achaea before 168, while he was still active in politics, and that this has been incorporated, with modifications, in the larger *Histories*. This is not impossible. But in the form in which we have it, his major work was certainly the fruit of his enforced leisure in Rome.

Pondering on what had happened, he resolved to recount the history of the fifty-three years which separated Hannibal's attack on Saguntum in 220 from the battle of Pydna in 168. These years, in which the rise of Rome had as its counterpart the fall of the power of Macedonia, reminded him[31] of a prophecy made by the Athenian philosopher and ruler, Demetrius of Phalerum, who at the time of Alexander's overthrow of the Persian Empire had observed that only fifty years earlier its downfall would have seemed inconceivable, and had foretold a similar fate for the Macedonians in their turn—an almost godlike example of pre-vision, Polybius thinks, and an outstanding proof of the power exercised by Fortune (*Tyche*) over human affairs. How far the work had gone by 150, when Polybius returned home from his internment, is uncertain; but in all probability he had written down to book XVI,[32] which reaches the end of the Hannibalic War, and had published at least the first six books. However, the events culminating in the destruction of Carthage and Corinth in 146, and the prominent part played by Polybius himself in those immediately afterwards, persuaded him to extend his original scheme. In the opening chapters of book III[33] we can read the introduction to a revised edition, which envisages carrying on the *Histories* from 168, the year of Pydna, to 146 and its aftermath. The ostensible purpose of this addition is to allow readers to pass judgment on the Romans' achievement by considering the manner in which they exercised their world-wide dominion, 'for', Polybius adds,[34] 'contemporaries will thus be able to see clearly whether Roman rule is acceptable or the reverse, and future generations whether this government should be considered worthy of praise and admiration or rather of blame'.

This remark is interesting for its implications, which are clearly that an ethical criterion is relevant to our judgment of an imperial power. Polybius nowhere specifically enunciates this principle; but his attitude, which forms so remarkable a contrast to the criterion of self-interest recognized by Thucydides, plainly foreshadows the idea later formulated by Scipio's other Greek friend, the Stoic philosopher Panaetius, and adopted in due course by the Romans themselves, that the true justification of Roman world dominion could only be one which took into account the good of both the rulers and the ruled.[35]

After 146, then, Polybius went on working at his *Histories*, and in the end they occupied forty books, of which the last (now lost) was an index. An 'obituary' incorporated in the penultimate book[36] suggests that the complete work was published posthumously, perhaps to include the revised version of books I to VI. Unfortunately only fragments now survive—books I to V complete, and enough of the rest to make up about a fifth of the original, and to give the reader a clear picture of the general plan, purpose and character of the whole work. It is loosely constructed, and in its length reminds us rather of Ephorus' twenty-nine books than of the unfinished eight of Thucydides. There is thus plenty of room for digressions, which were not only a traditional feature in Greek historical writing, but also suited Polybius' own purpose. For in addition to his concern with his subject and the need to enlighten his fellow-countrymen about the Romans, he also held strong views about the character of history-writing, which did not coincide with those generally popular at that time.

III

One of the striking features of Polybius' work is the large number of digressions in which he indulges in polemic against his predecessors. The reasons behind this are mixed. Sometimes Achaean or Arcadian patriotism comes into the picture. His outspoken attack on Theopompus,[37] for instance, for his severe criticism of Philip II of Macedonia is connected with Philip's services to

Arcadia; at the same time he censures Theopompus for abandoning his *History of Greece* in order to write a work centred around Philip, since this led him to omit the very years in which Epaminondas had founded Megalopolis and set up the Arcadian League.[38] Criticism of Phylarchus[39] cannot be divorced from that historian's partiality for Cleomenes of Sparta, the enemy of Achaea and of its hero Aratus, especially since the passages in Phylarchus on which Polybius comments concern events in which he himself was emotionally involved—the execution of Aristomenes of Argos, a renegade from Achaea,[40] the Achaean punishment of Mantinea,[41] and the courageous behaviour of the Megalopolitans when Cleomenes captured their city.[42] The Roman historian Postumius Albinus, whom Cicero praises as a good scholar,[43] is held up to contempt in Polybius' pages as loquacious and boastful,[44] no doubt because in his public capacity, as praetor in 155,[45] he had been responsible for having the proposal that the Achaean exiles should be allowed to return to Greece rejected. These examples, which could be multiplied,[46] reveal a human side to Polybius' character, and not perhaps a very attractive one; but they should not be allowed to obscure the fact that in much of his polemic against earlier writers he is concerned with something more important—the purpose and proper form of historical writing.

Especially since the fourth century Greek historians had come to concentrate on emotional writing, and the vivid presentation of sensational material in a way which would arouse the excitement and sympathy of the reader. Ephorus and Theopompus, brought up in the school of the rhetorician Isocrates, are criticized by the third-century historian Duris of Samos[47] for failing to give their material a vivid turn, and for concentrating on the mere formal aspects of composition to the detriment of the reader's enjoyment. Duris himself, along with the historian Phylarchus, is one of the most outstanding examples of this emotional manner of writing history, which Polybius criticized as being 'tragic'. Duris does not directly cross Polybius' path; but, as we have seen, Phylarchus, who recounted the rise and fall of Cleomenes III of Sparta from a Spartan point of view, is a direct object of his polemic. 'Being eager to stir the hearts of his readers to pity,' he writes,[48] 'and to enlist their sympathies by his story, he talks of women clinging to altars, tearing their hair, and exposing their breasts; and again of the tears and lamentations of men and women led off into captivity with their children and aged parents.' But Duris and Phylarchus were not alone in this fault. The association of history and tragedy was of long standing, and hard to break—for a number of reasons. Both tragedy and the history of the early days of Greece drew their subject-matter from the epics; for both Homer and the other epic poets were universally regarded as writing about real people. It never occurred to either Thucydides or Aeschylus to doubt that Agamemnon was the name of a real king, who had lived and reigned in Mycenae and had led the Greek host to Troy. In addition to this, history and tragedy both pursued a similar moral purpose; both were widely believed to offer consolation to those in trouble and to deter men from moral delinquency by displaying the fruits of evil doing. And finally there was a similarity in the effect which they created in their audience. The Greeks were especially sensitive to the spoken word—and history was normally read aloud—with the result that an outstanding rhapsode, or declaimer, like Ion in Plato's dialogue of that name,[49] could arouse the emotions of his audience in a manner little different from that of the tragic actor. That historical narrative did indeed create such an effect in readers or listeners is confirmed by the comments of Greek critics on the emotions aroused by such historians as Thucydides or Xenophon, whose work we nowadays regard as relatively restrained.[50] These various factors combined to encourage the Hellenistic historians to write in a manner which put vividness before truth and pleasure before utility, and it is against this trend that Polybius sets out to deliver a violent protest. He wrote at a time when history had come to mean largely the serving up of those wonder-stories which went back originally to the Ionian historians (including Herodotus), and for which there was a growing taste since the publication of the writings of the historians of Alexander's expedition into Asia, and of those of such authors as Pytheas of Marseilles, who circumnavigated Britain in about 300, and described his voyage in a way which aroused Polybius' unjustified distrust; while events nearer home were transformed in the melodramatic fashion of Phylarchus, so as to stress suffering, romantic incidents and harrowing reversals of fortune.

Consciously reacting against all this, Polybius reasserts the concept of history as a training-school for politicians and as a form of instruction for the ordinary man on how to bear those blows of Fortune, which can be seen illustrated in his pages as they befell others in the past. This is the programme which he sets out at the very beginning of his work,[51] and examples are easy to find. Thus in book III, at the end of a long interlude on the Gallic invasions of Italy,[52] he expresses the hope that it will help Greek statesmen to cope with similar attacks.[53] In book III his discussion of the difference between causes, pretexts and beginnings, in the analysis of such occasions as the outbreak of a war, is intended for the edification of statesmen, 'for,' he asks, 'what is the good of a statesman who cannot reckon how, why and from what source each event has originated?'[54] Similarly, the fate that befell Regulus in Africa during the First Punic War and the success of his opponent Xanthippus, a Spartan mercenary captain, illustrate the unexpected element in history and the victories that can come from sheer determination; these matters are treated at length 'in the hope of benefiting my readers'.[55] Statesmen too can correct their own conduct by studying the changes that occurred in the character of Philip V of Macedonia[56]; and statesmen will also profit from the detailed account of the Roman constitution.[57]

This utilitarian concept of history was not Polybius' invention. It was, on the contrary, well established alongside the notion of history as an entertainment, and is to be found particularly in the fourth-century historian Ephorus of Cyme, who asserted that it was the historian's duty to provide useful examples or patterns of behaviour.[58] Indeed, the contrast between the pleasurable and the useful seems to have been one of the regular antitheses stressed in the rhetorical schools, and their influence can be detected in the excessive emphasis on it in Polybius's more didactic passages.[59] He does not exclude pleasure from among his aims, for he has the wisdom to appreciate that the pill must occasionally be sugared; but the scales come down very decisively on the side of utility. This is a point he never tires of making, whether the subject under discussion is important or trivial. At one moment he is urging the value of geography,[60] at another the lessons implicit in biography—provided it is of the right kind, not mere panegyric[61] —and at another such a down-to-earth topic as the proper use of fire-signalling (introduced not without a glance at the fact that, as we saw above, Polybius had made his own personal contribution to this technique). Provided there is a lesson to be learnt, all is grist to his mill. But above all he underlines the general importance of history, a subject to which he returns again and again.[62]

Not all branches of history are equally profitable. There are several, he tells us, and they cater for various tastes.[63] There is that dealing with 'genealogies and myths'; he is thinking here of such writers as Hecataeus, Acusilaus and Hellanicus, whose histories involved a working over of epic material and the reduction of it to some kind of chronological scheme.[64] These contain much that is fabulous and false, and they appeal, Polybius says with a slight sneer, to the casual reader who likes a good yarn.[65] Then there are the works dealing with the foundations of cities, colonization and ties of kindred—topics which partly overlap the genealogical works, but also find a place in local and general histories, such as those of Ephorus and Timaeus.[66] These suit the man with antiquarian interests.[67] But the only history for the statesman is that which deals with 'the affairs of peoples, cities and rulers', in short political and military history, or to use Polybius' own term, 'pragmatical history'.[68] History of this kind is austere and factual, though indeed it may include anything that will help the statesman; as we saw, Polybius had no scruples about incorporating a digression on signalling, and he allows himself a good deal of latitude in book VI, with its theory of political evolution, its comparison between the constitutions of Rome, Carthage and other states, and its description of the Roman army and Roman camp, in book XII, which is devoted almost entirely to a critique of his predecessor Timaeus, with some polemic against Callisthenes and others thrown in for good measure, and in book XXXIV which consisted of a treatise on the lands of the western Mediterranean, in particular Spain, Gaul and Africa.[69] The important thing is to avoid exaggeration and sensationalism, and this is easier if one's canvas is wide. It is the authors of historical monographs who, in Polybius' opinion, are liable to indulge this vice—for example the historians who describe the reign of Hieronymus of Syracuse.[70] Their subject-matter is meagre and restricted, and in order to impress the reader they have recourse to inflated and rhetorical descriptions of places and accounts of sieges, whereas the writer of a universal history has no need of this kind of padding.[71] Moreover, it is only from a universal history that the reader can really gain a proper understanding of the causes and effects of events, estimate their true importance and so come to understand the workings of Fortune (*Tyche*) in human affairs.[72] The monograph puts things out of perspective, and obscures both the cause nexus and the role of *Tyche*; and this, as we shall see (pp. 56-8), takes on a special significance in Polybius' view of history.

In the past this fact had hardly been appreciated. No contemporary writer[73] and virtually none of Polybius' predecessors had attempted to write universal history; indeed the only exception appears to be Ephorus, whom Polybius praises on that account,[74] but who in fact merely attempted to combine in a single work the separate histories of the various Greek states.[75] Universal history in the fullest sense was of course only possible if the events throughout the world themselves formed some kind of whole; and this had become eminently true for the period with which Polybius was concerned. His *Histories* proper began with the one hundred and fortieth olympiad, 220-216.[76] 'Up to this time,' he observes,[77] 'the world's history had been, so to speak, a series of disconnected transactions, as widely separated in their origins and results as in their localities. But from this time forth History became a connected whole: the affairs of Italy and Libya are involved with those of Asia and Greece, and the tendency of all is to unity.' Thus from 220 onwards—the events from 264 to 220 which occupy books I and II are merely introductory to the main narrative—universal history is not merely the best kind of history, it is the only serious kind, since it corresponds to the objective situation in the contemporary world, all the parts of which were now, thanks to Rome, coalescing into a single organic whole.

IV

Polybius did not underestimate the difficulties of his task. He was well aware that to acquire and organize material over so vast an area needed hard work and special techniques. The historian's job is defined in an elaborate passage in book XII[78]: it is to study and collate memoirs and other writings, to acquaint oneself with cities, districts, rivers, harbours and geographical features in general, and finally to acquire a personal experience of politics. Of these the two last matter most. You can no more become a historian by studying documents than you can become a painter by looking at old masters,[79] but you must get out and see the sites, studying the accounts of the battle on the spot and, above all, cross-questioning wherever possible those who actually took part. Personal experience and personal investigation—these are at the very heart of the historian's task[80]; and, adapting Plato's famous remark about the philosopher-kings,[81] he observes that 'history will never be properly written until either men of action undertake to write it . . . or historians become convinced that practical experience is of the first importance for historical composition'.[82]

This programme implies hard work, and plenty of it. From 220 onwards Polybius was dealing with a period for which, he says,[83] 'I have been present at some of the events and have the testimony of eye-witnesses for others'; but for his introductory books he had to make use of the work of previous writers, Aratus the Achaean and Phylarchus who took the Spartan side, and for the First Punic War the Roman Fabius Pictor and the pro-Carthaginian Philinus of Acragas; but his critical discussion of these authors[84] shows that he used them in an independent spirit, balancing one against the other. Nor need we assume that they were his only sources. It seems certain that he used many other books whose authors' names he has not bothered to record. Adverse criticism too is not evidence that a historian's work was ignored. Even Timaeus, despite the bitter polemic in book XII, was probably Polybius' source for events leading up to the First Punic War; and he used Ephorus and Callisthenes for some of his digressions on fourth-century history.

However, for the period after 220 Polybius does not depend entirely on eye-witnesses. His derogatory remarks about Chaereas and Sosylus[85] show that he had read their works and he may have made use of these for the Second Punic War. For events in the east he mentions few sources but clearly had access to written accounts. Zeno of Rhodes, whom he criticizes along with Antisthenes for his inaccurate account of two naval battles fought by Philip V at Chios and Lade,[86] may well be his source for events in Crete and Sinope as well as for Rhodes. But one passage describing the death of Cleomenes of Sparta in Egypt,[87] which allows some analysis of the sources used, reveals so complicated a picture that we must clearly resign ourselves to ignorance concerning the written authorities which lie behind most of the *Histories*.[88]

Published histories were, however, only one part of Polybius' written material. He mentions using a letter sent by Scipio Nasica to some Hellenistic king describing the campaign against Perseus of Macedonia.[89] His information about Scipio Africanus was largely drawn from the latter's close friend C. Laelius,[90] to whom he could certainly talk, even if the existence of memoirs written by Laelius is merely conjectural; but in addition he had access to a letter sent by Scipio himself to Philip V, describing his campaign against New Carthage.[91] There were also some published speeches like that of Astymedes of Rhodes,[92] and various official archives. It is true, there is little to be said for the view sometimes asserted that Polybius used the archives of Rhodes, Aetolia and Macedonia, for it is difficult to see when he would have been given access to these. But he certainly had no difficulty in consulting those of Achaea, and after coming to Rome, thanks to his influential friends, he was probably allowed to see documentary material there. Examples are the senatorial decrees concerning the peace with Philip V,[93] and the terms of that made with the Aetolians or Antiochus III[94]; but it is uncertain whether he personally consulted the Carthaginian treaties which he says were filed in the 'aediles' treasury',[95] or merely saw a copy in private circulation. He quotes details of Hannibal's numbers from a bronze tablet which he found in the Temple of Hera on the Lacinian Promontory in south Italy[96]; but this is exceptional, for like most ancient historians he did not go out of his way to consult epigraphical material.

Indeed, it is fairly evident that he regarded the cross-examining of eye-witnesses as his main task. The details mostly elude us and it is unusual to be able to identify the individuals concerned—for instance C. Laelius, and Masinissa, who supplemented the information of Carthaginians who had known Hannibal with remarks about his avarice.[97] But in general Polybius' detention at Rome gave him unrivalled opportunities to carry out this part of his task, for apart from the vast concourse of internees and resident Greeks, he would there meet a constant stream of ambassadors and other visitors from all parts of the world. It is not difficult, as one reads the *Histories*, to note the individuals who played an important role in events and whose later presence in Rome can be attested, and so to make a guess at Polybius' sources for some parts at least of his narrative. But such guesses only touch on a small fraction of his probable informants and can only be regarded as illustrative of his oral sources in general. Their importance is as an indication of the vast number of possible informants on whom he could draw both during his years at Rome and afterwards during the decades following 146, when we know virtually nothing about his movements; and by this time it is reasonable to assume that he commanded a highly developed skill in interrogation. Hence, despite the anonymity of most of his sources, Polybius' readers are justified in approaching his narrative with confidence both in his facts and in the principles by which he selects them.

V

One reason for such confidence is his own emphatic insistence on the importance of truth. 'Just as a living creature is completely useless if deprived of its eyes, so,' he writes,[98] 'if you take truth from History, what is left but an unprofitable tale?' His utilitarian aims cause him to attach great importance to truthfulness, and he is awake to the many ways in which the historian can diverge from the narrow path. What is permissible in panegyric is quite out of place in history[99]; and he contrasts his encomium on Philopoemen with the more objective account of that statesman which he gives in the *Histories*.[100] Again, one of the main criticisms of sensational writing like that practised by Phylarchus is that it obscures the truth and so makes the whole story profitless[101]; and, as we saw,[102] the historical monograph is also criticized as liable to reveal the same fault.

Truth then was all-important; and in the main Polybius' practice seems to come up to his precepts. There are indeed exceptions. Two Polybius specifically concedes. The first is in a religious context. His views on miracles are those of an educated Greek rationalist: to believe things which are impossible 'argues a state of quite deplorable folly'.[103] But 'in so far as such tales tend to preserve the reverence of the vulgar for religion, a certain allowance may be made for some historians when they record these miraculous legends—provided they do not go too far'. In general this rather amiable and revealing concession has little relevance to Polybius' own history, except in the one case of Scipio Africanus, whom he depicts with approval as a man who made a cynical pretence to divine inspiration in order to render the men under his command more confident and more ready to face perilous enterprises,[104] a view of Scipio which hardly accords with what is otherwise known about him. The other concession is to patriotism. 'I agree,' he writes,[105] 'that authors should show partiality towards their own countries, but they should not make statements about them which are contrary to the facts.' The concession is well hedged about; but if Polybius does not in fact display obvious partiality in recounting the history of Achaea, his patriotic bias certainly leads him to neglect the rule of impartiality when he is dealing with states hostile to his own country. His hatred of Aetolia and of Aetolians is too patent to need illustration[106]; and though his hostile picture of the career of Cleomenes of Sparta, accompanied by a distorted account of Aetolian intrigue in the years immediately before his main period opens, goes back to the *Memoirs* of Aratus, he cannot escape the responsibility for having accepted this version uncritically. Political prejudice has also deformed his picture of conditions in third-century Boeotia, where he describes a state of social decadence which can be refuted from the evidence afforded by coins and inscriptions.[107] Sometimes too Polybius allows his assessment of a situation to be coloured by the attitude of those concerned in it towards Achaea or Rome. But it is fair to say that he is never deliberately untruthful and in general his narrative can claim a high degree of confidence.

The same claim can be made, though with slightly more qualifications, for the speeches which, following a tradition as old as the writing of Greek history—it goes back to the origins of history in the epic tradition[108]—he puts into the mouths of leading historical characters at critical points in the action. Thucydides had used this convention to introduce historical comments on a situation; but his successors in the Hellenistic period, writers such as Timaeus and Phylarchus, had preferred to compose mere rhetorical exercises.[109] This Polybius condemns. 'A writer,' he says, 'who passes over in silence the speeches made and the reasons for their success or failure, and in their place introduces false rhetorical exercises and discursive orations, destroys the peculiar virtue of history.'[110] Hence Chaereas and Sosylus are accused of purveying 'the gossip of the barber's shop'[111] because they invent versions of rival speeches supposed to have been delivered in the Senate on the eve of the Hannibalic War, though they had no authentic source for these. This Polybius regards as wholly culpable. He is sufficient of a traditionalist to accept the convention of including speeches, 'which as it were sum up events and hold the whole history together'[112]; but they must give what was actually said.[113]

Some thirty-seven reported speeches survive out of those Polybius included in his history; and though in a few[114] he appears to be repeating commonplaces, these may well go back to his source. For the most part he seems to have taken pains to have access to authentic versions, and often to be drawing on almost verbatim records, as in his account of the negotiations between Philip V of Macedonia and the Romans and their allies at Nicaea in 198.[115] In general, then, he appears to be asserting a return to more rigid standards, and any failure here and there springs rather from the shortcomings of his sources than from a deliberate betrayal of the principles he asserted. These qualities of serious purpose and truthfulness are not however inconsistent with one or two unpleasant faults. To the examples of his polemic already mentioned above (pp. 44-46) may be added his sustained and often disingenuous attack on the Sicilian historian Timaeus in book XII, which is only one example of a decided propensity for malice, often directed against his predecessors for causes other than the ones he alleges.[116] His dislike for Timaeus sprang from a number of reasons. He disliked a historian who made Sicily the centre of the picture, who spent his life in the library rather than in actively studying sites and questioning informants, and who was himself a harsh controversialist; but even more he disliked and resented an author who was widely regarded as the first Greek historian of Rome,[117] and so constituted a serious challenge to his own position. Polybius too was somewhat vain. In book XXXIV he gives disproportionate attention to the wanderings of Odysseus and the location of the places he visited; and if elsewhere[118] he explains that it is a man like Odysseus who is needed for the writing of history, there can be little doubt that it is he, Polybius, 'who underwent the perils of journeys through Africa, Spain and Gaul, and of voyages on the seas that lie on the farther side of these countries',[119] who is to fill that role.[120]

VI

These are human weaknesses, but they are not very important when measured against the solid achievement of his work, its serious purpose, its truthfulness and the great and impressive conception which lifts it above all incidental pettiness—a conception which also raises its author out of his familiar world of rational causes and utilitarian ends into another sphere, where a superhuman power directs the course of history to its own design. This change in attitude occurs in relation to Rome and the rise of Rome to world power, which is Polybius' central theme.

Rome is not of course Polybius' only topic and interest. Part of the attraction of his *Histories* lies in the width of canvas which embraces the history of the Greek confederations, the Seleucid monarchy, Pergamum, Rhodes, Macedon and Egypt as well as Rome. No doubt much of this went in largely because it interested its author; but it also went in because it formed part of the central story of how one by one the various parts of the inhabited world were subordinated to the power of Rome. As we saw (above, p. 43), Polybius interpreted the rise of Rome to control the whole world as the outward expression of the will of Fortune, *Tyche*, and it is in this sense that the achievement of Rome is unique. Other states had won empires: that is normal and frequent. But no other state before had become mistress of the inhabited world. If then Polybius' history was to be the useful work of statecraft that he intended, it must clearly give an answer to the question: how had Rome risen to such heights and such power within the space of fifty-three years?

What Polybius in fact says is: 'How and under what system of constitution have the Romans gained these ends?' The formulation is very typical of the Greek approach. For about three centuries Greeks had been busy discussing the nature of the state, the forms it could take, and which of these were best calculated to secure political stability and human happiness. Political success could not, in Greek eyes, be divorced from the kind of government a state enjoyed, and Polybius quite naturally regarded it as an important part of his task to describe the Roman constitution. He devotes a whole book, his sixth, to its analysis and to a description of the Roman army, the instrument of Roman success.

In it he sketches a general theory of the constitutional development of states, in the course of which monarchy, based on force, becomes kingship, based on moral superiority—the rule of the best individual—and then declines into tyranny; tyranny is overthrown by aristocracy which declines into oligarchy; oligarchy is overthrown by democracy which declines into ochlocracy or mob-rule; and in the conditions of mob-rule men turn once more to a monarch and the cycle begins afresh.[121] In its complete form book VI seems to have illustrated the working out of this schematic conception in the history of Rome down to the time of the decemvirate. But fortunately, Polybius went on to explain, in the middle republic the Romans were successful in putting a brake on the turning wheel of change by evolving the only stable kind of government—a mixed constitution in which the three elements of kingship, aristocracy and democracy, here represented by the consuls, the senate and the people, acquired an equal share in power and by a system of checks and counter-checks prevented any one element from gaining the upper hand. This best of all constitutions had been achieved, not as at Sparta by the genius of a single lawgiver, Lycurgus, but by a process of trial and error working out over a long period.[122] This mixed constitution was at its height at the time of the Hannibalic War, when the Carthaginians were already declining towards an excess of popular influence.[123] It could not of course last for ever—for it is the nature of all things to have their birth, growth, acme and decline—but at the time when Polybius was writing this decline had not (he thought) set in.

The mixed constitution, then, is part of Polybius' answer to the problem of Roman success, the political answer one might say. But there is another explanation on a different level. It was not simply Roman skill, foresight and ambition that explained the city's oecumenical role, but the working of *Tyche*, Fortune. Like most Greeks of his age Polybius was obsessed with the idea of *Tyche*, that intrusive power which seemed to play so great a part in human affairs. The trouble is that he uses the word *Tyche*, which we translate as 'Fortune', in a number of different ways.[124] Sometimes he will say that '*Tyche* brought something about', when he means no more than that 'something happened'; but elsewhere *Tyche* certainly seems to take on an existence of its own, which enables it to be invoked as a real factor in explaining why things happen. It remains, of course, something obscure and incalculable, and Polybius is well aware of the risk involved in appealing to it. Indeed he deliberately limits the sphere within which *Tyche* may be brought in. 'In the case of things of which it is difficult or impossible for mortal men to grasp the causes,' he writes,[125] 'one may justifiably refer them in one's difficulty to God and to Fortune;' such things are heavy and persistent rain, drought destroying the crops, outbreaks of plague, incidents, that is, which we also describe as 'acts of God'. He also includes completely incomprehensible situations, such as the support given by the Macedonian people to an impostor, the so-called false Philip, for this is also something which defies rational analysis.[126] But to invoke the power of Fortune to explain situations in which there are explicable causes, such as the achievements of Scipio Africanus,[127] the growth of Achaea[128], or the success of the Romans in battle[129], is a cheap and worthless device.

In practice Polybius is more ready to bring in Fortune than his sensible exposition would suggest. For instance he is apt to speak of Fortune when two lines of action, each explicable in rational terms, cross and by their interaction produce something new. Thus the elder Scipio is said to have been assisted by Fortune in Spain when the Spaniard Abilyx persuaded the Carthaginian Bostar to release some Spanish hostages and then handed them over to the Romans.[130] Abilyx's action was itself rationally motivated; but it fell outside the range of Scipio's calculations and so to him it was a stroke of Fortune. Fortune too appears as a power which originates events of a capricious and sensational character, often involving a sudden reversal of circumstances; and she allows no one to prosper indefinitely. Hence one of Polybius' objects is to school his reader in the exercise of moderation in time of prosperity, not because this will avert the inevitable blow, but because it may hereafter be remembered in one's favour.

All these slightly different concepts fuse in his writing and allow no firm boundaries to be laid down between them; and equally they are not clearly distinguishable from the aspect of Fortune which plays a central and in a sense illogical part in Polybius' *Histories*. As we have seen, he regarded the study of the past as essentially a means of learning lessons which would prove useful in one's own life; but the value of such lessons is necessarily reduced if the nexus of cause and effect is interrupted by the intrusion of an incalculable and capricious power. Nevertheless, such a power stands at the very centre of Polybius' historical scheme, where, looking more and more like Providence, *Tyche* directs the course of Roman expansion towards world dominion and ensures that in some fifty-three years the Romans shall become the masters of the civilized world.

This intrusion of *Tyche* into the world of cause and effect made the rise of Rome something unique, and virtually the expression of a divine plan. It had another result too. In later years the Romans acquired a clear picture of their own destiny, of the Roman place in history. 'I have given them empire without limit, *imperium sine fine dedi*,' is Jupiter's promise in the *Aeneid*.[131] But this picture involved some reshaping of the past. The early years of Roman intervention in the east were not in reality marked by any such ambitions. Careful analysis of Polybius' own scrupulous narrative[132] reveals that the Romans dealt with each emergency as it arose and that the various steps which took them to world dominion were neither consciously directed to that end nor yet consistent with any thought out imperial policy. Indeed in many of their wars the initiative came from the opponents of Rome, for instance in the Hannibalic War or that against Antiochus III. All this emerges clearly from Polybius' narrative. But it is contradicted by his own theory of Roman imperialism, which makes the expansion of Rome the fulfilment of the purpose of *Tyche*. For, obsessed by this belief he jumps to the conclusion that a process in which the Romans played so great and decisive a part must also be one which they themselves consciously designed. He therefore sees Roman expansion as a steady advance in which war leads to war in a regular process which is at once planned and inevitable, while his own narrative records a quite different sequence of events in which the initiative is frequently away from Rome and 'chance' in the modern sense plays a considerable part. Thus Polybius' belief that the rise of Rome was the handiwork of Providence gives his *Histories* a unity and justification of his claim that universal history is the only sort now worth writing. Despite the criticisms which can fairly be made of it, it furnished him with the drive and the inspiration to initiate and complete his work in the face of many handicaps. The result was a great history, inspired by an idea and written with passion; it is this which helps the reader over the many longueurs and across the wreckage of the later books. In his words we have the authentic voice of a contemporary recording the rise of Rome as it looked to the Greeks who had to suffer the uncomfortable process of conquest.

VII

Polybius' Greek style is not attractive. It is the general *koine*, the *lingua franca* of the Hellenistic age, reminiscent of the inscriptions, verbose and given to formulae, circumlocutions and a variety of abstract nouns used without precision. In addition, the influence of popular philosophy has helped to make the expression of his ideas prosy and didactic. Dionysius of Halicarnassus was no doubt not the only one of his readers to describe him[133] as an author no one could bear to read to the end. For all that men did read him Livy discovered his virtues soon after he reached the period of Rome's eastern wars, and Cicero drew on the political theory in book VI for his outline of the development of the Roman state in the *de re publica*. Polybius remained the ultimate authority for the period on which he wrote and most of his work still survived down to the tenth century, when the Byzantine emperor Constantine Porphyrogenitus produced his collection of classified excerpts from the ancient Greek historians. After that, unfortunately, the excerpts ousted the original work, and it is only in the last two hundred years that the careful work of scholars has reconstructed the *Histories* in the fragmentary form in which we now have them.

'The books of Polybius', wrote Mommsen, who was by no means blind to his failings, 'are like the sun shining on the field of Roman history; where they open, the mists which shroud the Samnite and Pyrrhic Wars are lifted, and where they end a perhaps even more vexatious twilight descends.' Mommsen wrote as a historian and to the historian Polybius is truly indispensable. But to the general reader who can find pleasure in seeing an age of transition and vital development through the eyes of a contemporary, who could claim to have lived through stirring events of which he was himself no little part, *quorum pars magna fui*, and who believed that they had a meaning, Polybius' *Histories* remain one of the great books in the Greek language and a splendid point of departure from which to set out on the study of Roman history.

NOTES

[1] See the convenient discussion of A. Momigliano, 'An interim report on the origins of Rome', *Journal of Roman Studies* LIII (1963), 96-8.

[2] Cf. F. W. Walbank, 'Polybius, Philinus and the First Punic War', *Classical Quarterly* XXXIX (1945), 15-18.

[3] Cf. M. Gelzer, 'Der Anfang römischer Geschichtsschreibung', *Hermes* LXIX (1934), 46-55 = *Kleine Schriften* III (Wiesbaden, 1964), 93-103.

[4] XXXIX, 1, 4. If not otherwise qualified, references are to Polybius.

[5] Dionysius, *Antiquitates romanae* I, 6, 1.

[6] Gellius XI, 1, 1, following Varro; cf. Momigliano, *Rivista storica italiana* LXXI (1959), 550; Walbank, *Journal of Roman Studies* LII (1962), 10-11.

[7] I, 14, 2-3.

[8] Cf. Walbank, *Historical Commentary on Polybius* I (Oxford, 1957), 1-2.

[9] Cf. IX, 20, 4.

[10] X, 45, 6.

[11] XII, 25, 6 (of Timaeus); XXXVI, 15, 5 (of Prusias).

[12] Plutarch, *Philopoemen*, 21, 5.

[13] X, 21, 4.

[14] Cf. XXX, 13, 1-11, 31, 1-12.

[15] III, 59, 7.

[16] IX, 25, 4.

[17] III, 48, 12.

[18] XXXV, 6; cf. Pausanias, VII, 10, 12.

[19] XXXVIII, 21-2.

[20] Cf. XXXIX, 3, 11.

[21] Pausanias, VIII, 37, 2.

[22] Pausanias, VIII, 37, 1.

[23] See the frontispiece to my *Commentary on Polybius*, with the description on pp. ix-x.

[24] XXXIV, 14, 6; XXI, 38, 7.

[25] Velleius Paterculus, II, 9, 3.

[26] Cicero, *ad familiares* V, 12, 2.

[27] III, 39, 8. Some, however, regard this passage as an interpolation; cf. P. Pédech, *La méthode historique de Polybe* (Paris 1964), 596.

[28] Ps-Lucian, *Macrobioi*, 22.

[29] XXXI, 14, 3, 29, 8.

[30] Cf. Gelzer, 'Die Achaica im Geschichtswerk des Polybios', *Abhandlungen der preussischen Akademie der Wissenschaften*, phil.-hist. Klasse, no. 2 (1940) = *Kleine Schriften* III, 123-54.

[31] XXIX, 21.

[32] Except, probably, book XII, which seems to be of later composition.

[33] III, 4-5.

[34] III, 4, 7.

[35] See my *Commentary on Polybius* on IV, 4, 4.

[36] XXXIX, 5.

[37] VIII, 10, 5.

[38] VIII, 11, 3-4.

[39] II, 56-63.

[40] II, 59-60.

[41] II, 56, 6 ff.

[42] II, 61.

[43] *Priora academica* II, 137, 'doctum sane hominem'.
[44] XXXIX, 1.
[45] XXX, 1, 5.
[46] See Walbank, 'Polemic in Polybius', *Journal of Roman Studies* LII (1962), 5, 11-12; and above, p. 54.
[47] F. Jacoby, *Fragmente der griechischen Historiker* II A (Berlin, 1926), 76 F 1 = Photius, p. 121 a 41; on this see Walbank, 'History and Tragedy', *Historia* IX (1959), 217-34.
[48] Cf. II, 56, 7.
[49] Plato, *Ion*, 535 C.
[50] Cf. Dionysius, *de Thucydide*, 15 (on Thucydides); Plutarch, *Artaxerxes*, 8, 1 (on Xenophon); fuller discussion in *Historia* IX (1959), 229-31.
[51] I, 1, 2.
[52] II, 14-35.
[53] II, 35, 9.
[54] III, 6, 5.
[55] I, 35, 6.
[56] VII, 11, 2.
[57] III, 118, 12.
[58] Strabo VII, 3, 9 = *Fragmente der griechischen Historiker* II A, 70 F 42.
[59] Cf for example I, 4, 11; VII, 7, 8; IX, 2, 6; XI, 19 a 1-3; XV, 36, 3; XXXI, 30, 1.
[60] III, 57, 9.
[61] Cf. X, 21, 3 ff (Philopoemen); XV, 35 (Dionysius and Agathocles of Syracuse).
[62] Cf. II, 56, 10; V, 75, 6; XII, 25 g 2; XXXIX, 8, 7.
[63] IX, 1-2.
[64] Jacoby, *Atthis* (Oxford, 1949), 134.
[65] τὸν φιλήκοον, IX, 1, 4; cf. VII, 8, 7.
[66] Cf. XII, 26 d 2 (Timaeus); XXXIV, 1, 2-3 = Strabo X, 3, 5 (Ephorus).
[67] τὸν πολυπράγμονα καὶ περιττόν (IX, 1, 4).
[68] πραγματικὴ ἱστορία.
[69] On book XXXIV see P. Pédech, 'La géographie de Polybe: structure et contenu du livre XXXIV des *Histoires*', *Les études classiques* XXIV (1956), 3-24.
[70] VII, 7, 6.
[71] XXIX, 12, 4-5.
[72] Cf. III, 32; VIII, 2, 1-11; IX, 44.
[73] I, 4, 2.
[74] V, 33, 2.
[75] Cf. E. Mioni, *Polibio* (Padua, 1949), 23.
[76] I, 3, 1.
[77] I, 3, 3-4.
[78] XII, 25 e.
[79] XII, 25 e 7.
[80] XII, 25 h 4 ff, 27-28, 28 a.
[81] *Republic* V, 473 C-E.
[82] XII, 28, 3-5.

[83] IV, 2, 2.
[84] I, 14-15; II, 56, 2; III, 26, 3-4.
[85] III, 20, 5.
[86] XVI, 14, 5-15, 8.
[87] V, 35-9; see my *Commentary on Polybius* ad loc.
[88] For full discussion see my *Commentary on Polybius* I, 26-35.
[89] XXIX, 14, 3.
[90] Cf. X, 3, 4-6.
[91] X, 9, 3.
[92] XXX, 4, 10-11.
[93] XVIII, 44.
[94] XXI, 32, 2-14, 43, 1-27.
[95] III, 26, 1.
[96] III, 33, 17-18, 56, 1-4.
[97] X, 25, 2-4.
[98] I, 14, 6; cf. XII, 2, 3.
[99] VIII, 8, 5-9.
[100] X, 21, 6-8.
[101] II, 56, 12.
[102] Above, p. 48.
[103] XVI, 12, 3-11.
[104] X, 2, 12-13.
[105] XVI, 14, 6.
[106] Cf. J. V. A. Fine, 'The beginning of the Social War of 220-217 B.C.', *American Journal of Philology* LVI (1940), 129-65.
[107] Cf. XX, 5-7; with the discussion of M. Feyel, *Polybe et l'histoire de Béotie au IIIe siècle avant notre ère* (Paris, 1942).
[108] See above, p. 46.
[109] Cf. XII, 25 b 4; II, 56, 10.
[110] XII, 25 b 4.
[111] III, 20, 5.
[112] XII, 25 a 3.
[113] Cf. II, 56, 10; XII, 25 b 1; 25 i 8; XXXVI, 1, 7.
[114] E.g. III, 63-4, 108-111; XV, 10-11.
[115] XVIII, 1-9.
[116] See Walbank, 'Polemic in Polybius', *Journal of Roman Studies* LII (1962), 1-12.
[117] See above, p. 40.
[118] XII, 27, 10 ff.
[119] III, 59, 7.
[120] See Walbank, 'The geography of Polybius', *Classica et mediaevalia* IX (1948), 171-2.
[121] See for discussion C. O. Brink and F. W. Walbank, 'The construction of the sixth book of Polybius', *Classical Quarterly* IV (1954), 97-122.
[122] VI, 10.
[123] VI, 51.
[124] See the discussion in my *Commentary on Polybius* I, 16-26.
[125] XXXVI, 17.

[126] XXXVI, 17, 5.
[127] X, 5, 8.
[128] II, 38, 5.
[129] XVIII, 28, 5.
[130] III, 97, 5-99, 9.
[131] Virgil, *Aeneid* I, 279.
[132] Above all in the various writings of Maurice Holleaux; for discussion of his thesis see Walbank, 'Polybius and Rome's eastern policy', *Journal of Roman Studies* LIII (1963), 1-13, and other works quoted there.
[133] Dionysius, *de compositione verborum*, 4.

III

Caesar: the 'Gallic War'

T. A. DOREY

CAESAR'S *Gallic War* has been for many years what stockbrokers would term a 'bear' point in the academic market. As a model for writing pure Latin with a strict adherence to established grammatical rules, his works are perused with diligence in the Middle Forms of schools, and then discarded. A recent attempt to get a book of Caesar placed on the Advanced Level syllabus of one of the Examination Boards was unsuccessful: he is an author, it was felt, only suitable for Ordinary Level, at which level, as most teachers and examiners would have to admit, he is 'crammed' rather than studied. One might almost feel that the *Gallic War* has reached its lowest depth in the scale of literary appreciation when it was published as a pictorial strip-cartoon as part of a series entitled 'Classics Illustrated'.

It is particularly unfortunate that Caesar is only read by students at a very early stage in their acquaintance with Latin literature. He is an author who is best appreciated when read as a great narrative writer always should be read—at speed. To be read only by beginners, many of whom have to puzzle out the meaning and construction of every word and soon find the process inexpressibly tedious, results in a failure to understand his great merits. Tacitus, on the other hand, is normally read only by people who already have sufficient command of Latin to appreciate the finer points of his style.

Another reason for the general lack of appreciation of Caesar's merits is that his style, his subject-matter and his handling of his theme are too unsophisticated ever to be in the literary fashion. This is particularly the case at the present time, when there is little interest in pure narrative, and the writer who concentrates on recording events, and avoids characterization and the interpretation of motives, is utterly out of favour. Yet Caesar handled a theme that was just as important as anything in Livy or Sallust, and the style in which he wrote is in no way inferior to that of those writers. No one would wish that Livy's account of the conquest of Gaul had survived and Caesar's had perished; an account of the Catilinarian conspiracy written by Caesar might have been more valuable than the account that we now have by Sallust.

In his book '*Caesar as Man of Letters*'[1] Sir Frank Adcock places the *Commentarii* in a special category of literary work, representing a first-hand account that will provide material for a man of letters to work up into a full-scale history (*historia*). Among parallels of this type of work, Adcock suggests the *commentarius consulatus sui* that Cicero sent, without success, to Posidonius to write up in the form of a proper history, a similar work by Atticus, and *commentarii* on his Eastern campaigns offered by the co-emperor Lucius Verus to Cornelius Fronto, the leading literary figure of the age of the Antonines. This is a very attractive theory, but not completely convincing. It may be admitted that Aulus Hirtius, in the preface of book VIII of the *Gallic War*, says that Caesar's *commentarii* were published in order to give writers a knowledge of those great events, but they gained such universal commendation that other writers found they had lost, rather than gained, a field for their talents (*qui sunt editi, ne scientia tantarum rerum scriptoribus desit, adeoque probantur omnium iudicio, ut praerepta, non praebita facultas scriptoribus videatur*). Cicero, too, in *Brutus* 75, 262, says that while Caesar wanted to provide potential historians with a readily available source of material, though he did a favour to fools he scared off sensible men from writing (*sed dum voluit alios habere parata, unde sumerent qui vellent scribere historiam, ineptis gratum fortasse fecit: sanos quidem homines a scribendo deterruit*).

Yet in spite of these two authoritative statements that clearly indicate the belief of his contemporaries that Caesar wrote his *Commentarii* for the purpose of providing adequate primary source-material for some literary man to work up into the form of a *historia*, it seems very doubtful whether Caesar really had this purpose in mind at all.

In the *De Oratore* II, 12, 54, Cicero makes it one of his chief criticisms of the earlier Roman historians that they were merely *narratores rerum* and not *exornatores*, that is, that they set out their facts in a bald, unadorned manner, without any literary embellishments. The whole of this passage contains references to the necessity for *ornatio* and *ornamenta* in the composition of history. This was the fundamental principle of the Isocratean school of history that came to dominate Roman historiographical thought. But Caesar scorned this principle. As Cicero said in the *Brutus*, 75, 262, his *Commentarii* were stripped of all oratorical ornamentation (*omni ornatu orationis tamquam veste detracta*). It is likely that in the *Commentarii* Caesar was deliberately rejecting the Isocratean ideals and reverting to the traditions of the best Greek historians, Thucydides and Polybius. If this interpretation is correct, Caesar's *Commentarii* were from the very start intended to be as much a finished historical product as the works of Sallust or Livy. Before he went to Gaul, Caesar was an orator of the first rank, and had a particularly high reputation as a master of language (this is what is meant by his *elegantia verborum* and *sermonis elegantia*). It is unlikely that such a man would deliberately set out to write something merely for a rival to improve.

In the De Oratore II, 15, 62, Cicero sets out the fundamental rules for writing history. First, the historian must never say what is false (*ne quid falsi dicere audeat*); secondly, he must never suppress the truth (*ne quid veri non audeat*). There must be no inkling of partiality, and no venting of hatred (*ne quae suspicio gratiae sit in scribendo, ne quae simultatis*). These are the basic laws (*fundamenta*), but though they are laudable in themselves, they call for the display of moral qualities rather than for any skill, critical judgement, or practical knowledge. But to many of the Romans the writing of history was either a form of literary entertainment or a means of moral teaching.

Cicero goes on to give the secondary rules for historical composition. In the description of an incident, the writer should express his own opinions on the plans to be put into practice, or the strategy to be adopted (*de consiliis significari quid scriptor probet*); when the action itself is related, he should describe not only what was said or done, but how it was said or done (*non solum quid actum aut dictum sit, sed quo modo*); and in describing the outcome of an event, he should explain the cause of that particular outcome, whether it be praiseworthy (*sapientia*), blameworthy (*temeritas*), or neutral (*casus*); and he should not merely tell of what men did but also of the careers and characters of all the men who gained a notable reputation (*non solum res gestae, sed etiam, qui fama ac nomine excellant, de cuiusque vita atque natura*). Caesar, on the other hand, rarely discusses his plans beforehand, he lets the actions speak for themselves, he seldom expresses praise or blame, and gives only the bare minimum of information about the men whose activities he describes. In his whole technique he seems to take up a position directly opposed to the Isocratean principles expounded by Cicero.

There were, however, other older established principles. Thucydides preferred his history to be judged on its permanent contribution to knowledge rather than on any temporary literary qualities:

> κτῆμά τε ἐς ἀεὶ, μαλλον ἢ ἀγώνισμα ἐς τὸ παραχρῆμα ἀκούειν ξύγκειται. (I. 22)

His standards of veracity were very high, and he insisted that whatever facts he recorded should have been obtained by careful investigation and where possible, vouched for by eye-witnesses:

> οὐκ ἐκ τοῦ παρατυχόντος πυνθανόμενος ἠξιώσα γράφειν οὐδ' ὡς ἐμὸι ἐδόκει, ἀλλ' οἷς τε αὐτος παρῆν καὶ παρὰ τῶν ἄλλων ὅσον δυνατὸν ἀκριβείᾳ περὶ ἑκάστου ἐπεξελθών. (I. 22)

This tradition was carried even further by Polybius. In his discussion of the necessary qualifications of a historian (XII, 25-28), he stresses the importance of practical acquaintance with military and political affairs and first-hand information about the places described, not only to make the work valuable, but also to make it more vivid to the reader:

> ὅτι οὔτε περὶ τῶν κατὰ πόλεμον συμβαινόντων δυνατόν ἐστι γράψαι καλῶς τὸν μηδεμίαν ἐμπειρίαν ἔχοντα τῶν πολεμικῶν ἔργων οὔτε περὶ τῶν ἐν ταῖς πολιτείαις τὸν μὴ πεπειραμένον τῶν τοιούτων πράξεων καὶ περιστάσεων. (25g. 1)

Again, after emphasizing the importance of personal activity in the investigation of facts, which he describes as the most essential part of historical composition:

> ἡ δὲ πολυπραγμοσύνη πολλῆς μὲν προσδεῖται ταλαιπωρίας καὶ δαπάνης, μέγα δέ τι συμβάλλεται καὶ μέγιστόν ἐστι μέρος τῆς ἱστορίας (27.6),

he concludes by saying, in adaptation of Plato's famous dictum, that history will never be properly written until either men of action undertake to write it, not as a side-line but as a task of primary importance, or else historians become convinced of the necessity of obtaining practical experience.

> *τὰ τῆς ἱστορίας τότε ἕξει καλῶς ὅταν ἢ οἱ πραγματικοὶ τῶν ἀνδρῶν γράφειν ἐπιχειρήσωσι τὰς ἱστορίας, . . . ἢ οἱ γράφειν ἐπιβαλλόμενοι τὴν ἐξ αὐτῶν τῶν πραγμάτων ἕξιν ἀναγκαίαν ἡγήσωνται πρὸς τὴν ἱστορίαν.* (28. 3-5)

Judged in these lights, Caesar's *Gallic War* would be accounted history of a very high order. Whether he deliberately followed the principles enunciated by Thucydides and Polybius cannot be ascertained with absolute certainty, but as one of the leading exponents of the 'Attic' school of oratory he was influenced by Thucydides in that sphere. That he knew Polybius cannot be definitely proved, but can almost certainly be assumed, as Brutus and Cicero, whose literary interests were similar to those of Caesar, both had a wide knowledge of Polybius. It is a fair conclusion, then, that Caesar, in writing the *Gallic War*, did so as a firm adherent of an established, but not very fashionable, school of historiographical thought.

Whether the first seven books of the *Gallic War* were composed all at once, possibly in 50 B.C., or at intervals, and whether, in the latter case, they were published together or by instalments, is a controversy that, has, to use the classic phrase, generated more heat than light.[2] There is insufficient evidence to come to any firm conclusion. Certain points, however, can be observed. First, as Adcock points out, the progressive development of Caesar's style, the loosening of the rigidity in the sentence structure, and the changes in the writer's preference for certain words, is more natural if we suppose that the books were written over a period of years than if we assume that they were begun and finished in a matter of months. Secondly, the changes of style appear more marked after the end of book IV. The later books give the impression of having been written more quickly; there are indications of haste about their composition, and not quite the same careful choice of words. The narrative is more diffuse, and there has not been the same ruthless pruning of inessentials. Now it is a possible assumption that Caesar started to write his *Commentarii* each winter when in Cis-Alpine Gaul. On this assumption, he could have completed the first four books in the four successive winters of 58/57, 57/56, 56/55 and 55/54. But in the winter of 54/53 he remained in Gaul, and the revolt of Ambiorix kept him on the alert. The following winter the Gallic revolt under Vercingetorix compelled him to return to Gaul in mid-winter, and during such time as he was in Cis-Alpine Gaul he was kept busy by the critical political developments at Rome. The next two winters he remained in Gaul, and it is possible that he did not have a suitable opportunity to finish books V-VII until the spring of 50 B.C. The need to complete these three books in a very short space of time would give point to Hirtius's remark about the speed with which Caesar wrote (*de Bello Gallico*, *Praefatio*, 6: *nos etiam quam facile atque celeriter eos perfecerit, scimus*).

The time of publication is also uncertain. One might expect, even if we reject the Mommsenian theory that the *Commentarii* were 'the report of the democratic general to the People', that the various books would be published as soon as they were ready, in order to keep Caesar's exploits continually before the public. On the other hand, Caesar, as a master of self-advertisement, would appreciate the value of holding them back and publishing them all at one time, when they would make the greatest possible impact, at a moment carefully chosen, when such an impact might be needed. All we know for certain is that they were published by 46 B.C., when Cicero mentions them in the *Brutus*. But it is hard to believe that Caesar would not have made the necessary effort to get them published before the outbreak of the Civil War. If so, it is likely that they were all published then for the first time. Writing to his brother Quintus in the autumn of 54 B.C., Cicero makes no mention at all of the *Commentarii*. As Adcock says, an argument *ex silentio* is not a very strong one; but in this case the circumstances are such as to make it almost conclusive. Cicero is doing his best, in these letters, to compliment and impress Caesar; he says a great deal about literary matters, his own poems, for example, and his brother's Tragedies; he hopes to get a full description of Britain, but it is from the pen of Quintus that he expects it, and not from that of Caesar. It is in these letters that we would expect to find some reference to the *Commentarii* if any section of them had been published. That no mention of them occurs makes it inconceivable that they had vet appeared.

To return to the consideration of Caesar's *Commentarii* as major works of literature, the *Gallic War* has as its subject some of the most striking events in Roman imperial history, the conquest, and, to a large extent, the pacification, in the short space of eight years, of one of Rome's most important provinces, that in later times was to become the hinge of the Western Empire; and also the penetration of Roman arms for the first time outside the continental land-mass, not once but in two successive years, and the subjugation, though nominal and temporary, of parts of a country that lay beyond the encircling limits of the Ocean; furthermore, the passage of the Roman forces across the other great natural limit, the River Rhine, not by boats, like some hit-and-run raiding party, but by the means employed by men who claimed the right of entry as and when they pleased, by a bridge. And yet, as a comparison between the various memoirs produced by statesmen since the last war must show, a great theme does not inevitably produce great writing; it is to Caesar's credit that in his case it did.

A comparison can be drawn between Caesar's *Gallic War* and the *Jugurtha* of Sallust. Both works describe important wars of conquest, that were, too, of approximately equal length. It is a curious coincidence that Caesar was, to some extent, the political heir of the hero of the *Jugurtha*. In the comparison Sallust is seen to suffer from two serious defects. First, his account of political events at Rome is highly tendentious and not completely credible; his repeated emphasis on bribery as the sole reason for the opposition to the war on the part of the leaders of the Senate vitiates his narrative at this point, and in his continual attacks on corruption in high places one can see his own frustrated personality showing through. His attempt to portray a society in decay is not wholly convincing; corrupt in many respects it may have been, but there was a splendour and brilliance about the last century of the Roman republic. One gets the impression that the picture of social evils that Sallust paints arises from a love of the sensational for literary effect rather than from a genuine belief in the validity of the portrayal. In spite of the recent attempt by Syme[3] to rehabilitate Sallust's character, the evidence clearly indicates that, though he was probably not much worse than the majority of his contemporaries, he was not sufficiently better to enable him to condemn the society in which he had moved without laying himself open to the charge of moral hypocrisy. Great writer though Sallust was

—and as a work of literature the *Catiline* is one of the greatest books produced by the ancient world—his political and social judgments should often be regarded as part of the literary ornamentation with which he enhanced his theme.

The second defect of the *Jugurtha* is one of style. The short, sometimes jerky, sentences, often with staccato phrases, the striving for brevity and variety, and the love of archaisms are unsuited for a prolonged military narrative, and by slowing up the pace make the whole work unduly tedious. Caesar's style, on the other hand, though simple and unadorned—or perhaps because of this—had the power to carry the reader rapidly through the narrative without loss of interest even when similar incidents were being told and retold.

Yet the *Gallic War* is not a mere catalogue of military events, however skilfully described. Apart from the major digressions—the geography of Gaul and Britain, the British methods of fighting, the comparison between Gallic and German customs and behaviour, the wonders of the Hercynian forest, the technical details, whether it be of the ships of the Veneti, the bridge across the Rhine, the construction of Gallic town-walls, or the complex fortifications round Alesia—Caesar provides considerable information about the contemporary political history of Gaul, especially in books I and VII, and the account he gives of the changing political situations and the motivation behind them is clear and credible.

Caesar differs from most other classical writers of history in one very important aspect, that he is primarily interested in the actions that take place rather than in the characters and personalities of the people who perform the actions. When he does discuss motivation, such as the *mobilitas* of the Gauls generally—their inability to persevere in a course of action they had undertaken—, the venality of the Aeduan leader Convictolitanis, who induced his people to revolt, the *cupiditas* and *temeritas* of the centurion L. Fabius and his comrades who, in their desire to win a rich reward for being the first men on the enemy walls, ignored discipline and helped to bring about the defeat at Gergovia, or the innate patriotism and love of freedom that made the Gallic chieftain Commius forget all the exceptional favours he had received from Caesar and his own loyal services to Rome in the past and become one of the leaders of the national revolt, it is not for the purpose of delineating the characters of the persons that he is describing but in order to illustrate and explain their subsequent actions. In any case, reference to men's motives or their characters occur very rarely. It is with the actions, the *res gestae*, that Caesar is concerned.

It is particularly significant that Caesar gives almost no information about the characters of his chief subordinates. There is nothing about C. Fabius, except an impression of general competence, which is greatly strengthened in *Civil War*, book I. Decimus Brutus is always referred to (perhaps affectionately—he was one of Caesar's heirs) as *adulescens*. About Publius Crassus we are told a little more: his youth, his initiative (I, 52.7) the affection and pride he inspired in his men (III, 21.1), his chivalry (III, 22.4). The picture is a pleasing one, and is confirmed by what we know of the deep friendship between young Crassus and Cicero. Cotta and Sabinus stand out in clear contrast in their behaviour against the Eburones, Sabinus capable of extreme self-delusion, eager to trust the good faith of the enemy up to the very moment when he himself was treacherously slain; Cotta resolute and uncompromising, even when wounded in the face by a stone from a sling, refusing to discuss terms with an enemy still under arms. There is also an interesting contrast in an earlier book between Sabinus and Crassus. Crassus and his men are eager to show what they can do in the absence of the commander-in-chief and the main body of the army (III, 21.1); Sabinus took the view that the initiative allowed to a subordinate in the absence of his supreme commander was strictly limited (III, 17.7). That this contrast anticipates the later one in book V is almost certainly accidental, but it is interesting. It is also a clear indication of Caesar's attitude towards the correct treatment of his theme that, in contrast to what most other Roman historians would have done, he portrays the clash between Cotta and Sabinus as a clash between two different policies rather than between two opposing personalities. Quintus Cicero is the only one of Caesar's *legati* about whose personality considerable information is available from other quarters, and what little Caesar says about him confirms most modern judgments of his character, that he was a brave and competent soldier and administrator with a strong sense of duty, who considered the welfare of the people placed in his charge. It is interesting to note that in his comments on the near-surprise of Cicero's camp by the Germans, Caesar uses the incident to illustrate the power of Fortune in warfare rather than to indicate any defect in Cicero's character (VI, 42). This is particularly significant in view of the fact that in a letter written at the time to Marcus Cicero, Caesar was strongly critical of Quintus for disobeying orders.[4] It is possible that on mature reflection Caesar decided that little blame should really fall on Quintus, especially since it seems that one of the reasons for Cicero's action in sending out a foraging party was that Caesar had not kept the rendezvous on time. Sulpicius Galba, an unsuccessful candidate for the consulship of 49 B.C., later one of Caesar's murderers and author of a letter to Cicero (Fam. X, 30) describing the battle of Forum Gallorum between Pansa and Antony in which he himself took part, does not appear to have been a commander of any great competence, and the position he chose for his camp at Octodurus soon proved untenable; but Caesar does not make any overt criticism of his military capacity on this occasion, he merely records his actions.

C. Volusenus, the one military tribune who achieved any real military prominence, who made a reconnaissance of the English coast in 55 B.C., and was one of Caesar's most trusted officers, is described as a man of great intelligence and courage (*vir et consilii magni et virtutis* III, 5.2).

Finally, little information is given about Caesar's second-in-command, Titus Labienus. Labienus was clearly a man of the highest professional skill and outstanding military judgment. What is significant is that on two occasions when he was operating independently, Caesar makes him encourage his troops before battle by telling them to imagine that Caesar himself is present (VI, 8.4; VII, 62.2). It is uncertain whether Labienus did in fact use this form of exhortation or whether Caesar is deliberately trying to associate himself with the credit of his subordinate's victories.

Little is told the reader about the men who served under Caesar, apart from what is necessary to clarify and explain their actions on each occasion. But Caesar's own personality is allowed to obtrude only to a very small extent.

Two examples can be given of how Caesar refers to people's background and ostensible reputation for the purpose of throwing into sharper relief their subsequent actions. In the opening campaign against the Helvetii, the officer who is sent out to make a vital reconnaissance, P. Considius, is described as a man of very great military experience (*qui rei militaris peritissimus habebatur, et in exercitu L. Sullae et postea in M. Crassi fuerat*). This short biographical note only serves to emphasize his subsequent cowardice, when he gave in a false reconnaissance report (*Considium, timore perterritum, quod non vidisset pro viso sibi renuntiasse*). Again, among the Belgae in the following year, Caesar mentions the outstanding military reputation of the Treviri cavalry who were accompanying him (*quorum inter Gallos virtutis opinio est singularis*). And yet, at the very start of the battle against the Nervii, they run away.

In the well-known letter to Lucceius, asking him to write a special history of his consulship, exile and triumphant return, Cicero says that nothing gives greater pleasure to a reader than changes of circumstances and reversals of fortune (*nihil est enim aptius ad delectationem lectoris quam temporum varietates fortunaeque vicissitudines* Fam. V, 12). Now Caesar had little sympathy with the ornate, rhetorical, didactic Isocratean style of historiography that was then coming into vogue at Rome, of which Cicero was a champion and Livy the great exponent. Concentrating as he did on men's actions rather than their characters, he saw history in the nature of a drama, and one of the methods that he frequently used to give force to the drama of events was the sudden reversal of fortune. In book II, for example, at the critical moment of the battle against the Nervii, when Labienus sends the Tenth Legion to the rescue, Caesar carries on the narrative with the words: '*Horum adventu tanta rerum commutatio est facta. . . .*' In book III, at Octodurus, when the Romans make a sudden sortie and take the enemy by surprise, Caesar says; '*Ita commutata fortuna eos, qui in spem potiundorum castrorum venerant, undique circumventos interficiunt.*' In book VI Caesar gives two examples of the workings of *fortuna*. When Ambiorix is almost captured by Minucius Basilus and the cavalry, who swoop down on his hiding-place without any warning, Caesar refers to the dominant power of fortune in war: '*Multum, cum in omnibus rebus, tum in re militari, potest fortuna*', and goes on to tell how the very circumstances that made the surprise possible (the denseness of the forest) enabled Ambiorix to escape. Later on, when Caesar has described the wholesale devastation inflicted upon the lands of the Eburones and is about to tell how, with the Gauls utterly demoralized and the Romans in a state of complete security, the Roman base is nearly captured by a marauding band of Germans, he introduces the incident with the words: '*Hic, quantum in bello fortuna possit et quantos adferat casus, cognosci potuit.*' In the account of the repulse at Gergovia in book VII, Caesar does not mention fortune specifically, but draws a vivid contrast between the behaviour of the Gallic townswomen at the start of the Roman assault, when they begged for mercy and even in some cases let themselves down from the walls to surrender to the Romans, and their later behaviour, when the arrival of the Gallic troops gave them fresh confidence and they began to urge on their men-folk to resist: '*matres familiae, quae paulo ante Romanis de muro manus tendebant, suos obtestari, et more Gallico passum capillum ostentare, liberosque in conspectum proferre coeperunt*' (VII, 48.3).

Shortly afterwards, the change of plans forced upon Labienus during his operations among the Parisii is described as a result of a change of fortune in the campaign as a whole: *tanta rerum commutatione* (VI, 59).

In the *Civil War* too, the same device is employed. When the two bridges over the river Segre are destroyed by a storm during the Ilerda campaign, Caesar describes the sudden change in the relative positions of himself and Afranius: '*et tam paucis diebus magna erat rerum facta commutatio ac se fortuna inclinaverat ut nostri magna inopia necessariarum rerum conflictarentur, illi omnibus abundarent rebus superioresque haberentur*' (I, 52.3).

Later on, when Caesar retrieves the situation by repairing one of the bridges, he says: '*simul perfecto ponte celeriter fortuna mutatur*' (I, 59.1). Another account of the power of fortune to bring about a sudden change in war is given in book III, when Caesar tells how an attack on one of the Pompeian forts at Dyrrhachium, at first successful, goes badly amiss when his troops become separated and are afraid of being cut off: '*Sed fortuna, quae plurimum potest cum in reliquis rebus tum praecipue in bello, parvis momentis magnas rerum commutationes efficit; ut tum accidit*' (III, 68.1). It is a result of this set-back that Caesar is compelled to abandon the siege of Dyrrhachium.

It is one of Caesar's most notable literary merits that he is able to intersperse and enliven a narrative that is generally told in sober, matter-of-fact tones and in a completely impersonal manner with sudden flashes of dramatic force and unexpected personal touches. At times Caesar's writing reaches very great heights:

the battle against the Nervii, with the chaos and confusion caused by a surprise attack gradually brought back to order by the discipline and training of the soldiers and the skill of their commanders; the landing on the British beach, under covering fire from the warships; the ambush in the cornfield, frustrated by the alertness of the sentries in the Roman camp who noticed the cloud of dust on the horizon; the whole story of Cotta and Sabinus; the defence of Cicero's camp; the hunting of Ambiorix; and finally, the last desperate struggle round Alesia, and the Roman counter-attack that succeeded with little to spare—all these passages are equal to the best in Livy, Sallust or Tacitus.

As has been already stated, Caesar gives little information about the personalities or characters of the men involved in the action, but from time to time he brings in details of incidents that are not essential to the main narrative, but arouse the interest and sympathy of the reader. In book I, for example, there are the details of the rescue of the interpreters Procillus and Mettius after the defeat of Ariovistus, and the story of how three times, in Procillus's presence, lots had been drawn to decide whether he should be burnt alive that day or left to the next (I, 53.7); there is the famous story of the standard-bearer of the Tenth Legion leaping ashore to shame his comrades into following (IV, 25.3); the Aquitanian noble, Piso, rescuing his brother from the German cavalry at the cost of his own life, and his brother's refusal to survive him (IV, 12); during the disaster among the Eburones, Titus Balventius, the senior centurion, a brave man of great authority, who had both thighs pierced by a lance, and Quintus Lucanius, another senior centurion, killed while trying to save his son (V, 35); the centurions Pullo and Vorenus daring each other to engage the enemy outside the walls of their beleaguered camp (V, 44); Marcus Petronius, a centurion of the Eighth Legion, holding off the enemy outside Gergovia to give his men time to escape (VII, 50); Publius Sextius Baculus, senior centurion of the Twelfth Legion, almost a mythical figure, who is mentioned on three separate occasions, fighting heroically against the Nervii until he can no longer stand up (II, 25), giving timely advice at a moment of crisis (III, 5), and, although weak from illness and lack of food, holding the Sugambri at bay in the gates of the Roman camp at Aduatuca (VI, 38); and finally, to take an example from the *Civil War*, the reservist Crastinus, who had been senior centurion in the

Tenth Legion, and who led the charge at the start of the battle of Pharsalus (III, 91, 99). Caesar knew all these men, and felt that his readers would want to know about them too.

It is interesting to note that there are more details given in those parts of the narrative where Caesar was not himself present, and which he wrote up from the reports of his subordinates. Where he is an eye-witness, his account tends to be more sober and bare. It seems that Caesar was a writer who derived a greater literary stimulus from things that he read than from things that he saw. Perhaps where he was an eye-witness he felt himself compelled to a stricter adherence to absolute veracity than when he was re-telling something second-hand. There would also be a tendency to cut down the accounts of the major campaigns, which Caesar would conduct in person, and allow some expansion of the subsidiary campaigns, in order to give the complete work a better balance.

The use of Direct Speech in the *Gallic War*, is, with one exception, confined to short statements. In almost every case it is used in reporting statements which were not made in Caesar's own hearing. The use of Direct Speech in these passages is a result of an attempt to give greater dramatic force to the utterance rather than to put on record the exact words of the speaker. In one instance, when the Eburones captive (VI, 35) diverts the raiding party of the Sugambri to the richer booty in the Roman base at Aduatuca, not only are the words fictitious but the incident itself may well be nothing more than an imaginative reconstruction of what Caesar felt may have happened. But the way the incident is treated makes it extremely vivid. The other occasions, too, where Direct Speech is used nearly always come at a dramatic point of the narrative, as where the standard-bearer of the Tenth Legion leaps into the water, or the quarrel between Cotta and Sabinus reaches its height, or the centurion Pullo challenges his rival, or Petronius orders his men to leave him to his fate beneath the walls of Gergovia, or Litavicus persuades the Aedui to turn against the Romans, or where Vercingetorix promises total victory to the Gauls at the beginning of the revolt. It is significant that the use of Direct Speech increases during the later books, indicating a greater willingness to experiment with new literary methods.

The one long piece of Direct Speech is the speech of Critognatus at the council of the Gauls in Alesia, which Caesar (VII,

77) purports to give verbatim because of the horrible nature of the measures—cannibalism—that Critognatus is suggesting. The actual proposal is given briefly; but the speech as a whole is a rhetorical exercise, with the argument skilfully developed by the clever use of antitheses. It serves to emphasize the desperate nature of the resistance which Caesar was soon to overcome. In these speeches Caesar is probably following the principle of Thucydides, of using words appropriate to the speaker on each particular occasion while keeping as close as possible to the gist of what was actually said (Thucydides I, 22).

The other long speeches are all in Indirect Speech, and in most cases constitute a straightforward exposition of what the speaker had in mind. There are, however, possible exceptions in book I. The arrogant statements of the Helvetii, reminding Caesar of a former Roman disaster suffered at their hands and threatening to inflict another (I, 13), and of Ariovistus, threatening Caesar with destruction (I, 36.6) and casting back into their teeth the Romans' friendship (I, 44.11), are probably exaggerated in order to appeal to Roman national pride and sentiment, that would welcome the humiliation of such contumacious enemies. It is likely, too, that the suggestion of Ariovistus that many men at Rome would welcome Caesar's death (I, 44.20-21) is put into his mouth by Caesar for the purpose of discrediting the leaders of the Optimate faction. The whole theme of the book, with its references to the deaths of L. Cassius and L. Piso in former disasters and Caesar's statement that to allow the Aedui to remain in a state of subjection was disgraceful to himself and to Rome (*in tanto imperio populi Romani turpissimum sibi et rei publicae esse arbitrabatur*, I, 33.2), is the due punishment of Rome's enemies for their crimes (*pro veteribus iniuriis populi Romani poenas bello repetisset*, I, 30.2); and by his repeated mention of the Cimbri and Teutones and finally of Marius himself Caesar shows that he is taking up the mantle of the great soldier whose political heir he already was.

If the theme of book I is *debellare superbos*, the keynote of the second book is *parcere subiectis*. The emphasis is on Caesar's clemency. The Bellovaci, supported by the Aedui, implore him to show them mercy and compassion (*ut sua clementia ac mansuetudine in eos utatur*, II, 14.5); after the defeat of the Nervii, Caesar does what he can to spare the remnants of the shattered tribe, in order to appear compassionate towards wretched suppliants (*ut in miseros ac supplices usus misericordia videretur*, II, 28.7); and the Aduatuci appeal to his clemency and compassion (*pro sua clementia ac mansuetudine*, II, 31.4), which they subsequently abuse—to their cost.

The next four books emphasize the expansion of Rome's power. First, there is the Roman triumph at sea in book III, over a noted maritime race, in the first sea-battle ever fought by Romans on the Ocean. Then, in books IV and V, the repulse of the German invaders, the invasion of Germany, and the two expeditions to Britain, with the subjugation, though nominal, of the south-east corner of the island. Finally, in book VI, Caesar makes up for the disasters and dangers recounted at the end of book V by describing with some emphasis a second penetration into Germany and giving an ostensibly first-hand account of the habits of the Germans, to which he appends a brief note on the remarkable animals found in the jungle of the Hercynian Forest. This, one feels, is an attempt to match Pompey's penetration beyond the shores of the Black Sea. In book VII the stress is continually placed on the burning desire of the Gauls to regain their liberty and their warlike valour, and on their resolute and desperate resistance—which Caesar was able to overcome.

Cicero, in *Brutus*, 75, 262, refers to Caesar's *pura et illustris brevitas*. *Brevitas* is one of the most important features of Caesar's literary style; it is not the slightly artificial brusqueness of Sallust, but rather a constant demonstration of economy and good husbandry in the use of words that Caesar showed in the use of all his resources. His language, though unadorned, is never stark, and the words always flow smoothly and with perfect balance.

Caesar's *brevitas* is displayed not merely in the use of words but also in the presentation of ideas. He rarely explains beforehand the stratagems that he is adopting, leaving them to be unfolded during the course of the action. In the sea-battle against the Veneti, for example, the existence of the special Roman weapon for destroying the enemy's rigging, the *falx*, is only mentioned when it comes into play at the vital moment of the fighting. In his manœuvres against the Helvetii, Caesar does not explain to the reader that he is planning a simultaneous attack from two sides by himself and Labienus; he merely uses the stock phrase: *quid sui consilii sit, ostendit* (I, 21.2) and lets the nature of the *consilium* emerge as the narrative progresses. This technique not only results in brevity, but also increases the suspense.

As is natural with a writer whose main interest is in the actions that he describes rather than in the men who perform them, the most important parts of speech in Caesar's sentences are nouns and verbs; it is around them that the narrative revolves. The verbs play a particularly vital part and are nearly always placed in the position of greatest emphasis. The main verb is usually at the end of the sentence, often isolated from the rest of the main clause by the interposition of a subordinate clause, so that it is heavily stressed, or else it is placed at the beginning of the sentence, in the next most emphatic position.

Caesar is sparing with adjectives, and confines his use of them to a restricted number. Apart from adjectives denoting number and size, the ones he most frequently uses are: *aequus*, *iniquus*, *patens*, *apertus* (to denote features of the ground significant from a military point of view); *turpis*, *pulcher* (to indicate blame or approbation); *perpetuus* (continuity); *egregius*, *eximius* (to show admiration or praise); *incredibilis* (a favourite word, used with *celeritas*—Caesar often emphasizes speed—and once with *lenitas*, to denote the sluggish flow of the Saone); *repentinus* (indicating the occurrence of the unexpected often with the idea of speed or surprise); and three rather emotive adjectives, *communis* (used with *libertas*, *periculum*, *salus*, *fortuna*, and generally conveying the idea of comradeship, of things shared for good or ill), and *pristinus* and *vetus* (usually used with *gloria* or *virtus* in exhortations and appeals to act with courage).

Skilful use is made of adverbs, which are nearly always made to convey some additional information relevant to the action that is being described. Sometimes the comparative is used, to denote some *change* in the circumstances: *audacius resistere ac fortius pugnare coeperunt* (II, 26.2); *hostes acrius instarent* (III, 5.1); *ob eam causam minus commode frumentum supportari* (III, 23.7); and *quod longius eius amentiam progredi videbat* (V, 7.2). The use of *parum*, *nimis*, and *satis* gives an air of exactitude to statements. There is a constant use of adverbs denoting speed (*celeriter*), advantageousness (*commode*), and above all, care and professional competence (*caute*, *industrie*, *diligenter*).

However, the most important feature of Caesar's literary style is his skill in using long and short sentences in appropriate combinations. Long sentences are used to convey a complex situation, or a series of simultaneous or interrelated occurrences, or to give a description of motives. But however complicated the sentences, often containing a number of ablative absolutes and subordinate clauses, they are developed in a manner so lucid and so logical that the meaning readily unfolds itself. The consecutive clauses are generally anticipated by *tam*, *tantum*, *ita* or *adeo*, the relative clauses by an appropriate demonstrative pronoun, and the temporal clauses by *prius*, so that the reader can form an adequate idea, early on in the sentence, of what is to follow. As a result, a considerable amount of information can be expressed in one sentence without causing the reader any difficulties of comprehension, and a very high pace can be sustained in the narrative. This is one of the most important aspects of Caesar's style, his ability to keep the story moving at a very fast rate.

From time to time, at a moment of climax or when it is necessary to make some strong impact on the reader, the long compound sentences give way to simple sentences that are short, sometimes very short. The most notable occasion is when the struggle outside Alesia reaches its height. The Gauls are on the point of breaking through the Roman lines; Caesar himself, having arranged a last desperate counter-attack with Labienus, enters the battle. The enemy attack once more. Then, the climax is told in a series of six short sentences, the last four of them consisting only of three words: '*Nostri, omissis pilis, gladiis rem gerunt. Repente post tergum equitatus cernitur; cohortes aliae adpropinquant. Hostes terga vertunt; fugientibus equites occurrunt; fit magna caedes*' (VII, 88). It is interesting to note that in the first five of these six sentences the verb is placed at the end, but in the last sentence, where the final climax is reached, the order is reversed and it is placed at the beginning.

There are other examples of this effective use of short sentences. The account of the fight between Caesar's cavalry and that of Vercingetorix begins with one short sentence: *Consistit agmen*, and ends with another: *Omnibus locis fit caedes* (VII, 67). In the description of the disaster to Cotta and Sabinus in book V, after a passage composed of long sentences telling about the behaviour of the Romans, a new paragraph dealing with the behaviour of the Gauls is introduced by the short sentence: '*At barbaris consilium non defuit* (V, 34.1), and the very shortness of the sentence helps to convey the great impact of the words. In book I, the description of the panic in the Roman camp at the thought of marching against Ariovistus is brought to a climax with the sentence: '*Vulgo totis castris testamenta obsignabantur*'—'all over the camp men were making their wills' (I, 39.5). But one of the most effective uses of a short sentence occurs when Caesar tells how, on hearing that Cicero is besieged by the Nervii, he sends word to his quaestor, M. Crassus, ordering him to join him without delay: '*Exit cum nuntio Crassus* (V, 46.3).

Caesar also achieves considerable effectiveness by the occasional use of irregularities of construction or by variations in his normal word order. In the description of the battle against the Nervii in book II, the scene of confusion on the Roman side is conveyed by a long and involved sentence containing an anacoluthon—the repetition of the verb *vidit* in the temporal clause that takes up most of the sentence (II, 25). Again, in book VI, the irresistible forward movement of the German raiders is expressed by the sentence: *non hos palus in bello latrociniisque natos, non silvae morantur* (VI, 35.7), with the pronoun *hos*, the nouns *palus* and *silvae*, and the negative *non* all being emphasized by their abnormal position.

Although free from the literary affectations that were becoming fashionable at that time, Caesar does employ certain devices to add grace to his style. One is the use of alliteration, one of the oldest stylistic devices in Roman literature. Typical examples are: *disparandos deducendosque*, *patienda et perferenda*, *praemiis pollicitationibusque*, *conquiruntur et conferuntur*, *diversos dissipatosque*, *sacrificia publica ac privata procurant*, *totis trepidatur castris*, and *ferventes fusili ex argilla glandes fundis et fervefacta iacula*. There are, too, very numerous examples of lighter alliteration.

Another device Caesar often uses is the frequent repetition, usually with slight alterations of words, of certain stock phrases to denote actions or ideas that are frequently repeated. Examples of this usage are: *quid sui consili sit*, *ostendit*; *quid fieri vellet*, *docet* (or *ostendit* or *praecipit*); *laborantibus auxilia* (or *subsidia*) *submittit*: and *pristinae* (or *veteris*) *virtutis memoriam retinere*. These, and other similar phrases, reappearing from time to time in slightly different forms throughout the work, strike a note of recollection in the mind of the reader, as if part of a remembered pattern.

Such, then, is Caesar's *Gallic War*, the story of the conquest of one of the great European countries, written in an easy, fluent style that keeps pace with the rapid movement of events in the narrative. It is not necessary to deny the work a claim to the title of 'history' merely because it bears the name *Commentarii*, or because it was a first-hand account, written contemporaneously with the events described. The *Gallic War* is a history with a limited scope, confined to a certain geographical area and a certain span of years. It deals in full with all relevant happenings within that restricted scope.

Caesar's contemporaries expected from his pen nothing more than the raw material for some armchair historian to embellish. They were surprised and disappointed. Caesar produced not raw-material but a finished end-product, written in the severe, unadorned Attic style of which he was one of the chief proponents in the field of oratory, the style which Quintilian characterized as concise, simple, and lucid (*pressus*, *tenuis*, *lucidus*, XII, x, 16-21).

NOTES

[1] Cambridge, 1956. See also Greece and Rome, *Julius Caesar* Bimillenary Number, March 1957 (Vol. IV, 1).

[2] See Rice Holmes, Roman Republic (Oxford 1923), Vol. II, pp. 271-81.

[3] *Sallust* (Cambridge 1954), pp. 269-71.

[4] Charisius, ed. H. Keil, 1957, p. 126.

IV
Sallust

G. M. PAUL

THERE must be few Roman writers of whom it can be said that a knowledge of their origins and social status would not contribute significantly to the understanding of their works. Such knowledge is particularly important in the case of Sallust, not only because he himself sharply contrasts his periods of political and literary activity, but also because misunderstandings about his political career and views have led to false judgments on his works. Sallust's origins as a municipal *novus homo*, and his experiences as he strove for social and political advancement, have coloured his historical judgment and, it can be argued, have had a formative influence on his style. The period of Roman history about which he chose to write, namely the last century of the Republic, was one of great economic, social and political change, and of those changes Sallust's public career is itself a symptom. A correct interpretation of his career can help us to evaluate his literary aims and achievements and can provide a useful corrective to assessments based on the *a priori* literary and historiographical categories which have occasionally bedevilled Sallustian criticism.

It must at once be confessed, however, that for much of Sallust's career we have no reliable information. His full name was C. Sallustius Crispus, and it is reasonably certain that he was born in 86 B.C. at Amiternum in the Sabine country, some fifty miles north-east of Rome. But after 86 there is no event in Sallust's life which can be indisputably dated until we reach 52, when Sallust was politically active, as a turbulent tribune of the *plebs*, in opposition to Milo and his advocate, Cicero.[1] We may go some little way towards filling in this gap, but in view of claims confidently advanced about Sallust's political allegiance (and therefore about the political bias of his historical works) it is important to emphasize that no solid fact is known about Sallust's life between his birth and his tribunate. Sallust's family seems to have had no earlier representative among Rome's magistrates, but it was probably influential locally, for at least by the historian's day it must have possessed considerable means; as his works testify, Sallust himself was given a fine education, both in Latin and Greek, and the fact that he embarked eventually on a political career indicates the possession of a large private income, public office at Rome being unpaid. Sallust probably came to Rome quite early in life; perhaps, like Horace, he was taught by a Roman *grammaticus*; in any case, one would expect to see him settled in Rome shortly after assuming the *toga* of manhood (thus about 70 B.C.), for he had intended to follow a literary career and that could best be pursued in Rome.[2]

But Sallust soon abandoned a literary career for politics:

> Sed ego adulescentulus initio, sicuti plerique, studio ad rem publicam latus sum. . . .[3]

Because of his tender years, 'imbecilla aetas', his integrity was corrupted in the struggles into which political ambition led him, so degraded were the morals of contemporary politicians. Yet even if we accept the tradition that makes the Sabine country one of the last strongholds of the sterling virtues of old Rome, it is difficult to believe that anyone entering upon political life at Rome shortly after the civil war between the Marians and Sulla, anyone who had heard of Pompey's ruthless rise to power, could be so innocent of the character of contemporary public life. One is tempted to believe, therefore, that Sallust's strictures on late Republican politics reflect his own later failures. His holier-than-thou attitude to his contemporaries is one of the less pleasing strains in Sallust's thought, but an important constituent in his historical judgments.

Since Sallust came from a family which was apparently not hitherto represented in public office at Rome and which presumably therefore lacked the necessary connections with politically influential families, he would have to make his own way by attaching himself to one of the great noble houses or joining the following of one of the *principes*, the leading statesmen of Rome. It is idle to assume, however, that Sallust at this period became a follower of Caesar; there is no evidence for Sallust's connection with Caesar before 50, and in the late 70's or early 60's Caesar, whose first notable political success was perhaps the securing of the chief pontificate in 63 over the head of Lutatius Catulus,[4] had not yet the eminence to attract an ambitious young politician. It has recently been suggested that Sallust was rather a follower of Crassus, the later triumvir: Crassus' political influence in the 60's was undoubtedly greater than Caesar's, but the evidence adduced in support of an actual connection between Sallust and Crassus is hardly sufficient. In later days Sallust was subject to the animosity of the Pompeian faction, but this ill-feeling perhaps originated in and after the events of 52 and need not reflect Sallust's allegiance at an earlier date. There is nothing to connect Sallust with Pompey in the early 60's, but it is not impossible he served in the east under Pompey. (Interestingly enough, Sallust nowhere explicitly appeals to his own evidence as an eye-witness of the events surrounding the Catilinarian conspiracy; this may indicate he was not at Rome in 63.[5] Sallust was undoubtedly interested in the geography of the eastern lands, as certain excursuses in his *Historiae* indicate; this interest was perhaps aroused during service in the region, if not in Pompey's army, then in that of Lucullus or Q. Marcius Rex. These latter possibilities gain some support from evidence for connections between Sallust and the aristocratic Claudii Pulchri.

The brothers Claudii Pulchri, Appius and Publius (the later Clodius), served in the east under their brother-in-law, Lucullus, though Publius later transferred to the staff of Marcius Rex. A passage in Suetonius,[6] which seems to refer to these brothers at this time, would indicate that they were accompanied by the *grammaticus*, L. Ateius Philologus; Suetonius also informs us that Ateius was afterwards a close friend of Sallust. Further, Sallust in his tribunate was a notable opponent of Milo and this presumably means, though Asconius does not say so, that Sallust had some earlier connection with Clodius, Milo's enemy. If so, we may perhaps trace the beginnings of Sallust's friendship with Ateius to an earlier connection with the Claudii Pulchri, established during military service in the east. The Claudii had interests in the Sabine land which might account for the original contact. An immediate objection to this idea is that it was Ap. Claudius who, as censor and leading Pompeian, was responsible for Sallust's expulsion from the senate in 50: the objection need not be decisive, however, if Sallust had been a closer associate of Publius, dead since 52, or if Sallust's breach with Appius or the other Pompeians arose out of the events of 52.

Sallust may therefore have seen service in the east in the 60's. There is a report in the *Invectiva in Sallustium* (in certain manuscripts foisted on Cicero but in fact the fabrication of a later rhetorician, one Didius) that Sallust's first office was the quaestorship, but this evidence is not very reliable and it may well be that Sallust's first public office was the tribunate and that this gave him entry to the senate.[7] Sallust's position in the disturbed events of 52 is not quite clear, but he was presumably acting in the interests of the dead Clodius. It is very likely that the same year saw some breach between Sallust and Pompey's faction; at any rate Sallust's riotous associates, who had previously been followers of Pompey, broke with their leader in consequence of the events of 52. In 50 Sallust himself was expelled from the senate by Ap. Claudius, the Pompeian censor, allegedly on moral grounds; the other censor, L. Piso, Caesar's father-in-law, intervened to save the Caesarian Curio, but apparently acquiesced in Sallust's removal, an odd fact if Sallust were already a noted partisan of Caesar's.

It is only after these events that we have any clear indication of Sallust's being a follower of Caesar. But if Sallust joined Caesar only then, we have no justification for assuming him to be an out-and-out Caesarian. Many who took one side or the other as the civil war approached or began did so simply from lack of a better alternative: many who joined Caesar were former partisans of Pompey; many, like Cicero at one point, felt there was little to choose between the two.[8] Sallust, at any rate, was placed in command of one of Caesar's legions in 49, though neither then nor in 47, when he was sent to quell a military mutiny in Campania, was he a noticeably successful officer. Sallust is said to have been restored to the senate by a quaestorship (in 49?) but our only authority for this is of doubtful worth.[9] and it may be better to assume that in these years Sallust acted as *legatus* without formal restoration of senatorial rank, obtaining this only after election to the praetorship in 47.[10] As praetor with the Caesarian forces in Africa in 46, Sallust was a moderately successful officer; when the province of Africa Nova was created, after the battle of Thapsus, Sallust was appointed its first governor.

Sallust returned to Rome in 45 or early in 44. He is said to have misgoverned and plundered his province to such an extent that he was put on trial on his return, escaping condemnation by bribing Caesar.[11] These reports are possibly exaggerated, but there is no reason to doubt that Sallust substantially enriched himself at the expense of his African province. Whether or not his conduct in Africa would have hindered his further advancement, however, his political career must certainly have been brought to a halt by Caesar's assassination. In the prologues to his two monographs, Sallust ascribes his non-participation in political life to a personal decision influenced by the nature and conditions of contemporary politics (i.e. in the Triumviral period), but it is unlikely that Sallust, once his patron, Caesar, was dead, could have made further progress, and it is perhaps significant that though Sallust would have been eligible for a consulship in 43, he seems not to have been considered for the office by Caesar.

In ch. 4 of his first monograph, the *Coniuratio Catilinae*, Sallust dates his resumption of literary work after the close of his political career. This fact by itself might seem to tell against the Sallustian authorship of the two *Epistulae ad Caesarem senem* (ostensibly written in or about 50 and 46 B.C.) which are transmitted in a manuscript along with the letters and speeches from the historical works. Even if the *Epistulae* are regarded as political pamphlets and it is claimed that Sallust, in the passage in question, is referring exclusively to historical works, it may yet be doubted whether the *Epistulae* can be accepted as genuine in view of the weighty literary, linguistic and historical arguments to the contrary.[12] The case for the Sallustian authorship of an *Invectiva in Ciceronem* is weaker still. None of these compositions is here regarded as authentically Sallust's; even if they were genuine, it is doubtful whether they would contribute much to an assessment of Sallust's aims and achievements as an historian.

Sallust himself explains his resolve to turn historian as the outcome of a desire not to waste his leisure, 'bonum otium', or to devote himself to farming or hunting, which he describes as 'servilia officia' (thereby, incidentally, revealing a lack of sympathy for the old Roman habits he is elsewhere eager to extol); his decision to write historical works, 'res gestas populi Romani carptim . . . perscribere', represented a return to a youthful ambition which he was the more ready to resume 'quod mihi a spe metu partibus rei publicae animus liber erat'.[13] The claim of impartiality can be ignored: it was a common-place of the Greco-Roman historiographical tradition, and in Sallust's case, at any rate, not substantiated from his works. It may be accepted, however, that Sallust had had literary ambitions as a young man; nevertheless, since the shape of these ambitions is not likely to have remained unchanged since his youth, in reconstructing Sallust's literary aims we must start from the works themselves, aided by what we know of his career and the circumstances of his time.

Some indication of his immediate motives in turning to history is provided by two aspects of his works, namely the censorious moral tone of his writing (remarked on even in antiquity) and his concern with *virtus*, which he regarded as the pursuit of *gloria* by the performance of outstanding deeds (particularly in the service of the *res publica*). In his treatment of these aspects Sallust may be thought to go beyond the moral preoccupations which are common to most Greek and Roman historians, and it seems likely that an explanation may be found in the events of his own public career. For Sallust, the pursuit of *gloria* was a fact of human experience, natural, self-evident and unquestioned; for Romans of his class and time the most obvious, one might even say the required field in which to obtain this distinction was service of the state, that is, politics. When in 44, or even a little earlier, Sallust's political career was brought to an end, he can only have been disappointed (he was no doubt already disillusioned), though at the same time his desire for distinction spurred him on to pursue it in another field, namely historiography.

Disappointment and ambition will not, of course, by themselves produce historical works, even from a man with literary aptitudes. It would seem, however, that Sallust came to regard his own experiences as symptomatic of the political *malaise* of late Republican Rome; as he turned to historical writing, he began to investigate the pathology of the body politic. At the same time, he could not remain faithful to traditional Roman ideals if he diverted his striving for distinction from the accepted path, service of the state:

> Pulchrum est bene facere rei publicae, etiam bene dicere haud absurdum est.[14]

The close connection between *gloria* and service of the state can be seen also in the remarks of a contemporary, Cicero, writing only shortly before the date of the *Coniuratio Catilinae*:

> si quidem gloria est illustris ac pervagata magnorum vel in suos civis vel in omne genus hominum fama meritorum,

or again:

> carum esse civem, bene de re publica mereri, laudari, coli, diligi gloriosum est.[15]

Sallust believed therefore that his history-writing, which was to soothe his bruised ambitions and win him distinction and which was to analyse the ills of the Republic, would also be of service to the state. This idea he expresses vigorously in the prologue to his second work, the *Bellum Iugurthinum*, when he claims that the state will gain more advantage from his *otium* than from the *negotium* of contemporary politicians.[16] On this point, however, one may feel some reserve in view of Sallust's general pessimism.

Surprise has sometimes been expressed at Sallust's choice of theme for the first monograph. Was the Catilinarian conspiracy really a political phenomenon of sufficient importance to warrant Sallust's attention? Cicero regarded the conspiracy as a dire threat to the life of the *res publica*,[17] but of course his evidence might be impugned, for the greater the danger the greater would appear the glory of the consul who claimed to have detected and suppressed the conspiracy. Yet at the same time, the fact that the state was to undergo greater perils and endure greater miseries in the civil wars which brought Republican government to an end, and that the conspiracy itself was suppressed without too much difficulty, should not obscure from us the realization that Catiline's attempt could have been extremely dangerous, had it not been met with resolution. Even if Catiline's own intemperate utterances, threatening widespread destruction,[18] cannot be taken as a statement of policy, it is clear that there was a common belief at the time of the conspiracy that Catiline, if thwarted, would involve the state's destruction in his own—for if Cicero got a hearing for his views there must have been many who shared his estimate of the threat posed by Catiline—and this would justify Sallust's statement that he thought the conspiracy an event which was particularly memorable 'sceleris atque periculi novitate'.[19]

Further, the conspiracy revealed what, but for Sallust, might almost have escaped record, widespread discontent throughout Italy, reaching even the upper classes, provoked by the high level of debt and social and economic dislocation deriving from hasty and ruthless arrangements for the settlement of Sulla's veterans.[20] Cicero, it is true, mentions the debtors and the Sullan veterans in his catalogue of Catiline's supporters,[21] but his attitude to these is that they are simply guilty of moral failings and once these 'perditissimi cives' have been removed all will be well. He has no understanding of, or will at least not acknowledge, the social and economic ills which created support for Catiline. It may of course be unfair to judge Cicero's grasp of the situation on the basis of a speech which, as originally delivered, aimed at an immediate, practical effect and was not a sober, factual account of the conspiracy; however that may be, there is neither in Cicero's Catilinarian orations nor elsewhere in his writings an analysis of the situation which approaches the historical value of, for example, the excursus in Sallust, *Cat.* 36, 4 ff. The Catilinarian affair therefore merited historical treatment since it could be regarded as a symptom of the social and political ills which plagued *res publica*. It is for this reason, it would seem, that Sallust has taken such pains to place the conspirators in their social setting and to compose a portrait of Sempronia as a complement to that of Catiline, both being types of the corrupt and dissolute nobility.[22]

The conspiracy, then, was regarded by Sallust as a symptom of the political decay that had visited the *res publica*, beginning perhaps with the complete destruction of Carthage,[23] but intensified after the dictatorship of Sulla and the restoration of the tribunes' powers in the first consulship of Pompey and Crassus.[24] But though the monograph naturally concentrated on the events of the conspiracy and its immediate antecedents, since Sallust had set out to write the history of the Roman people, he was also obliged to set the events within a larger historical framework. If this is understood, the introductory chapters on the early history of Rome will seem less of an artistic blunder (whatever may be thought of their historical value). In any case, the idealistic recreation of Rome's past might almost be said to be a psychological necessity for Sallust; his own disappointments, even discontent, found expression in moral censoriousness towards his contemporaries, to whom an ideal past of simple virtues and civic integrity provided the perfect foil. By inventing this past which had room only for the traditional Roman virtues, Sallust was able to sharpen his attacks on the *avaritia*, *ambitio* and *luxuria* of those around him. There was also just sufficient truth in the contrast to make the ideal past plausible to those contemporaries who were concerned at signs of apparent moral decline. Sallust himself, despite his awareness of social and economic problems, tended to see the political crisis of his day as essentially a moral crisis; the portrayal of ancient virtue might therefore also be intended as an encouragement to any contemporaries who yearned for reform, for history could be regarded as an incitement to virtue, serving the same function as ancestral portrait-busts in the halls of the leading families.[25] One may wonder, however, whether Sallust is not more at home in denunciation than in protreptic; the impression created by his works is that his outlook on society was fundamentally and perhaps increasingly pessimistic. This has been denied, but Sallust's very idealisation of the remote past tends to suggest a hopelessness for the present and future.[26]

The conspiracy, it must also be said, lent itself readily to monographic treatment, especially given Sallust's diagnosis of the situation. The important events were few and easily related, the principal personalities involved were colourful and called for historical evaluation, the clash of parties was immediate and required no subtle distinctions, and senate and *plebs* could be represented as opposing forces. Further, there was ready-made drama in the senatorial debate over the punishment of certain conspirators who had been arrested. In these events Sallust could discern the action and reaction of forces which were rending the *res publica* apart; and, by epitomizing historical trends, the conspiracy allowed Sallust to sharpen his analysis of the political crisis. In addition, it is no doubt true that material for the history of the conspiracy lay ready to hand, above all in the Catilinarian speeches of Cicero but also in other of his writings,[27] not to mention the possibility of oral reports from eye-witnesses of the events. The posthumous publication of Cicero's *De consiliis suis* may well have been the final influence on Sallust's choice of subject, though few now accept the view that the monograph was designed as a counter-blast to Cicero's memoir.[28] Nor should it be accepted that Sallust, in spite of obligations to Cicero's evidence, was unfair or slighting to his memory in the way he reported his actions; in particular, he was not grudging in his report of Cicero's First Catilinarian, for, as has been pointed out, since the speech had been published by Cicero himself, it was unnecessary to cite it, and to offer a synopsis of it might have been offensive to Cicero. In any case, when Sallust describes the speech as 'utilis rei publicae', he is using language which in his own world of values denotes high praise.[29] The choice of subject was influenced by the suitability of the material itself, not by the desire to denigrate Cicero.

Sallust's observation of the clash of forces in the events helps to account for an apparently puzzling feature of the monograph. In a work dealing ostensibly with the conspiracy, the amount of space allotted to the speeches of Caesar and Cato, and the comparison between them, may seem excessive[30]; is the internal balance of the work not thereby endangered? In fact, of course, the senate reached its decision to punish the conspirators on a motion of Cato's (much as Cicero would have liked to deny it[31]) and Caesar's was the view most opposed to the final decision. Yet it is still striking that the speeches of Caesar and Cato and the appended comparison appear to form the high point of the whole monograph. Considerations such as these might seem to lend support to the contention that Sallust, known follower of Caesar in the civil war, is really more concerned to show Caesar in a favourable light than to give a balanced account of the conspiracy; alleged evidence of the tendentious falsification of details in order to favour Caesar has been found. Yet this view will hardly stand: the evidence of tendentious falsification diminishes on closer inspection,[32] and in any case, after Caesar's death and the pact of Bononia between Antony, Octavian and Lepidus, the whole face of political life had changed, and justifications of Caesar, recently dead though he was, were almost pointless.[33] Indeed it may be wondered whether it was not realization that the old order was gone that inspired Sallust to devote so much space to Caesar and Cato. These men, in Sallust's view, were exceptional in their time because of their possession of *virtus*, yet neither of them, so divergent in character and views, had been able to save the *res publica* from falling into the hands of the Triumvirs,[34] and one might well feel that ruinous civil strife was likely to break out again.[35] If the conspiracy was genuinely symptomatic of the political crisis, it was important also to emphasize the healthful but, in the last resort, powerless elements in the situation. A method of isolating and emphasizing important historical factors had been devised by Thucydides, namely to work them into a speech given to some participant in the events or, better still, to set before the reader two opposed speakers; one may compare the two contrasting pairs of speeches at Sparta on the eve of the Peloponnesian War, those of the Corinthians and the Athenian ambassadors and those of Archidamus and Sthenelaidas.[36] In Thucydides the important, contrasting factors are embedded in the speeches; Sallust has gone further, and made his meaning more explicit by appending the two contrasted characterizations, which, incidentally, reaffirm Sallust's own standards of value. The senate debate, therefore, is both a central event in the history of the conspiracy, and is exploited by Sallust, through historical references in the speeches themselves and through the following comparison, to place the conspiracy once more in a wider historical framework, and to record his own historical assessment of the political crisis.

Sallust himself had participated in turbulent political activity as tribune in 52. Though that aspect of his life was decisively ended when he wrote his first monograph, inflammatory oratory and mutinous political passions, secret assembly and the threat of violence, all formed a congenial topic for the historian. Further, Catiline, the dissolute and recklessly ambitious patrician, recalled one with whom Sallust had been in all probability closely associated, namely Publius Clodius. The *Coniuratio Catilinae* might therefore not only offer scope to a talent that delighted in the artistic portrayal of spirited action and dramatic conflict but also afford an opportunity to pillory the type of the degenerate but dangerous *nobilis*. In this, as in so many other ways, the monograph can be related to Sallust's own career and to the ideas which he had at least partially formed as a result of his personal disappointments.

When Sallust chose to write a monograph rather than annals, he was adopting a form that had already been domesticated in Roman historiography by Coelius Antipater, who had some distinction though his style was uncouth.[37] Sallust's style, on the other hand, was the product of care and time; this view was traditional by Quintilian's day, and that critic added that the works themselves revealed the pains Sallust took. If, then, the first monograph was begun in 43, say, it might even be as late as 41 before it was completed. Yet whatever stylistic development may be observed from one work to the next,[38] the essentials of the Sallustian manner had been created in the *Coniuratio Catilinae*. It seems likely, therefore, that Sallust began work on his second historical monograph fairly soon, and we are probably justified in supposing that the *Coniuratio Catilinae* had been an immediate success. Certainly the tone of the prologue to the second monograph, the *Bellum Iugurthinum*, seems more confident, particularly in pressing the claims of history-writing over politics. It is tempting to conclude that Sallust was immediately recognized as conferring that distinction on Roman historiography, the absence of which Cicero had marked.[39] There is, it is true, no strictly contemporary, direct evidence for the recognition of Sallust's achievement, but it is significant that Sallust was already asked to write a speech for the triumph of P. Ventidius in 38.[40] The Sallustian manner, at any rate, speedily found imitators, even if not always successful ones; the historian, L. Arruntius, probably consul in 22 B.C., exploited to excess certain of the rarer Sallustian expressions.[41] Sallust's influence is early apparent in matter also; for example, Velleius Paterculus, an historian of Tiberian date, when he is putting forward the view, common in itself, that the destruction of Carthage (146 B.C.) marked an epoch in Roman history, closely follows the language which Sallust uses of this event.[42] When he came to write the second monograph, therefore, beginning perhaps in 41 or 40, Sallust was probably already confident of his powers. Certainly it conveys the impression of greater assurance: the prologue, which is almost as long as that of the *Coniuratio Catilinae* and similar in content, is nevertheless more crisply written, with more confident assertion of the value of historiography; the theme of the work covers a field that is more extensive in time and place, allowing digression not only into historical analysis,[43] but also, a new feature, geographical description[44]; the narrative, without losing concentration when requisite, is more clearly outlined, though this may be partly accounted for by the nature of the events described; finally, the work itself is almost twice as long as the first monograph.

In his earliest historical work Sallust was concerned with the moral degeneracy of the Roman state, particularly of its ruling class, the *nobiles*, but also of the *plebs*: he had concentrated on the period after Sulla's domination, epitomizing in Catiline the most vicious type of *nobilis* but not refraining from denunciations of the whole senatorial class, all the more piquant when delivered by Cato, the defender of traditional senatorial rule.[45] In the *Bellum Iugurthinum*, going back to events at the end of the second century, Sallust's censoriousness fastens particularly on two features of Rome's political decay, the inefficiency and venality of senatorial government, especially in foreign affairs, and the refusal of the oligarchs to admit outsiders, *novi homines*, of talent to a share in the responsibilities and privileges of office. Both iniquities are hinted at already in the *Coniuratio Catilinae* and both may be related to Sallust's own experiences; in view of his own doubtful reputation as a provincial governor, he may have been eager to emphasize the shortcomings of traditional, imperial government in general, and certainly, as a *novus homo*, he is likely to have suffered from noble exclusiveness (note the 'multa advorsa' he claims to have experienced in public life). The weakness of the senate's handling of the succession-problem in the client-kingdom of Numidia is the dominant theme of the first part of the monograph; the struggle for recognition on the part of *novi homines* comes into greater prominence in the second part, as Sallust relates Marius' canvass for the consulship and reports his post-election speech.

Sallust declares that he intends to write about the war which the Roman people waged against Jugurtha, king of the Numidians (the date is 111-105 B.C.):

> primum quia magnum et atrox variaque victoria fuit, dein quia tunc primum superbiae nobilitatis obviam itum est; quae contentio divina et humana cuncta permiscuit eoque vecordiae processit, ut studiis civilibus bellum atque vastitas Italiae finem faceret.[46]

This passage indicates, what has not always been appreciated, that the words after the semi-colon, 'quae contentio . . .', are also part of Sallust's reason for writing, and that he is not simply recording, in partisan fashion, an attack on noble exclusiveness, but is interested in this attack since it heralded the civil strife which was to be ruinous to the state.[47] That is, Sallust is seeking an explanation of civil dissension of which the Catilinarian conspiracy had been such a notable expression. To return, however, to the first of Sallust's reasons: since the actual narrative of the war is patchy, uneven, imprecise and weak in chronology and geography, it has readily been assumed either that Sallust was not genuinely interested in the war or that his shortcomings are intentional, tendentious distortions designed to win favour for the *novus homo*, Marius, at the expense of his noble predecessors in the command.[48] As in the case of the *Coniuratio Catilinae*, however, suspicions of tendentiousness must be mitigated on closer inspection of the work; for example, the noble general, Q. Metellus, by no means suffers in comparison with Marius.[49] It may be granted that with the exception of some set-pieces, notably battle-scenes, the narrative of the war is less compelling than the descriptions of political intrigue and agitation in Rome, yet Sallust's readers probably looked for the artistic treatment of a few events rather than a complete and analytical account of the whole; and secondly, Sallust is unlikely to have had access to sources dealing with the whole war. The indications are that Sallust found the bare framework for his narrative in some earlier work, perhaps the *Res Gestae* of Sempronius Asellio,[50] and that he filled this out, as he could, with information from the autobiographical writings of certain contemporaries of the events, Aemilius Scaurus, Rutilius Rufus and L. Cornelius Sulla. If this was the method forced on Sallust, it will go a long way towards explaining the unevenness of the narrative.

It has been claimed that Sallust, out of hostility to the *nobiles*, has exaggerated Jugurtha's bribery of senators, that he has obscured the real reasons for the senate's unwillingness to embark on a Numidian war, and that the war was really fought in the interests and at the instigation of the equestrian order, those wealthy non-senators whose far-reaching commercial activities included links with the Roman and Italian merchants in N. Africa and interested them in the possibility of war-contracts.[51] Now it cannot be doubted that Sallust, for reasons already suggested, is hostile to noble exclusiveness, but he is not opposed to senatorial government as such; he takes, for example, the 'senatorial' view of the *senatus consultum ultimum*, thus revealing a difference between his own ideas and the 'popular' political tradition[52]; and, as has already been noted, he is generous in his judgment of the *nobilis*, Metellus (whose only recorded vice is *superbia*), and not unfavourable to Sulla.[53] Moreover, bribery was surely practised by Jugurtha on a large scale; there is considerable evidence for the venality of at least some senators in the second century, and Jugurtha's widely reported taunt of leaving Rome, 'urbem venalem et mature perituram, si emptorem invenerit', would lose all point if bribery had not been practised.[54] One may also doubt whether the equestrian order could have taken the leading part claimed for it in bringing on the war; that order had no official organs of opinion, and it was therefore more difficult for it than has sometimes been assumed to give influential expression to its views as a class. It is not denied that Marius, after the war had started, had the backing of many equestrians, duly noted by Sallust, in his canvass for the consulship, but it was much easier for the order to demonstrate its class-interests at the annual elections than it was for it to influence imperial policy at other times; unless, that is, a significant number of magistrates and ordinary senators shared its views. Even the massacre of the Italian merchants at Cirta might have been ignored but for Memmius' hostility to the *nobiles*. Sallust has perhaps, however, obscured the possibility that other reasons may account for the senate's initial unwillingness to go to war with Jugurtha, for example, the difficulty and costliness of a war in N. Africa for no obvious advantage, or the threat of another war in the north against the restless Cimbri. Yet, though such considerations may have weighed with some senators, the real issue was probably one of factional strife. Sallust's narrative allows us to discern such strife in the senate in the decade before the outbreak of the war, between a group led by Opimius which favoured Jugurtha's claims, and a group, presumably the Metellan faction, led by Aemilius Scaurus.[55] These senators may have divided over questions of policy, but there is a strong possibility that the real issue was a struggle for power in the senate, one faction favouring Jugurtha as a client and potential addition to their prestige.[56] If, in this way, questions of foreign policy were liable to become subservient to the issue of factional strife, Sallust's attack on senatorial government is quite intelligible. It is also understandable that Sallust should put in the mouth of the anti-noble tribune, Memmius, a speech that is concerned as much with domestic politics as with foreign affairs[57]: the burden of Memmius' attack is that all political questions are settled in accordance with the selfish interests of the oligarchs. Memmius is not made to impugn the senate as an institution, in fact one of his charges is that 'hosti acerrumo prodita senatus auctoritas', but he attacks the 'superbia paucorum', 'pauci nobiles' and 'pauci potentes' who have formed a *factio* which subordinates the honour of the whole Roman people (and not only in foreign affairs) to its own selfish desires and ambitions. Allowing therefore for the possibility that Sallust as a *novus homo* had a particular relish in retailing the iniquities of the *nobiles*, one may still claim that Sallust's interpretation of events was not unjustified; further, that while the student of today may feel the need of more detail and a juster distribution of emphasis, the conclusions to be drawn from Sallust's narrative about the senate's bungling, venality and factionalism, not only over the Numidian question but also in other fields of government, are not so very different from those a disinterested enquirer might draw.

If, however, Sallust's representation of senatorial misgovernment and noble iniquity is not without a basis in the facts, some of his particular judgments may be questioned. For example, his portrait of M. Aemilius Scaurus is clearly prejudiced. Scaurus was no doubt not a wholly admirable figure—very few successful party-men are[58]; but the assertion that Scaurus changed his policy towards Jugurtha for a bribe, when the narrative itself reveals the likelihood that the change was induced by familiarity with the real difficulties of a N. African campaign, is sufficient indication of Sallust's bias. It was Scaurus' adaptability, among other qualities, that earned him his position as leader of his faction and pillar of the senatorial oligarchy; by Sallust's day his memory was revered, at least on Cicero's evidence, as that of a 'grand old man' of senatorial government. Possibly Sallust was consciously seeking to show the idol's feet of clay; certainly, in view of his own experiences, he was not likely to be sympathetic to a successful *nobilis* who also proved an astute politician. He may also, in the tangled politics of his own day, have become embroiled with Scaurus' son. Perhaps even as Catiline, in the first monograph, represented the type of dissolute and reckless young *nobilis*, so Scaurus stood for all that Sallust had come to detest in the *nobilis* who had power and respectability (Catiline and Scaurus, both patricians, recalled the patrician Claudii). Detestation of the type has coloured the assessment of the man.

In the *Bellum Iugurthinum* the narrative is constantly enlivened by changes of scene between N. Africa and Rome; events in Numidia impinge upon and are influenced by events in Rome. It was not only for artistic reasons that Sallust found this action and re-action attractive; for if he was interested in the war itself, as far as his sources allowed, and worked up certain set-pieces, such as the sieges of Zama and Thala,[59] he was even more interested in the events at Rome which influenced the course of the war, particularly since these events had a wider historical significance as aspects of the *contentio* which increasingly racked the state. As in the *Coniuratio Catilinae*, Sallust does not ignore other social or economic factors that have contributed to the *contentio* (see, for example, in the excursus on parties, references to poverty, the demands of military service and the ruthless greed of powerful landowners),[60] but he has chosen to concentrate on a particular source of trouble, the exclusiveness, arrogance, selfishness and lust for power of the 'pauci nobiles'. Their vices are recalled at various points in the narrative; during the preliminaries to the war and in its opening stages, the conduct of many senators and of generals in the field is seen as governed by *avaritia* and *ambitio* (faults which are mirrored in the intrigues of the Numidian princelings), while the *superbia*, which is the noble Metellus' sole fault, is nevertheless 'commune nobilitatis malum'.[61] It may be imagined that it was the *superbia* of the *pauci nobiles* which was particularly distasteful to Sallust; the theme occurs at all three points where he pauses to summarize the iniquity of the nobles, namely the speeches of Memmius and Marius and the excursus on parties.[62] Each of these passages approaches the question from a slightly different standpoint, but there is no significant difference in outlook between the excursus on parties (where Sallust develops an ostensibly detached analysis of the problems of party-strife) and the views expressed by the anti-noble speakers. In the excursus itself, Sallust does not exempt the *plebs* from all blame, and other passages in the monograph suggest that he was by no means an uncritical admirer of the *plebs*[63]; but the *nobiles* had the power, which they sustained by *factio* (a recurring object of Sallust's disapproval) and therefore must take the major share of the responsibility. The *contentio* was maintained by nobles and non-nobles alike, but it originated in the 'superbia nobilitatis'.

The excursus on parties has a structural function in the monograph, marking the break between the period of venality and bungling in the conduct of the war, and the period of serious campaigning introduced by the appointment of the efficient and incorruptible general, Metellus. Other digressions serve a similar structural purpose; the description of Africa[64] marks a pause in the narrative at the first ostensible settlement by the Romans of the

Numidian question; the narrative is resumed with a report of Jugurtha's fresh ambitions. The note on the Syrtes with the digression on the Altar of the Philaeni[65] marks the end of one phase of the war, when Jugurtha seems to have suffered a severe blow in the loss of Thala, but the narrative is resumed with fresh efforts on Jugurtha's part (to raise support among the Gaetuli and from Bocchus). This digression is probably also intended to mark the end of the campaigning season of 108 B.C., as the character-sketch of Marius marks the end of that of 109.[66] Digressions, of course, could have artistic point in their own right; an historian, in the Hellenistic tradition at any rate, might be expected to adorn his narrative with some 'egregium atque mirabile facinus' such as the story of the Philaeni.[67] The digressions embodying ostensible geographical descriptions need serve no more sober purpose. Certainly the blend of mythology, false ethnology and geographical commonplace which enlivens the 'Africae situs' cannot have contributed much to the reader's understanding of the narrative. Such passages catered for the reader's appetite for interesting detail, revealed the author's out-of-the-way knowledge and his ability to display it artistically. The Romans in general were poor geographers, and Sallust is no exception, as is made plain enough by mistakes in the *Bellum Iugurthinum* itself.[68] The larger compass of the *Historiae* offered even more scope for geographical excursuses, such as those on the Taurus and the notable digression 'De situ Ponti'[69]; only fragments of these survive, but enough of the latter to indicate that it also contained a fair amount of mythology and doubtful ethnology. They are not likely to have contained much valuable geographical information, however much their literary excellences received, and deserved, the compliment of imitation.[70]

Distressingly little of the *Historiae* survives: the known fragments, from five books, deal with events in the years 78-67 B.C. Since there is no obviously suitable terminus in the events of 67, it is likely that the advance of the work, begun perhaps *c.* 39, was interrupted by the author's death in 35 B.C.; possibly Sallust had intended to continue the work either to the time of the Catilinarian conspiracy or, a grander design, to embrace the events leading to the civil war between Pompey and Caesar, thus showing the fatal progress of *contentio*. It is likely enough that the vicissitudes of Pompey's career were to form a central theme.[71] The most substantial surviving fragments are certain letters and speeches, excerpted from the body of the work at some period for use in the classroom. The speeches may have had a structural function; certainly in other ways they recall the speeches inserted in the monographs. They show no obvious differences in style among themselves, nor any obvious attempt to adapt the style to the speaker (one may compare Caesar's speech in the *Coniuratio Catilinae* which is certainly not Caesarian in style) but seem all to have been freely composed by Sallust.

The practice of inserting speeches in the narrative was common in ancient historiography, though not without its critics; Pompeius Trogus is said to have blamed both Livy and Sallust for exceeding the proper bounds of history in this way.[72] But the practice could hardly be offensive where the conventions were known; Thucydides, for example, plainly stated his own conventions and used speeches to good effect as essays in historical analysis. Learning from Thucydides and others Sallust also used speeches to set forth historically important causes, e.g. in the *contio* of Memmius in the *Bellum Iugurthinum* or in Marius' speech after his election to the consulate. Speeches are particularly used to develop attacks against the rule of the nobles, thus permitting the exposition of Sallust's own views under cover of what is appropriate to a given historical situation: such are the tribunician speeches of Memmius and Licinius Macer, the speeches of noble renegades such as Catiline and the consul, Lepidus, and even, by a congenial irony, of Cato in the senate itself.[73] Sometimes the speeches deal particularly with immediate events, as for example that of Philippus in the senate, setting forth the danger to be feared from Lepidus and his followers; more often, especially by enumerating historical *exempla*, they remind the reader that the narrative is always to be set against the background of the history of the Roman people. They may also be used to document one another; for example, when Catiline uses the slogan, *libertas*, to rally his fellow-conspirators, case-book evidence is provided for Cato's contention, 'nos vera vocabula rerum amisimus'[74]; Cotta, 'ex factione media consul', in his plausible speech to the people recalls Memmius' claim, in the *Bellum Iugurthinum*, that the people are imposed upon by the *pauci potentes*.[75] As far as is known, Sallust never repeated the experiment of composing *in extenso* two contrasting speeches such as those of Caesar and Cato: in the negotiations between Bocchus and Sulla for the surrender of Jugurtha, replies to speeches are cast in indirect statement; possibly Sallust had come to feel that full citation of a debate slowed up the pace of the narrative.

The letters included in the works are hardly to be distinguished in effect from the speeches: Adherbal's letter to the senate virtually repeats the arguments of his speech to the same body,[76] while his plea for just treatment as a client-king recalls Sallust's own statements that the rights of the *socii* are neglected. More pointed attacks on Roman imperial government are made in the letter of Mithridates, the language of which recalls Jugurtha's harangue (reported in indirect speech) to Bocchus.[77] Most of the letters also appear to be free compositions. Two, however, in the *Coniuratio Catilinae*, purport to be copies of actual documents, namely the letter of Catiline to Q. Catulus and that of Lentulus to Catiline.[78] There is perhaps a *prima facie* case for accepting the first as a genuine copy; it is not notably Sallustian in style and contains expressions not found elsewhere in Sallust.[79] The second, however, in the opinion of competent judges, has been remodelled by Sallust; the same letter is cited by Cicero in different words which, however, seem closer to the customary colloquial, epistolary style.[80]

Letters and speeches both may be employed to characterize a critical situation or a prominent actor in the events. The conventional maxims of the death-bed speech of Micipsa to the Numidian princelings[81] contrast dramatically and ironically both with his own earlier conduct and suspicions and with the actual course of events after his death. The speeches of Cato and Marius admirably reflect the contemporary image of these two worthies, the stern upholder of ancient morality and the bluff, blunt but rather unpolished soldier. In this way, the speeches and letters fill out and supplement the portraits presented in Sallust's masterly character-sketches. These sketches, swift, bold, incisive, immediate, aimed to please as well as instruct the reader, emphasize the dramatic elements in the narrative and sum up in individual characters Sallust's view of historical forces. Mention has already been made of the portraits of Catiline, Sempronia, Caesar and Cato in the *Coniuratio Catilinae*. In the second monograph, the sketch of Jugurtha, comparable as it is to the idealizing ethnography of barbarian peoples,[82] acts as a foil to the vices of the Roman nobility; the senatorial nobility is attacked more directly in the person of its 'grand old man', Aemilius Scaurus, damned in a lapidary phrase, 'homo nobilis, inpiger, factiosus, avidus potentiae, honoris, divitiarum, ceterum vitia sua callide occultans'.[83] The contrasting merits of the later rivals, Marius and Sulla, find due commemoration, in each case the chronicle of their early virtues rounded off with a condemnation of their later careers.[84] Not enough of the *Historiae* survives to trace the further development of these artistic and imposing portraits, but a fragment referring to Sertorius, and the famous judgment on Pompey, 'oris probi, animo inverecundo', suggest that the connoisseur of the form would not have been disappointed.[85]

The characteristics of Sallust's style are so marked that opinion about it was fixed at an early date.[86] Among the features most commonly noted are brevity (leading sometimes to obscurity), the use of archaisms and Greek constructions, the coinage of new words and of new meanings for old words, abrupt language with phrases ending unexpectedly, yet at the same time careful and artistic composition. Contrast and antithesis are apparent not only in the use of words and sentence-structure but seem to be a natural element in Sallust's thought; there is something in the idea that the mind-body dualism, so prominent in the prologues of the monographs, though it is by Sallust's day a philosophical commonplace, is nevertheless for him a particularly congenial way of regarding human activity. Contrast is above all a feature of the *sententiae*, pithy, gnomic utterances which occur frequently in the works, often embodying a wry, rather cynical comment on human conduct. Comment on the gulf between appearance and reality is implicit in the style as well as explicit in the judgments: the reader is provoked to closer attentiveness by unusual expression, while the theme of the cleft between public profession and political reality occurs in all three works.[87] It may not be fanciful to see in this bent of Sallust's the effect not only of his own experiences of political life but even of the contrast between his early hopes and later disappointments; moreover, a certain dichotomy of view is perhaps not to be wondered at in a man who enriched himself at the expense of his province yet adopted so censorious a tone towards similar conduct by others. The general effect of the writing is of speed, restlessness, discordancy, admirably adapted to the tangled and violent events which are Sallust's chosen theme.

There is a purposeful striving after disharmony, the so-called *inconcinnitas*, totally at variance with the dominant contemporary, oratorical style. Apuleius wrote of the 'parsimonia' of Sallust and the 'opulentia' of Cicero[88]; the real contrast lay deeper, in a fundamental difference of attitude to the public life of the late Republic. When Sallust came to write history, in the words of Sir Ronald Syme, 'smooth phrases were suspect, their authors in discredit'[89]; Sallust sought to pierce the facade, revealing corruption in high places. It is no accident that Augustus, the master of the official phrase, adopted canons of style that damned Sallust.[90] The historian of Republican decline rejoiced in exposing the unpleasant realities with startling and vivid phrase.

Two features of the style merit further comment, the archaism and the Grecisms. Though additional sources may be found, it is not seriously misleading to state that these features are owed to admiration and imitation of two predecessors in particular, the elder Cato and Thucydides. Sallust was early taxed with theft of 'prisca verba' from Cato whom he himself described as 'Romani generis disertissimus'.[91] In fact, it is not easy to demonstrate any considerable dependence by Sallust on the vocabulary of Cato; there were in any case other sources on which Sallust might draw for an antique expression to lend dignity to his prose. Certain phrases, however, and certain figures, notably alliteration, seem to be modelled on Cato's writings. Alliteration is, of course, a feature of most literary Latin up to late antiquity, but there seems to be a particularly close correspondence between some of Sallust's alliterative phrases and those of Cato.[92] In both authors alliteration results in increased energy and concentration, even if Sallust occasionally, forsaking *brevitas*, adds a word principally for alliterative effect, e.g. 'neque modum neque modestiam'.[93] It is also possible that Sallust was reproached not so much with the theft of vocabulary as with the theft of *sententiae* from Cato.[94] One can readily imagine that Sallust would be greatly attracted by Cato's pithy expression of an ancient morality, especially since Cato was famed for his attacks on the vices of the senatorial class. It is no surprise, therefore, that echoes of Cato have been detected especially in the speeches Sallust gives to the younger Cato, Memmius and Marius; in the elder Cato then not only the writer but also the moralist was attractive to Sallust's taste.

In the case of Thucydides also both writer and thinker proved worthy of emulation. His influence, too, was early noted in antiquity; it seems reasonable, therefore, to derive certain Greek turns of syntax (e.g. 'quae ira fieri amat' or 'uti militibus exaequatus cum imperatore labor volentibus esset') from Thucydides rather than from any other Greek author.[95] It is known that in the late Republic a cult of Thucydides was maintained by the Atticists: Cicero strongly disapproved; Thucydides was no model for oratory.[96] History was quite another matter, as Sallust proved. The harshness, speed and archaic colouring of Thucydides were exactly to Sallust's taste. He set out to emulate the Greek historian in Roman letters and Quintilian, at least, did not shrink from matching the two, 'nec opponere Thucydidi Sallustium verear'.[97] Though the name of Thucydides is not in fact mentioned, Sallust's aim might almost be said to be announced in ch. 8 of the first monograph where he commemorates the advantages the history of Athens has derived from 'scriptorum magna ingenia' in that city. Moreover, Sallust found it possible to apply some of Thucydides' historical conclusions to Rome; he had clearly studied Thucydides' remarks on party-strife, *stasis*; verbal reminiscences, especially of the concluding section of the well-known chapter, III, 82, are frequent in Sallust; and many other well-known passages, especially from the speeches and excursuses of Thucydides are echoed in the Roman author.

There can be no doubt of the immediate success and extended influence of the Sallustian style.[98] That style was susceptible of development and enrichment, as was to be demonstrated by Tacitus (whose indebtedness to the 'rerum Romanarum florentissimus auctor'[99] recently received fresh and full commemoration in Syme's volumes), but in Sallust's own day it was already an artistic achievement of the first rank; terse, swift, energetic yet dignified, provoking attention, in passages brilliant, a vehicle apt to the theme, it won for its author the *gloria* he so passionately coveted. Yet Sallust would not have been content to be remembered only as a stylist, for he believed he had truths of moment to reveal about Roman politics, Roman society and Roman history. And certainly he succeeded in communicating his forceful moral judgments; his attitudes had powerful influence on Tacitus again, but also, significantly, on Christian writers of the fourth and fifth centuries who found in Sallust confirmation of their own views about pagan society; above all, he is quoted extensively by

Augustine to whose 'De civitate Dei' we owe our knowledge of some important passages from the *Historiae*. We have less sympathy now for the moralizing strain in an historian, but praise and blame were an essential part of Roman historiography, 'ne virtutes sileantur utque pravis dictis factisque ex posteritate et infamia metus sit'[100]; and if Sallust's moralizing had a sharper edge, it was a result of his own experiences of political life and his disappointments. The Romans in any case tended to use the same terminology for morals and politics; witness the terms *boni* and *improbi*. And there was perhaps some justification for seeing the political crisis of the late Republic in moral terms; in a basically aristocratic society, such as Rome's, it was almost inevitable that the historian should concentrate on the activities of the ruling-class, and the old ideals of the class had been abandoned or had become mere catchwords as the old economic community broke up and the struggle for political power intensified. On the other hand, Sallust's moral vision was bounded by these old, aristocratic ideals (saving his insistence on a place in the sun for *novi homines* of merit); he was not unaware of social and economic problems, but in so far as he did genuinely seek reforms, and was not simply

> difficilis, querulus, laudator temporis acti,

he envisaged it as the 'restoration' of a state of society which was itself an ideal.

Finally, it must candidly be confessed that Sallust as an historian does not meet the rigid requirements of a later day. If it is no longer possible to accept the view that Sallust resorted to malicious or tendentious falsification for party-political ends, he is nevertheless careless in chronological or geographical detail, vague as to numbers, dates and distances, impressionistic rather than factual, concentrating on personalities rather than on more general causes; and at the same time, even if he is free from party-bias in the narrow sense, his historical judgment is coloured by his personal hostility to the senatorial nobility. It might indeed be claimed that our judgment on these questions is formed on the basis of the two monographs and that in these the monographic technique itself encouraged the grouping of facts for artistic effect or to bring out underlying causes not immediately apparent in a bare narrative of the events; nonetheless, what little survives of the *Historiae* also reveals deficiency in historical judgment, e.g. in the view that 'maxima concordia' prevailed between the Second and Third Punic Wars, though Sallust must have had access to evidence that demonstrated the contrary. What must, however, be put down to his lasting credit is that he has recorded for us what might be called the 'anti-establishment' view of late Republican political life; as a man who knew politics from the inside, who had sat, if briefly, in the senate and had commanded, if not altogether successfully, legions, he was able to provide the necessary corrective to the official view of public life and the recent past as recorded in the oratory and even in the history[101] of the senatorial class.

NOTES

[1] Cf. Asconius 37; 45; 49 Clark (i.e. Asconius' commentary on Cicero, *Pro Milone*).

[2] Cf. Sallust, *Coniuratio Catilinae* 4, 2. (References to Sallust's works are to the Teubner editions of A. Kurfess (Leipzig, 1957) for the monographs and of B. Maurenbrecher, fasc. I-II (Leipzig, 1891-93), for the fragments of the *Historiae*. The abbreviations *Cat., Jug.* and *Hist.* will be used in citing the works.) Copious information on Sallust's career and works will be found in the article by G. Funaioli in Pauly-Wissowa-Kroll, *Realencyclopädie der classischen Altertumswissenschaft*, I A, 2 (Stuttgart, 1920) 1913-55 s.v. Sallustius; for an extensive bibliography see A. D. Leeman, *A Systematical Bibliography of Sallust* (1879-1950) (Leiden, 1952). (This chapter was completed before the publication of Sir Ronald Syme's Sather Lectures on *Sallust* (Berkeley and Los Angeles, 1964). References to that work have been incorporated, where appropriate, in the following notes.)

[3] Sall. *Cat.* 3, 3.

[4] *Cat.* 49, 2.

[5] *Cat.* 36, 4, 'ea tempestate mihi imperium populi Romani multo maxume miserabile visum est' *might* be interpreted to mean that Sallust was then in Rome; note, however, *Cat.* 48, 9, 'ipsum Crassum ego postea praedicantem audivi. . . .' K. Büchner, *Sallust* (Heidelberg, 1960) 34-6, sees in the latter passage evidence that Sallust was a follower of Crassus.

[6] Suetonius, *De grammaticis* 10.

[7] The case of M. Caelius Rufus, one of Sallust's colleagues, may be similar; see the remarks of R. G. Austin in his edition of Cicero. *Pro Caelio*, 3rd ed. (Oxford, 1960), 145-6. See also Syme, *op. cit.*, 28.

[8] On the composition of the Caesarian party see R. Syme, *The Roman Revolution* (Oxford, 1939) 61-77; among those who joined Caesar were two other enemies of Ap. Claudius, namely C. Scribonius Curio and M. Caelius Rufus, *op. cit.*, 63.

[9] *Invectiva in Sallustium* 6, 17.

[10] Dio XLII, 52, 2.

[11] Dio XLIII, 9, 2-3; *Invectiva* 7, 19.

[12] There is a considerable bibliography on these writings; convincing arguments against authenticity have been brought by R. Syme, 'Pseudo-Sallust', *MH* XV (1958), 46-55; 'The Damaging Names in Pseudo-Sallust', *MH* XIX (1962), 177-9; and see now *Sallust* 318 ff. References to other recent literature will be found in these works.

[13] *Cat.* 4, 1-2.

[14] *Cat.* 3, 1.

[15] Cicero, *Pro Marcello* 8, 23; I *Phil.* 14, 33.

[16] *Jug.* 4, 4.

[17] Cf. Cicero, III, *In Catilinam* 10, 24-5.

[18] Cf. Sall. *Cat.* 31, 9; Cicero, *Pro Murena* 25, 51.

[19] *Cat.* 4, 4; on the question of Sallust's choice of themes in the monographs see W. Steidle, *Sallusts historische Monographien: Themenwahl und Geschichtsbild* (Wiesbaden, 1958).

[20] Cf. Syme, *The Roman Revolution*, 89.

[21] Cicero, II, *In Catilinam* 8, 17 ff.

[22] *Cat.* 5, 1-8 (Catiline); 25 (Sempronia). There is no reason to accept the view, originally advanced by E. v. Stern, *Catilina und die Parteikämpfe in Rom der Jahre* 66-63 (Dorpat, 1883), 124, n. 1, that the sketch of Sempronia is motivated by the desire to abuse D. Brutus, one of Caesar's murderers, in the person of his mother. See further now Syme, *Sallust*, 134. The sketches naturally have artistic value as well as historical point.

[23] Cf. *Cat.* 10, 1; the importance of the destruction of Carthage as a turning-point in Roman history is stated even more firmly in the later works, cf. *Jug.* 41, 2-3; *Hist.* I, 12. The idea of the salutary effect of a 'metus hostilis' was a commonplace of ancient historiography. Sallust's application of the theory to the particular case of Carthage was perhaps derived from the famous debate between the elder Cato and Scipio Nasica on the fate of that city; cf. D. C. Earl, *The Political Thought of Sallust* (Cambridge, 1961), 47-9, with references to earlier literature. Sallust may have found the view enunciated in the writings of P. Rutilius Rufus rather than in the Greek author, Posidonius.

[24] Cf. *Cat.* 5, 6; 11, 4 ff; 38, 1 ff.

[25] Cf. *Jug.* 4, esp. 5-6.

[26] Pessimism is denied for example by Steidle, *op. cit.* (n. 19), 9 ff; note, however, the language of *Cat.* 39, 4; 53, 5; *Hist.* I, 12; 13; 16.

[27] Cf. Steidle, *op. cit.*, 14-5.

[28] For this view see E. Schwartz, 'Die Berichte uber die catilinarische Verschwörung', *Hermes* XXXII (1897), 554-608, esp. 580-1; this article was mainly responsible for the contention that the *Coniuratio Catilinae* was a party-tract designed to attack the oligarchy and defend Caesar, and that errors in Sallust could be explained as tendentious falsifications.

[29] *Cat.* 31, 6.

[30] *Cat.* 51-4.

[31] Cf. Cicero, *Ad Atticum* XII, 21.

[32] Evidence against the thesis of Schwartz (n. 28 above) and his followers is discussed by O. Seel, *Sallust von den Briefen ad Caesarem senem zur Coniuratio Catilinae* (Leipzig/Berlin, 1930) 46 ff; cf. also Steidle, *op. cit.* (n. 19), 91 ff.

[33] There are in any case those who hold that Cato emerges superior from

the comparison of *Cat.* 54; cf. Earl, *op. cit.* (n. 23), 101; Syme, *Sallust*, 134. If Sallust says of Cato 'esse quam videri bonus malebat' (54, 6), it is difficult not to feel that Caesar is being tacitly condemned.

[34] The phrase 'potentiae paucorum' at *Jug.* 3, 4, probably refers to the Triumvirs. See further Syme, *Sallust*, 216.

[35] Cf. Hirtius, *De bello Gallico* VIII, praef. 2.

[36] Cf. Thucydides I, 68 ff; see also the analysis in J. H. Finley, *Thucydides* (Cambridge, Mass., 1947), 121-36.

[37] On Coelius Antipater see Cicero, *De oratore* II, 12, 54; *De legibus* I, 2, 6.

[38] On the development of Sallust's style see A. Kunze, *Sallustiana* III, 1 (Leipzig, 1897), 49 ff; E. Löfstedt, *Syntactica* II (Lund, 1933), 290-4; Syme, *op. cit.*, 266 ff, 305 ff.

[39] Cf. Cicero, *Brutus* 64, 228.

[40] Cf. Fronto II, p. 136 Haines.

[41] Cf. Seneca, *Epistulae* 114, 17-9.

[42] Cf. Velleius Paterculus I, 12; II, 1, and n. 23 above.

[43] The digression on party-strife, *Jug.* 41-2, is foreshadowed by that at *Cat.* 36, 4-39, 4.

[44] Cf. the 'Africae situs' of *Jug.* 17-9; cf. *Jug.* 78-9 on the Syrtes and the brothers Philaeni.

[45] Cf. *Cat.* 10; 12-3; 52, 7 ff.

[46] *Jug.* 5, 1-2.

[47] On this point see, recently, Steidle, *op. cit.* (n. 19), 34-5.

[48] Cf. C. Lauckner, *Die künstlerischen und politischen Ziele der Monographie Sallusts über den Jugurthinischen Krieg* (Leipzig, 1911). Lauckner applies the interpretation of Schwartz to the second monograph.

[49] Cf. K. Vretska, *Studien zu Sallusts Bellum Jugurthinum* (Vienna, 1955), 94-101.

[50] On the character of Asellio's work see Aulus Gellius V, 18, 9; cf. II, 13, 3.

[51] See, for example, G. De Sanctis, *Problemi di Storia Antica* (Bari, 1932), 187-214; K. v. Fritz, 'Sallust and the Attitude of the Roman Nobility at the Time of the Wars against Jugurtha (112-105 B.C.)', *TAPhA* LXXIV (1943), 134-68.

[52] Cf. *Cat.* 29, 2-3; on the *senatus consultum ultimum* see Ch. Wirszubski, *Libertas as a Political Idea at Rome during the Late Republic and Early Principate* (Cambridge, 1950), 55-61.

[53] Cf. *Jug.* 95, 2.

[54] *Jug.* 35, 10.

[55] Cf. *Jug.* 15-6.

[56] Cf. *Jug.* 15, 4; cf. 29, 2; the influence of senatorial faction is indicated by Sallust's reference (*Jug.* 8) to Jugurtha's connections with certain Romans in Scipio's following at Numantia; see also W. Allen, 'The Source of Jugurtha's Influence in the Roman Senate', *CPh* XXXIII (1938), 90-2.

[57] Cf. *Jug.* 31.

[58] For a hostile modern view of Scaurus see P. Fraccaro, *Opuscula* II (Pavia, 1957), 125-47, 'Scauriana'; cf. also A. R. Hands, 'Sallust and *Dissimulatio*', *JRS* XLIX (1959), 56-60.

[59] Cf. *Jug.* 57 ff; 75 ff.

[60] *Jug.* 41, 7-8.

[61] *Jug.* 64, 1.

[62] Cf. *Jug.* 31; 41-2; 85; see especially 31, 12; 41, 3; 85, 38.

[63] *Jug.* 41, 5; cf. 40, 5; 66, 2; cf. *Cat.* 37, 1-3.

[64] *Jug.* 64.

[65] *Jug.* 78-9.

[66] Cf. *Jug.* 63, 3-6. On the chronology of the war see H. Chantraine, *Untersuchungen zur römischen Geschichte am Ende des 2. Jahrhunderts v. Chr.* (Kallmünz, 1959), 29-62; Syme, *Sallust*, 143 ff.

[67] E. Bolaffi, *Sallustio e la sua fortuna nei secoli* (Rome, 1949), 130, cites an interesting parallel from Diodorus IV, 20, 2-3 (i.e. Posidonius) where a story is recounted mainly, it seems, as 'a strange and surprising occurrence'.

[68] Sallust errs notably in his view of the topography and position of Cirta, *Jug.* 21.

[69] Cf. *Hist.* II, 82-4; III, 61-8.

[70] For the influence of Sallust's excursuses on Tacitus see R. Syme, *Tacitus* (Oxford, 1958) I, 353-4; cf. 125-6; II, 728-30; cf. *Sallust* 294.

[71] Cf. Syme, *Tacitus* I, 134; *Sallust*, 192.

[72] Cf. Justin, *Hist. Phil.* XXXVIII, 3, 11; cf. Gran. Licin. p. 33 Flemisch. On the speeches and letters in Sallust see H. Schnorr v. Carolsfeld, *Über die Reden und Briefe bei Sallust* (Leipzig, 1888).

[73] Cf. *Hist.* III, 48 (Macer); *Jug.* 31 (Memmius); *Cat.* 20 (Catiline); *Hist.* I, 55 (Lepidus); *Cat.* 52 (Cato).

[74] Cf. *Cat.* 20, 6; 14; cf. 52, 11.

[75] Cf. *Hist.* II, 47, for Cotta's speech.

[76] *Jug.* 24; cf. 14.

[77] *Hist.* IV, 69 (Mithridates); cf. *Jug.* 81, 1.

[78] Cf. *Cat.* 35; 44, 5; note the use of 'exemplum' in each case, *Cat.* 34, 3; 44, 4.

[79] See the note, *ad loc.*, in the edition of *Cat.* by A. M. Cook (1901) 118.

[80] For Cicero's version see III *In Catilinam* 5, 12; on the contrasting styles see K. Latte, *Sallust* (Leipzig/Berlin, 1935) 19-20; see, however, J. B. Hofmann, *Lateinische Umgangssprache*, 3rd ed. (Heidelberg, 1951), 208, who suggests both versions may differ from the original.

[81] Cf. *Jug.* 10.

[82] Cf. *Jug.* 6, 1, for the sketch of Jugurtha; 89, 7-8, is a good example of the influence of idealizing ethnography.

[83] *Jug.* 15, 4.

[84] *Jug.* 63, 2-6; 95, 2-4.

[85] Cf. *Hist.* I, 88 (Sertorius); II, 16; cf. 17 (Pompey).

[86] On Sallust's style, in addition to the works of Kunze, Löfstedt, Latte and Syme (cited in nn. 38, 80), see L. Constans, *De sermone Sallustiano* (Paris, 1880) 244-59; E. Norden, *Die antike Kunstprosa*, 5th ed. (3rd ed. repr.) (Stuttgart, 1958) 200-4; W. Kroll, 'Die Sprache des Sallust', *Glotta* XV (1927) 270-305; E. Skard, *Sallust und seine Vorgänger* (Oslo, 1956); see also 'Remarks on Sallust's Style' on pp. xxix-xliii of Cook's edition of *Cat.* (n. 79 above). I have not had access to S. L. Fighiera, *La lingua e la grammatica di C. Sallustio Crispo*,

3rd ed. (Savona, 1905). For ancient judgments see the testimonia on pp. XXII ff of Kurfess' Teubner edition.

[87] Cf. *Cat.* 10, 5; 38, 3; cf. 52, 11; *Jug.* 41, 5; *Hist.* I, 12; cf. 13; III, 48, 11.

[88] Cf. Apuleius, *Apologia* 95.

[89] Syme, *Tacitus* I, 135; cf. 197.

[90] Cf. Suetonius, *Divus Augustus* 86.

[91] *Hist.* I, 4.

[92] Cf. Skard, *op. cit.* (n. 86), 80.

[93] *Cat.* 11, 4.

[94] Cf. Skard, *op. cit.*, 104-5.

[95] Cf. *Jug.* 34, 1; 100, 4. The question of Sallust's Greek models has been investigated by P. Perrochat, *Les modèles grecs de Salluste* (Paris, 1949), though he has sometimes been too confident in detecting influences.

[96] Cf. Cicero, *De optim. gen. orat.* 5, 15-6; *Brutus* 83, 287; *Orator* 9, 30.

[97] Quintilian X, 1, 101.

[98] On Sallust's influence see Bolaffi, *op. cit.* (n. 67); Syme, *Sallust*, 291 ff.

[99] Tacitus, *Annals* III, 30.

[100] Cf. Tacitus, *Annals* III, 65.

[101] See, for example, Sallust's remarks on Sisenna, *Jug.* 95, 2.

V
Livy

P. G. WALSH

'I am convinced that there never, never existed such a nation, and I hope for the happiness of mankind that there never will again'. GIBBON, in a letter to his father (Norton I. 61)

'. . . nulla umquam res publica nec maior nec sanctior nec bonis exemplis ditior fuit, nec in quam tam serae avaritia luxuriaque immigraverint, nec ubi tantus ac tam diu paupertati ac parsimoniae honos fuerit.' LIVY, *Praef.* 11

IN Britain and America Livy is enjoying a modest revival amongst scholars after years of neglect.[1] The full-throated condemnation of the great German historians of the last century has given way to the more moderate and constructive estimates of scholars like De Sanctis. It is recognized that from the viewpoint of the scientific historian Livy must be criticized on many counts; but his achievement is to be measured in the context of a 'rhetorical' tradition of history quite alien from ours, and the difficulties which his ambitious theme presented are increasingly acknowledged. It has been noted that he had to rely in part on authorities who were as dishonest as they were inventive[2]: the prevailing standards of historiography, after a century and a half of Latin endeavour in the shadow of the Greeks, encouraged 'fine writing' and slipshod research[3]: and the rudimentary historical tools available put an almost intolerable premium on strenuous personal experience, of which Livy was wholly innocent. The wonder is that being neither Senator nor soldier nor avid traveller he got so much right.

Since Livy's account of first-century Rome has not survived, it is useless for us to construct a league-table amongst the Roman historians, to compare him with Sallust or Tacitus. Both these historians circumscribed their work by choice of themes of immediate relevance to the Rome they knew. A more rewarding comparison would be with a similarly panoramic work such as Gibbon's *Decline and Fall*. Even this works to Livy's disadvantage; for since his surviving books (I-X and XXI-XLV, covering the years 753-293 and 219-167 B.C.) are all in the first third of the *Ab Urbe Condita*, we read all that is most idealized and least critical.

Both historians write under the stimulus of a central thesis. For Gibbon it is the conviction that conditions of political and spiritual freedom are essential for the maintenance of civilized life; and the *Decline and Fall* is the description of the disastrous chain-reaction which ensued upon the Romans' abdication of freedom. This central thesis, constantly present in the historian's mind, guides him in the choice of salient topics and ensures the cohesive structure of the whole. Tacitus was the model: 'Tacitus is the only writer I know', wrote Gibbon, 'that comes up to my idea of a philosophical historian. He employs the force of rhetoric only to display the connexion between the links forming the chain of historical events.'[4]

Livy too had his cohesive vision to lend shape to his writing. It is outlined in the Preface. Rome, after the acquisition of empire under the guiding hand of Providence for four hundred years, has undergone first a gradual decline and finally headlong degeneration. For Livy the turning point may have come not so much with the fall of Carthage as with the subsequent challenge thrown by the Gracchi at the Senatorial government.[5] The great Republican leaders before the watershed, from Brutus the Liberator to the second-century Scipio Aemilianus, are set before the reader's eyes as national *exempla virtutis*:

> ad illa mihi pro se quisque acriter intendat animum, quae vita, qui mores fuerint, per quos viros quibusque artibus domi militiaeque et partum et auctum imperium sit.[6]

The account of the early and middle Republics is indeed largely a parade of Roman civic and military virtues. Gibbon likewise was guilty of overidealizing the Rome of the Republic, but he did not make the mistake of choosing it as his main theme. In the books which have survived Livy lacks the critical incisiveness (and indeed the cynicism) of a Gibbon; without the idiosyncratic vision to organize the source-material, often subscribing to the traditional attitudes of his authorities, his thesis and his dominance of interpretation strike us by comparison as slack and at times insipid.

Because of this limitation in Livy of a lack of shaping control, there is something to be said for the view that he is pre-eminently an industrious compiler. This label immediately forces us to make the necessary qualifications; he is certainly not content to play the role of a Diodorus, to retail the accounts of others virtually untouched. He overlays the presentation of his sources with his moralizing views, and with the political and religious motivation which we must shortly consider. Further, he is more than a compiler in the sense that he has a large literary talent, which preoccupies itself particularly with psychological interpretation, both in narrative and in the composed speeches which are the most conspicuous feature of the 'rhetorical' tradition.

But his rhetorical power does not, as Tacitus' does, take control of the whole with the authority of a panoptic vision. An immense obstacle here was the annalistic presentation to which he was by tradition committed; it is significant that Tacitus later in the *Annals* abandoned this close annalistic form.[7] Lacking the analyses in depth which are a feature of Gibbon's later chapters, Livy's literary powers are devoted to the depiction of a succession of vividly drawn scenes, frequently studded with speeches of a remarkably Ciceronian virtuosity. These episodes have frequently the function of illustrating one or other of the Roman virtues; 'time and again episodes are given a self-contained unity by being turned into moral parables'.[8] And the anecdotes of the first decade pre-eminently serve this purpose, attesting the *fides*, *disciplina*, *concordia*, *virtus* or *pudicitia* of the Roman patron saints.

Livy's strength as historian lies in the comprehensiveness of his information. Any history of Republican Rome must be chiefly a study *quibus artibus domi militiaeque et partum et auctum imperium sit*, and such political and military considerations form the main lines of Livy's account. But there is also a large amount of economic and social information; far more indeed than in any other Roman historian.[9] The interest which Livy devotes to Roman religious feeling and cult-practices, especially in the first decade, makes him a most important source for the religious history of the Republic.[10] Though the extant books do not cover the period when Latin literature flowered, literary historians find Livy useful for the history of the early genres.[11] Unfortunately, for factual information of all kinds he is almost invariably at the mercy of his sources, the study of which accordingly assumes outstanding importance in any estimate of the value of his history.[12]

I

The biographical detail[13] which has survived concerning Livy is jejune, and has little import for the surviving sections of the *Ab Urbe Condita*. Born, according to Jerome, in 59 B.C. (but possibly in 64), he must have spent his first thirty years in his native Padua without experience of war or politics, a man of severely literary interests. He may have come to Rome about 30 B.C., after Octavian's final victory at Actium; but his studious life, within his literary family-circle of wife and at least three children, has left no clinching evidence of the background to his activities. But he was certainly in Rome by about 5 B.C., when he was on sufficiently intimate terms with Augustus to be rallied for showing pro-Pompeian bias in his history. About A.D. 8 he was encouraging the studies of the future emperor Claudius—doubtless to the relief of Augustus, for whom the cripple's public appearances would have been a strain. He died, again according to Jerome, in A.D. 17, though the date is wreathed with doubt.[14]

II

Of greater importance for the history are his political views. The assumption that has held the field for many years, that Livy sought to recommend the principate of Augustus by historical interpretation, is being slowly discarded.[15] His political standpoint is in fact abundantly clear in the first pentad. The ideal is a Senatorial government which seeks to establish *concordia ordinum*, and treats the plebs with courteous equity. Kingship at Rome, under whatever guise, is anathema. *Libertas* is fundamental; the rule of law must transcend the political power of individuals, and the supreme office must not remain indefinitely in the hands of a single person.

By espousing these principles, the Senate of the early Republic achieved concord and popularity; such concord in the state is Rome's greatest need for the new era of peace.[16]

The standpoint is in effect that of Cicero's later years. Livy's Preface, the credo of a young and naif idealist, asserts the familiar doctrine of the Golden Age; the early Republic embodied the ideal polity. Against the background of Augustus' 'restoration of the Republic' in 27, he urges a return to the old institutions and the old moral outlook: 'inde tibi tuaeque reipublicae quod imitere capias'. We can trace, through the Periochae of the lost books and the writers of the Livian tradition, how this yardstick dominated his presentation of the last century of the Republic. He is highly critical of the Gracchi: he justifies the Sullan party and holds Marius wholly responsible for the Civil War: he labels the First Triumvirate 'conspiratio', and attacks Julius Caesar's design for usurping power. Like Cicero, Livy did not shrink from criticizing Pompey at several points of his career; and when Augustus called Livy a Pompeian, the word indicated not a cult of personality but an interpretation supporting the lawful Senatorial government against Caesar.[17]

Livy indeed walks in Cicero's shadow. He did not hesitate to criticise Cicero's human weaknesses, but his definitive judgment reflects his admiration: 'Vir magnus ac memorabilis, et in cuius laudes persequendas Cicerone laudatore opus fuerit'.[18] He is a Ciceronian at many points. His history, as has often been suggested,[19] is the flesh of Cicero's theory of historiography. His philosophical outlook—and Livy wrote philosophy as well as history, again with Cicero as model—reflects basic similarities, for though Cicero proclaimed himself an Academic, he repeatedly adopted a Stoic position on matters of ethics.[20] Livy's speeches are elegant models of Cicero's. But above all the political attitudes are Ciceronian. Livy described the death of Cicero, and the spoliation of his corpse, with transparent sympathy and indignation, though he was well aware that Augustus remained hostile to his memory. This passage above all attests his political independence:

> ita relatum caput ad Antonium, iussuque eius inter duas manus in Rostris positum, ubi ille consul, ubi saepe consularis, ubi eo ipso anno adversus Antonium, quanta nunquam humana vox cum admiratione eloquentiae auditus fuerat. vix attollentes prae lacrimis oculos homines intueri trucidata membra eius poterant.[21]

So too in his later narrative Livy pursued his 'Pompeian' line, characterizing Brutus and Cassius, whose memory Augustus execrated, as 'insignis viros'. In the long struggle between Octavian and Antony, Livy is firmly biased in favour of Octavian. But in the final ten books, which cover the principate of Augustus, there appears to be a curious absence of reference to domestic affairs. When we recall that the last twenty-two books were not published until after the death of Augustus, we are justified in suspecting that they may have lain completed for years, and that Livy showed prudence in postponing publication, but resolute independence in his writing.[22]

III

Nowhere does Livy draw aside from his history, as Tacitus does briefly at one point,[23] to discuss his fundamental philosophical attitudes. Tacitus, more typically Roman in this respect than Cicero was, regards overenthusiasm for philosophical speculation as unbecoming in the Senatorial politician.[24] Livy had never aspired to politics, and though none of his philosophical writings has survived, his interest in philosophical issues and his own philosophical attitudes may be inferred from the *Ab Urbe Condita*. Antagonism towards Epicurean dogma is manifest.[25] He is a living exemplar of Roman piety, recounting the detail of Roman myth and ritual with an engaged zeal transcending the academic interest of a mere antiquarian; yet at the same time we observe a rationalizing mind at work, quietly dissenting from the more ludicrous elements in the canon of religious legend.[26]

This combination of piety and rationalism is characteristic of Roman Stoicism. We cannot be certain that Livy was a Stoic, but if he was it would go far to explain the curious problem of the prodigy lists. For, in an age in which historians had ceased to report these catalogues of superstition,[27] Livy regularly reproduces them, but often with caustic commentary on individual claims. This is precisely the ambivalence of the Stoic—the admission of the theoretical relevance of divination and augury, combined with scepticism of many allegedly miraculous events.[28] For our purpose the label of the philosophical school is not so important as the realization that Livy approached his authorities, crammed as they were with detail of supernatural occurrences chiefly in the Roman interest, with a divided mind. On the one hand he is convinced that Rome survived its early crises and grew by divine Providence[29]; but alleged revelations of the divine Mind he handles with caution and frequently with scepticism.[30]

IV

Livy's moral, political and religious attitudes are the basic preconceptions with which he approaches his sources. Since he has asked his readers to investigate the leading Romans and their manners, his presentation is dominated by moral judgment of individuals according to the criteria of the traditional Roman virtues. Much of this is in essence a recapitulation of earlier accounts. But the happy survival of one of his main sources, the Greek second-century historian Polybius, allows fascinating comparisons. Livy's portrayals of the hero of the Hannibalic War, Scipio Africanus, and the 'liberator' of Greece in the early second century, Quinctius Flamininus, reveal a subtle reorganization of the source-material. Scipio, the *fatalis dux*, becomes in Livy more *pius* in the traditional Roman sense and less the unorthodox mystic: his qualities as general and soldier are enhanced: his personal qualities of *comitas*, *modestia*, *temperantia* are emphasized. Flamininus is the genial but dignified father-figure, venerated by the Greeks whom he so altruistically liberated. Evidence which calls these idealized portraits into question is suppressed. And likewise on occasion when the Senate or a Roman army has behaved shabbily, Livy has overlooked it.[31]

The changes are, however, mostly marginal. For the main lines of his narrative Livy relied on his literary sources. The large scope of his subject, as well as the prevailing standards of Roman historiography, makes it in the highest degree unlikely that he consulted documents or other primary evidence.[32] Instead, he chose secondary authorities wherever possible in whose factual accuracy he could place confidence; or where he could find no reliable source—a dilemma particularly frequent in the early books—he took the trouble to scrutinize the interpretations of two or three writers of radically different viewpoints.[33] The care and fidelity with which he transcribed these accounts represents a noble advance in Roman historical standards. But it is a recurrent cause for complaint that he does not always evaluate the merits of opposing statements, being content to present differing interpretations and to leave the onus of choice to the reader.[34]

In the first decade, as Livy knew well, the theme of the struggle of the orders had offered boundless temptations to historians of the second and first centuries who wished to further the Optimate cause or to reinforce the claims of the Populares. He sought to steer a fair course by choosing authorities of opposed views, Valerius Antias and Licinius Macer. The reconstruction of Roman history was an especially lively weapon of propaganda in the hands of Licinius, a vehement supporter of the Populares. Valerius on the other hand favoured the Sullan interest, as well as seeking the maximum glory for the Valerii and their allies. Livy's early books do not always avoid the dangers; at their worst they represent not so much a reconciliation of opposed views as a combination of distortions from the two polar positions.[35]

So also in the third decade Livy utilized contrasting viewpoints, those of Coelius Antipater and of Valerius Antias. Coelius' history, as we have seen,[36] is a remarkable phenomenon at Rome, and its literary vices should not distract attention from its historical virtues. The historian's consultation of the work of Silenus, writing from the Carthaginian standpoint, provided Livy with detailed information about the activities of Hannibal's army in Spain and in Italy. To counterbalance and complement this view of the fighting, Livy relied on Valerius, whose annalistic presentation centred on Rome, providing important detail of political, diplomatic and military administration by the Senate and the magistrates. Finally, the great Polybius was consulted for Greek, African and Sicilian affairs; and it is a tribute to Livy's recognition of a major historian that he was usually content to accept Polybius' version of events without recourse to other authorities.[37]

Polybius becomes still more important in the fourth and fifth decades, which cover the events of 201-167. Livy follows his version with great fidelity, occasionally offering clarification on points of geography or constitutional procedure, occasionally making minor changes of a moral or patriotic nature, and regularly reshaping his source in the interests of literary effect. Only rarely, however, does he challenge the Greek historian on a major issue of fact or interpretation; in fifteen books there are only sixteen occasions when he appends citations from other authorities to the version adopted from Polybius.[38] For information about events in Italy and Spain during these years, he turns again to Valerius Antias and to the contemporary of Antias, Claudius Quadrigarius.[39]

In all likelihood this technique of choosing sources with varying backgrounds and viewpoints continued in the lost books. A recent analysis of Livy's account of Sulla has convincingly revealed the disharmony of two sources—the one pro-Sullan, probably the *Commentarii* of the man himself, and the other representing the Senatorial view, Sisenna's study of the Social and Civil Wars.[40]

Livy's method of handling this source-material stands out clearly at numerous points of the narrative. The careful choice of sources suggests that he first made a general survey of those apposite to his purpose. Then in the actual composition he followed the single source already established as best suited for a particular topic; and when he changed topics or shifted the focus of his narrative he often changed his main source. For example, early in the third decade Coelius is regularly followed for details of the fighting in the Hannibalic War; but when the Roman scene is introduced, Livy has usually turned to Valerius. Then at the end of each section of narrative, when the version of his main source was controverted, he appended other views in what are virtually footnotes. This technique allowed him to build up his own literary structure on the basis of a single account.

By the standards of a modern historian, whose desk and shelves are piled high with volumes for consultation, this Livian method seems primitive. By comparison with the careful research of Gibbon's earlier volumes it is slipshod. It requires an effort of the imagination to visualize the difficulties of simultaneous consultation of different *volumina*, with the laborious unwinding and rewinding of each roll. And the framing of a narrative completely independent of the sources was too large a task for a historian whose schedule demanded the publication of a pentad every twelve to eighteen months for over thirty years. Those who compose regular lectures (and some who write books) are aware of the time and labour saved by glossing another man's presentation rather than constructing one's own. At Rome this was unfortunately the regular practice; and even Tacitus, writing the specialized history of a shorter period, is in places guilty of it.[41]

With this picture in mind of Livy's attitudes and methods of research, we can proceed to examine the value of the extant sections of his history.

V

For many, reliving their experiences of inky school-texts and Macaulay's *Lays of Ancient Rome*, Livy's name evokes no more than romantic stories of courage and chastity, standing out like islands in an ocean of carnage. Lucretia's suicide, Brutus the Liberator's execution of his son, Horatius on the *pons sublicius*, Cloelia's swimming the Tiber, Verginia and the lustful Appius Claudius—it is tempting to use these as evidence against Livy and to banish him for ever from the fold of real historians.

But almost all of these fables occur in the first pentad, which is no more than a prologue to Livy's serious history, and which occupies only a thirtieth of the whole area. Further, Livy was well aware of the historical dubiety of much of this early material; he took pains to present it to the reader as *poeticis magis decora fabulis quam incorruptis rerum gestarum monumentis*.[42] But should he have presented it at all? His dilemma was shared by other historians, some of whom declined to treat such shadowy themes.[43] Livy could have followed their example, or presented a bald summary of what probably happened. The decisive factor in rejecting these courses was probably his patriotic pride; he decided to indulge the tradition *ut primordia . . . augustiora faciat*.[44] The scientific historians like Mommsen and Pais had no doubt that this was the wrong answer, and they rejected the early books as a tissue of fiction. But modern scholars applaud Livy's decision. They allow that the written and oral traditions suffered distortion and accretion, and that Livy's authorities manipulated these traditions in a spirit of chauvinism, party-politics, gentile glorification and literary elaboration. Yet 'in every sphere of ancient history modern research is revealing the solid core of historical reality which lies beneath legendary traditions', and Livy is being studied by archaeologists with enhanced respect.[45]

Livy's account of Rome's foundation is, of course, utter myth, being derived from Greek versions which go back to the fifth century.[46] In fact, habitation of the Palatine hill goes back well beyond the eighth century; monumental building in the Forum Romanum and the Forum Boarium began about 575 B.C.[47] In

Livy's first book, whilst Romulus must be dismissed as a personification of the city, the three ensuing kings (Numa Pompilius, Tullus Hostilius, Ancus Marcius) can be accepted as historical figures, but shadowy leaders of the primitive village-community on the Palatine hill.[48] The traditional date of the first Etruscan king is 616 B.C., and this change in the disposition of power at Rome clearly coincides with the first building in stone; the literary dating may be a little early, but the names of Tarquin and Tanaquil have been found on tomb-inscriptions, and can be accepted. The 'achievements' of Tarquinius Superbus are, however, largely a duplication of those of Tarquinius Priscus[49]; we can establish from Livy's account only the limits of Etruscan control. It is possible that the reign of Servius Tullius represents an interlude of autonomy between eras of this control, and that the 'Servian' reforms, the original Servian wall, the cult of Diana do go back to the late Regal period. The modern historian is uncomfortably aware that innovations and general policy attributed to individual kings were still being politically 'slanted' in the middle of the first century B.C.[50]; and there are numerous examples of Greek myths being introduced in adapted form to Roman circumstances.[51] But there is no reason to reject the bare outline, and Livy's sensible commentary is useful at many points.[52]

Liberi iam hinc populi Romani res pace belloque gestas. . . .[53] How reliable are the other nine books of the first decade? As Livy knew well, the written evidence for the first century of the Republic, before the sack of Rome by the Gauls, was slight and mostly perished in the conflagration.[54] But it is perfectly possible that bare records of magistrates and *res gestae* survived from the fifth century, even if the pontifical annals were compiled in systematic form only a century later. This material was brought together into *volumina* in the second century: it was incorporated into their histories by second-century annalists such as Piso: taken over by the late annalists Valerius and Claudius, who exercised their inventive talents to forge further archival material *ad maiorem patriae gentisque gloriam:* and Livy finally got the material (at best at third hand and perhaps at fourth) in its augmented form. With this list of yearly magistrates and events he collated another, the *libri lintei*; this list on linen, which I believe may have been compiled in the fourth century,[55] was read by Livy not in the original but in the account of Licinius Macer. However derivative the end-product is, the outstanding scholar in this field believes that the list of magistrates in Livy is superior to that found in other historians or documents.[56]

Within this reliable framework Livy recounted his interlocking themes—Rome's military advance towards the hegemony of Italy, and the domestic struggles out of which the plebs won an honourable role in the seat of government. In the military sphere, no more than the outline can be accepted—the struggle with the Latin league, the interminable campaigning against the mountain-tribes to the east and north-east, the struggle with the Etruscan cities of the north, the Gallic catastrophe and the ensuing Roman revival, the Wars with the Samnites. In all these operations as described by Livy the distortions caused by Roman chauvinism are blatant. Livy's authorities palliate Roman defeats by emphasizing the divine anger, the discriminating weather, and the headstrong failings of Roman individuals. After Roman defeats, there are invariably Roman recoveries and still more crushing victories. Individuals are glorified. We recognize the contributions of Fabius Pictor (and perhaps of Licinius[57]) in the splendid deeds of Fabii, of Valerius Antias in the achievements of Valerii, of Licinius Macer in the prominence of Licinii.[58] In recounting these glorious sagas and the courage of Roman leaders, Livy and his sources often adapted the *motifs* and language of Greek epic.[59] A similar judgment can be passed on the depiction of the domestic evolution. The outline of the decisive stages can be accepted; but the detail was largely written into the framework by historians and legal authorities in the late second and first centuries. Later constitutional and legal practices are given ancient precedents.[60] And as in the accounts of external achievement, family-glorification is a prominent feature. So is the projection into the past of the fame or disgrace sustained by *gentes* in the events of the third and second centuries.[61] Some famous careers have been wholly invented; Coriolanus is a case in point.[62]

VI

Livy devoted the other twenty-five surviving books (XXI-XLV) to the half-century between the outbreak of the Second Punic War and the battle of Pydna. This is in general far more reliable as detailed history, reflecting the choice of superior sources, Polybius and Coelius Antipater, as well as the greater abundance of available facts. But since Valerius Antias and Claudius Quadrigarius are also employed for most items of political history and some of military campaigns, the dilemma of what is fact and what is invention in these 'annalistic' sections still plagues the historian.

These fifty years are a period of almost continuous warfare. Livy is no military expert, and it would be easy to catalogue many of the deficiencies in the accounts of campaigning in Italy, Spain, Greece and Asia.[63] But if we flank Livy's history with Sallust's *Bellum Jugurthinum* and with Tacitus ('the most unmilitary of historians' in Mommen's acid comment) it becomes clear that precision of topography and tactical movement had low priority in the Roman conception of *historia*, which was more concerned with the psychology of the combatants and their leaders.

Much of this period is also described in the extant books of Polybius. Comparison with this excellent authority confirms that whilst Livy steers clear of Valerius and Claudius, his account is in general reliable, and there are places where he is more accurate in detail than the Greek historian.[64] But the 'annalistic' sections are vitiated by errors of chronology,[65] moralizing distortion,[66] patriotic bias,[67] anti-plebeian sentiment,[68] and that idealizing of Roman leaders which Livy extends to all parts of his work.[69]

The political sections of these decades reflect the strengths and weaknesses of the annalistic sources. The strengths reside in the framework they provide of the central administration of the wars, with an extraordinary amount of administrative detail, especially prosopographic, in both political and military contexts. It is possible to obtain from Livy's account an almost complete list for this half-century of elections to the higher magistracies and of appointments of magistrates and ex-magistrates to their spheres of duty. Again, from information supplied by Livy an almost complete chart of legionary dispositions in the various theatres of war can be assembled, and this type of information on strategic planning is often more significant than details of military tactics for an understanding of the outcome of campaigns. There was less temptation on the part of Livy's sources to manipulate this kind of information, because their evidence could be checked against available records.

Detail of Roman diplomacy is also copious, with accounts of the dispatch and reception of embassies; and treaties are set down in detail. Unfortunately, patriotic feeling frequently affected the annalists' presentation of such treaties. For example, if we compare Livy's account of the peace-terms imposed on Carthage after the Hannibalic War with those in Polybius,[70] we find a general correspondence except on two issues. Livy says that Carthage was to make a *foedus* with Masinissa about their common boundary; Polybius does not mention this, and indeed such permissiveness on Rome's part would have been a remarkable departure from her diplomatic techniques. Secondly, Livy maintains that Carthage could not wage even defensive war in Africa under the treaty; these alleged clauses, which probably never existed, allowed Livy's sources more comfortably to assign responsibility for the Third Punic War to Carthage, when that city retaliated against constant Numidian infiltration. Many other examples of such problems in Livy's account caused by such chauvinistic distortions could be cited.[71]

In spite of these defects, Livy's picture of Senatorial activity and procedure is of considerable value. Another valuable contribution lies in the social and economic sphere. An outstanding example of his usefulness lies in the copious information he provides on Italian colonies founded by Rome between 200 and 170. He does not provide a concentrated analysis of this programme, but the information can be assembled from the annalistic entries under each year.[72] Again, the depth of his demographic information is impressive; the population-statistics of citizens enrolled at each *lustrum* are regularly recounted. One can also glean a surprising amount of information about state-income; for example, in the Hannibalic War there is detail of the direct tax on citizens, the purchase-taxes on salt and slaves, the income derived from booty, the money raised from sale of public lands.[73] The efforts made by the citizens are also noted; the liturgies imposed on the rich to equip the navy, the loan of trust-funds to the state by widows and minors, the collections of gold, silver and jewellery from patriotic persons.[74] There is an important list of towns which made contributions in kind before the Roman invasion of Africa, together with the commodities offered—providing precious information about local industries.[75] And in general these details give us a larger view of the sustained patriotic sacrifices, enabling us to understand how Rome recovered after Cannae from the earlier crushing disasters.

In this sense, therefore, the comprehensiveness of Livy's account surpasses in breadth that of other ancient historians.

VII

In spite of these solid virtues, by the criteria of the modern historian Livy's performance must be criticized on many counts. Such criticisms are partially an indictment of the aims of 'rhetorical' history. Whilst the Romans recognized the obligation to tell the whole truth,[76] for them *historia* was also a literary category, visualized by some theorists as the written counterpart to oratory, by others as closely related to poetry.[77] It is not concerned with the evolution of political institutions, nor with economic 'laws', nor with scientific disquisitions on warfare, but with men and manners —the deeds, words, and thoughts of communities and their leaders. It is Livy's aim to demonstrate that mental and moral qualities have a decisive impact on events, and by the dramatic quality of his writing, in which the techniques of Tragedy are prominent, to engage the reader in the attitudes and decisions of the participants at critical junctures of history.

Livy's history, then, is pre-eminently psychological history. In warfare he constantly interprets the outcome of events by analysis of the state of mind of the troops, of the plans and moral qualities of their commanders.[78] In description of political activities he tries to account for attitudes or decisions by depicting group-motives.[79] Speeches are composed to delineate the thoughts of individuals, and their impetus is conveyed in the comments and thoughts of the by-standers. Livy invariably uses *oratio obliqua* to achieve his psychological aim of evoking the secret thoughts of communities. In Quintilian's view[80] Livy was the outstanding Roman exponent of such psychological techniques, and Tacitus' exploitation of them undoubtedly owes much to study of Livy's methods.

At this point historical vision and literary talent converge, reflecting the 'mira iucunditas' and 'clarissimus candor' of his narrative and the 'ineffable eloquence' of the speeches (these would be curious criteria of a historian's excellence, but Quintilian[81] is writing for students of rhetoric). In the narrative, the annalistic form dictates the presentation. Livy must reproduce for each year the lists of magistrates, army commanders, sacerdotal appointments, and prodigies; the Latin is neat but simple and often paratactic, echoing the jejune sentences of the original registers.[82] But in the description of military campaigning or political discussion, Livy seeks to mould the material into separate episodes.[83] Time after time one observes how the scenes are constructed on a trinity of introduction, psychological observation, action[84]; time after time one notes how he moulds the attitudes and activities of opposing groups into a unified narration. The description of the Roman capture of Veii is a good example:

> cuniculus delectis militibus eo tempore plenus in aedem Iunonis, quae in Veientana arce erat, armatos repente edidit, et pars auersos in muris inuadunt hostis, pars claustra portarum reuellunt, pars, cum ex tectis saxa tegulaeque a mulieribus ac seruitiis iacerentur, inferunt ignes. clamor omnia uariis terrentium ac pauentium uocibus mixto mulierum ac puerorum ploratu complet. momento temporis deiectis ex muro undique armatis patefactisque portis cum alii agmine inruerent, alii desertos scanderent muros, urbs hostibus impletur; omnibus locis pugnatur; deinde multa iam edita caede senescit pugna, et dictator praecones edicere iubet ut ab inermi abstineatur. is finis sanguinis fuit.[85]

Within the structure of such alternation of standpoint, one notes how Livy can summon all the resources of dramatic description which the Latin language affords. As so often, the suddenness of the onset is stressed; '*repente* edidit . . . *momento temporis* urbs hostibus impletur'. The technique of 'divided description' shows the sections of the army at work attacking the defenders in the rear, breaking open the gates from the inside, throwing torches into recalcitrant houses; and the use of historic presents brings the scene closer to our eyes. Though Livy describes the shouting of both sides, he draws our attention more particularly to the Veientines by the alliterative phraseology, 'mixto mulierum ac puerorum ploratu'. Then the entry of the main Roman force, again described in sections (alii . . . alii); and chiastic antithesis is sought between the actions of the mining force (deiectis ex muro undique armatis patefactisque portis) and that of the main army ('some rushing in . . . others climbing the abandoned walls'). There is that tint of poetic language throughout which is appropriate to *historia*[86]; the tunnel is said to 'bring forth' armed men, a powerful metaphor reminding us of Ennius' 'grauidus armatis equus': the mingled cries 'omnia complet'—this use of the neuter plural is especially common in dramatic contexts[87]: and after much slaughter the battle 'grows old' or 'loses its vigour'.

Quintilian claims that the speeches in Livy are perfectly adapted to both circumstances and speakers.[88] This is true not only of the formal orations but also of informal conversations. The historian was well aware of the potentialities of the dialogue both for characterization and for high drama.[89] We may cite as example the conversation after Cannae between Hannibal and his cavalry-commander Maharbal; it has been noted that this anecdote appeared in more basic form in Cato and Livy's source Coelius.[90] Livy sets the scene by contrasting the attitudes of other Carthaginian leaders, urging rest, with that of Maharbal, who

> minime cessandum ratus, 'immo ut quid hac pugna sit actum scias, die quinto' inquit 'uictor in Capitolio epulaberis. sequere; cum equite, ut prius uenisse quam uenturum sciant, praecedam'.
>
> Hannibali nimis laeta res est uisa maiorque quam ut eam statim capere animo posset. itaque uoluntatem se laudare Maharbalis ait; ad consilium pensandum temporis opus esse.
>
> tum Maharbal: 'non omnia nimirum eidem di dedere. uincere scis, Hannibal; uictoria uti nescis'.
>
> mora eius diei satis creditur saluti fuisse urbi atque imperio.[91]

By comparison with the version of Coelius, Livy's Latin makes few concessions to archaism or colloquialism, *immo* being the only gesture in that direction. But he has shaped the story to sharpen the psychological interpretation: *nimis laeta res est visa*—Hannibal cannot contemplate the possibility of dining on the Capitol. (Similar observations are found in other Livian dialogues to account for attitudes or decisions).[92] Livy uses *oratio obliqua* for Hannibal's reply in extension of the psychological portrait, and also to lend additional rhetorical effect to the *oratio recta* of the celebrated *sententia* of Maharbal. The purpose of the anecdote, in Livian elaboration, is not merely to characterize Hannibal as a great general and a poor politician, but also to stamp the *occasion* of the decision as uniquely significant; 'that day's delay, we can safely assume, saved Rome and saved the empire'.

Such psychological depiction of leaders and of armies, in the various complexities of victory and defeat, stale-mate and massacre, forms the staple of Livy's literary approach. In political contexts too the same probing of motives and the same elucidation of character is to be observed. Assemblies can be described to reflect national characteristics[93]; and the extended speeches are usually placed in the mouths of prominent persons whom Livy desires to characterize. Not that he wholly invents the speeches when authentic records of what was actually said were available; but he shapes the material into the appropriate 'deliberative' structure, and in the *tractatio*, the section of the speech which discusses the utility and morality of the issue under judgment, the arguments can be edited or developed to draw attention to the speaker's main attitudes.[94] For example, Cato's speech delivered in 195 B.C., in opposition to the proposed repeal of the Oppian law,[95] contains no echo of the surviving fragments of that speech; the Latin is that of Augustan prose, and the anti-feminist arguments and apothegms intensified—'quia singulas non continuimus universas horremus', 'simul pares esse coeperint, superiores erunt'. Livy characteristically juxtaposes this long speech with the counter-speech of the tribune Lucius Valerius, and the effective contrast adds force to the characterizing arguments which are attributed to Cato himself.

VIII

Livy's strengths and limitations may be seen in microcosm by the brief survey of a single book. Book XXI will admirably serve our purpose, for here the historian has everything in his favour. With the experience of the composition of two decades behind him, he has here the theme of the Hannibalic War, which moved him deeply as a patriot, and recourse to reasonably adequate sources. With characteristic neatness the book is divided into three approximately equal sections—Spain and the outbreak of the war, Hannibal's invasion of Italy, and the first operations in Italy.

In the section on Spain, overshadowing all else is the chronoogical error by which the siege of Saguntum was dated to 218 instead of 219. This was a mistake which Livy need not have made, for he reveals that he has read the correct chronology, and later tacitly accepts it.[96] This deliberate falsification by his source,[97] which palliates the Roman failure to help Saguntum, affects the whole of Livy's version of the diplomatic dialogue of 219 between Carthage and Rome, much of which is fiction.

A second source of distortion here is Livy's version of the two treaties of Lutatius Catulus (241) and of the Ebro (?226-5) as they affect Saguntum. According to Livy's version, the freedom of the Saguntines was protected by both these treaties; whilst dispute is possible in the first case, the second appears to be a complete falsification introduced by Livy's source, and again the error is pervasive throughout the account of the debates before the declaration of war.[98]

Tendentious source-material also distorts Livy's version of Hannibal's military operations in 221-20, which are presented as a chain-operation with the ultimate aim of destroying Saguntum. With characteristic vagueness of geography, he calls the Olcades, Vaccaei, and Carpetani 'neighbours' of Saguntum (*finitimae gentes*).[99] Hannibal's aim was in fact to extend Carthaginian dominion to the Ebro. All these are typical examples of how Livy swallows whole the fabricated or tendentious versions of his less reliable sources. His inexperience of warfare results in confusion in the description of the battle of the Tagus, where he states that the Carthaginians pitched camp on the north bank instead of south of the river; Polybius' account is overwhelmingly more probable.[100]

Livy seeks to concentrate the reader's attention initially on Hannibal as the most menacing exponent of Barcine imperialism. A character-sketch in the Sallustian manner is reinforced by speeches from Hanno; so far from being historical, these speeches are an expression of the traditional Roman view of Hannibal as the *furia faxque huius belli*.[101] The portrait is further rounded by recounting his popularity with his troops. This depiction is lent further vividness by the account of Hannibal's famous dream, in which the Carthaginian leader is represented as a huge dragon devastating Italy. Livy's source has here happily survived, and we can clearly observe how the psychological and dramatic elements are sharpened. A storm-cloud is made to hover over the scene ('cum fragore coeli nimbum'), and a more ominous answer given when Hannibal enquires the meaning of the portent: 'sineretque fata in occulto esse'.[102]

The second feature which here fired Livy's imagination was the siege of Saguntum, the detailed treatment of which unfolds like the acts of a drama. The mundane issue of where the attack was mounted obtains little mention[103]; the interest is focused on the psychological sector. The Saguntines win the first round, causing *trepidatio* amongst the enemy: in the second stage, the city is almost in Carthaginian hands when *desperatio* animates the defenders, and they dramatically (*repente*) rout the enemy: the third section describes how Carthaginian hatred of the enemy and prospects of booty (*ira . . . spe*) bring them close to success ('adeo accensi omnes sunt ut nulla vi resisti videretur posse') and the morale of the Saguntines sags. Finally, after Alorcus the Spaniard advises surrender comes the dramatic denouement. Suddenly (*repente*) treasures are flung into the forum and ignited; the inhabitants fling themselves into the flames or 'enclosed themselves with wives and children inside their houses, which they burnt over their heads'. For those who remained, 'death alone brought an end to the conflict'.[104] Livy's description of the *Saguntina rabies*[105] does full justice to its noble theme.

Thirdly, one should note how Livy analyses the Roman reaction to the Saguntine tragedy. 'Such boundless grief (*maeror*) and pity (*misericordia*) at the unmerited slaughter of their allies, such shame (*pudor*) at their own failure to bear assistance, such anger (*ira*) at the Carthaginians and fear (*metus*) for the safety of the state oppressed the Senate, as though the enemy were already at the gates, that overwhelmed by this simultaneous concourse of emotions they panicked rather than coolly deliberated'. The favourite device of *oratio obliqua* is employed to elaborate upon the source of their fear; they ponder the contrast between the lively, warlike Carthaginians and the sluggish, inexperienced Roman troops. 'The war would have to be waged against the whole world in Italy, before the walls of Rome.'[106] This brilliantly-drawn picture, so persuasive as an imaginative reconstruction, provides a salutary instance of the dangers of such *post hoc* psychological analysis. For the following chapter (a clear, concise account of Roman commands and legionary dispositions, reflecting one of Livy's greatest merits as historian), shows clearly enough that no defensive campaigning in Italy was yet envisaged, and that Spain and Africa were anticipated as the battlefields.[107]

A detailed discussion of the problems of Hannibal's route from Spain to Italy would be inappropriate here. Livy's version attempts to be accurate and topographically informative, and in its defence it should be noted that as far as the notorious 'Island' on the Rhone it not only squares with Polybius but supplies extra topographical precision.[108] Moreover, Livy's account of the final stage of the journey has persuaded most modern scholars to reject the Little St Bernard as Hannibal's pass, as proposed by Polybius, in favour of Mt Genèvre or one of the Mt Cenis passes.[109] But Livy's account of the journey from the Rhone to the main Alpine range is not only inconsistent with Polybius but also self-contradictory, and it appears certain that he has introduced dissonant material from a second source, which will be Valerius, into the account as provided by Coelius.[110]

Livy's main purpose here is to unite, in a memorably dramatic narration, a psychological depiction of the emotions and moral courage of Hannibal and the Carthaginians with vivid word-pictures of their hazards and privations. First there are the hostile Volcae on the banks of the Rhone: 'occursant in ripa cum variis ululatibus cantuque moris sui, quatientes scuta super capita vibrantesque dextris tela'.[111] Their discomfiture is described, as they are suddenly assailed in the rear by a Carthaginian detachment, by Livy's favourite 'deus ex machina' device.[112] Next follows the lively description of how the elephants are shipped across the Rhone on rafts, 'urgentes inter se, cedentibus extremis ab aqua . . . donec quietem ipse timor circumspectantibus aquam fecisset'.[113] Before the Carthaginians resume their journey, Hannibal addresses them; Livy has rearranged the order of events and reorganized the speech itself to provide the maximum rhetorical impact.[114] Next comes the celebrated depiction of the Alps, 'montium altitudo nivesque caelo prope immixtae, tecta informia imposita rupibus, pecora iumentaque torrida frigore, homines intonsi et inculti, animalia inanimaque omnia rigentia gelu. . . .'[115] In describing the emotions of the Carthaginians, Livy constantly reminds us that they are southerners in a strange world; so when they reach the main Alpine range they are stupefied by falling snow: 'nivis etiam casus . . . ingentem terrorem adiecit. per omnia nive oppleta, cum signis prima luce motis segniter agmen incederet, pigritiaque et desperatio in omnium voltu emineret. . . .'[116] The narrative of the descent is equally memorable by its evocation of 'pity and fear' for the participants.

With Hannibal's arrival in Italy, the war proper is fittingly inaugurated in Livy's account by two of the finest of his orations, the battle-speeches of Scipio the elder and of Hannibal before the skirmish at the Ticinus. They are carefully balanced in length and content, with beginnings and ends notably parallel; but the *tractatio* has in each case been utilized to contrast the essential religious attitudes of the Roman with Hannibal's over-reliance on fortune, which he is later to admit brings him low.[117]

This section is a nightmare for the scientific historian seeking detailed evidence of the events of late 218. The battle of the Ticinus is placed too far north near Victumulae: in his description of the aftermath of the battle, the rivers Ticinus and Po are confused: the battle of the Trebia is hopelessly confused topographically, and the Roman defeat is seen to incorporate face-saving elements: there is a most unlikely account of the capture by the Carthaginians of Victumulae, apparently wholly invented to brand Hannibal as a treacherous and cruel tyrant, for it makes no military or diplomatic sense. There is a description of an unsuccessful attempt to cross the Apennines and of subsequent fighting around Placentia, both of which look suspiciously like duplication from a second source. And finally the operations of Cn. Scipio in Spain are presented in two consecutive stages, with peaceful negotiations preceding all warfare against resisting towns; Polybius shows that the two were concurrent, as indeed the late date of the campaigning-season demanded.[118] At some points, however, Livy is more reliable than Polybius, as in the greater detail of Sicilian operations and his account of Sempronius' journey by sea to Ariminum; and again at some points of the campaigning in northern Italy.[119]

Livy's basic preoccupation here, however, is to produce moral criteria to account for Carthaginian successes. The *temeritas* and *ferocitas* of Sempronius are sharply contrasted with Hannibal's *prudentia*. This version of the battle of the Trebia was traditional, but Livy makes the judgment sharper and more emphatic. The thoughts and words of Sempronius at the bedside of his sick colleague and in the *praetorium* are tellingly juxtaposed with the reflections of Hannibal. The artistic balance of these contrasting attitudes (both culminate in *oratio recta*) is reinforced by emphasis on the unpreparedness of the wet, cold and hungry Romans confronted by Carthaginians who are warm, dry, well-fed, and supple with the application of olive-oil.[120] So too in the final chapters of the book the characterization of C. Flaminius sets the scene for the disaster at Lake Trasimene; his *impietas* and *discordia* are presaged by a long list of prodigies, which creates the ominous atmosphere of divine disfavour.[121]

Characteristic, too, is the emphasis on the shocked reaction at Rome to the defeat at the Trebia: 'Romam tantus terror ex hac clade perlatus est . . .'. This psychological interpretation is developed by expressing in *oratio obliqua* the Roman desperation at the defeat of the two consular armies. As earlier, the drama is achieved at the expense of the facts; for according to Polybius Sempronius was able initially to conceal the defeat, the realization of which came too slowly for sudden panic.[122]

Such detailed analysis reveals the gulf between ancient and modern historiography. Above all, the exclusive concern with human motivation leads to an excess of moralistic interpretation, of over-imaginative psychological analysis; and the 'rhetorical' tradition encourages manipulation of 'what really was said' in favour of character-building and stirring oratory. And even in the context of ancient historiographical theory, Livy cannot be regarded as a great historian; it is no accident that Sallust was widely preferred *as historian* by ancient critics.[123] On the other hand, the classification of Livy as a non-historian, as a 'prose Virgil', as a 'Roman Sir Walter Scott' (to quote two common if incompatible formulae), does little justice to the astonishing range of prosaic but precious facts which this essay earlier emphasized. Livy is a second-class historian, who raises an abysmally bad historiographic tradition to more respectable levels; lacking the critical faculties of a Gibbon, he is that historian's equal only in the versatility of his literary genius, which is equal to all the demands placed upon it.

NOTES

[1] Mr R. M. Ogilvie's important *Commentary* on I-V has appeared, and a revised text of this pentad will, it is hoped, follow. Dr T. A. Dorey is working on a new Teubner text of XXI-XXV. The new Oxford text of XXXI-XLV is in the hands of Dr A. H. McDonald. In America the much-needed Lexicon of Livy is under way. A stimulating survey of the biographical problems has recently been published by Sir Ronald Syme ('Livy and Augustus' in *HSCP* 64 (1959), 27-87). The present writer's *Livy* (C.U.P., 1961) attempts a general evaluation; some repetition is inevitable in this essay if it is not to become eccentrically selective.

[2] See the earlier chapter of Dr E. Badian.

[3] Livy, *praef.* 2; Pliny, *Ep.* V, 8.

[4] I have found Harold Bond, *The Literary Art of Edward Gibbon* (Oxford, 1960) to be the most useful guide here.

[5] See *Per.* LX; Orosius V, 8.3-4, 12.3; Florus II, 3.

[6] *praef.* 9.

[7] Unlike Syme (see the interesting comment in *Tacitus*, 269) I would regard his reasons as primarily an attempt at more coherent presentation.

[8] Ogilvie, *Commentary*, 18.

[9] A glance at Tenny Frank's first volume of the *Economic Survey of Ancient Rome* will demonstrate this.

[10] As such handbooks as G. Wissowa's and K. Latte's clearly show.

[11] Notably the discussion at VII, 2, for the origins of drama and satire.

[12] Note 2 above.

[13] See, most recently, R. Syme's article (n. 1 above) and Ogilvie, *Commentary*, 1 ff. For earlier bibliography, see *Livy*, 1-19.

[14] The dates of birth and death are recorded by Jerome in *ad Euseb. Chron. ad ann. Abr.* 1958 and 2033. But the second or both these dates may be five years too late, through grouping Livy with Messala Corvinus. This thesis is propounded by Syme and Ogilvie; for an intelligent defence of the traditional dating, see G. V. Sumner, *AUMLA* (1961), 191-3, quoting Hanslik, s.v. 'Messala Corvinus' in *RE* VIII A 1.

[15] The earlier view is enshrined in such important works as Cochrane's *Christianity and Classical Culture* (Oxford, 1940) and Syme's *Roman Revolution* (paperback, 1960). For the reaction, Walsh, *Livy*, 11 ff, and *Proc. Afr. Class. Assn.* (1961); H. Petersen, 'Livy and Augustus', *TAPA* 92 (1961), 440 ff; Ogilvie, *loc. cit.*

[16] See Livy II, 1.1; III, 39.8; II, 9.7-8; IX, 19.7, etc.

[17] For the Gracchi, n. 5 above; Sulla and Marius, *Per.* LXIX, LXXX; Florus II, 9.6 (see Badian, *JRS* 52 (1962), 48 ff). On Caesar, *Per.* CIII; Sen. *N.Q.* V, 18.4. Criticism of Pompey, *Per.* XCII; Flor. II, 13, 16, 20; Dio 41.13.4.

[18] Sen. *Suas.* VI, 17.

[19] See, e.g., R. Heinze, *Die augusteische Kultur*[2] (Leipzig, 1933); H. Bornecque, *Tite-Live* (Paris, 1933); M. Rambaud, *Cicéron et l'histoire romaine* (Paris, 1953).

[20] See the excellent book of H. A. K. Hunt, *The Humanism of Cicero* (Melbourne, 1954). Cicero mirrors largely the position of Antiochus, who sought to reconcile the philosophies of Academics, Peripatetics, and Stoics; see *Fin.* V, 22; *Ac.* I, 17, II, 15, etc. E. Zeller's *History of Eclecticism* is still most useful as a guide here.

[21] Ref. at n. 18.

[22] On Brutus and Cassius, Tac. *Ann.* IV, 34; Octavian and Antony, *Per.* LXXX; Eutropius VII, 7. Some manuscripts of the Periochae state that book 121 was published after the death of Augustus.

[23] *Ann.* VI, 22.

[24] Tac. *Agric.* 4.4.

[25] III, 56.7; X, 40.10, 14.

[26] See I. Kajanto, *God and Fate in Livy* (Turku, 1957).

[27] Livy XLIII, 13.1.

[28] See *AJP* 79 (1958), 355 ff; M. L. W. Laistner, *The Greater Roman Historians* (Berkeley, 1947), 68 ff.

[29] See, e.g., I, 4.1.

[30] *Livy*, 62-3.

[31] For further detail, on Scipio and Flamininus see *Livy*, 93-101; the constructive criticisms of J. E. A. Crake (*Phoenix* 16 (1962), 212) persuade me that my criticism of Livy is unfair in one or two places, though I think his apologia for the late annalists is misguided. For conscious suppression of Senatorial intrigue, see notably XLV, 19-20, against the source Pol. XVIII, 43; for army-truculence unmentioned by Livy, see XXXIII, 10, against Pol. XVIII, 27.4.

[32] Useful source-discussion is unfortunately almost all in German. See especially A. Klotz, *Livius und seine Vorgänger* (Leipzig, 1940-1); on the first books, the useful comments of Ogilvie's *Commentary*; on the third decade, G. De Sanctis, *Storia dei Romani* III, 2 (Turin, 1917); and for the fourth and fifth, H. Nissen, *Kritische Untersuchungen* (Berlin, 1868), and U. Kahrstedt, *Die Annalistik von Livius* (Berlin, 1913).

[33] With the noteworthy exception of Coelius Antipater, none of the Latin sources consulted by Livy reveal this impressive impartiality.

[34] See, for example, XXI, 38.2-3; XXVII, 1.13; XXXIII, 23.5, etc.

[35] This emerges repeatedly from Ogilvie's *Commentary*. Also cited in these earlier books are Q. Aelius Tubero, whose legal and antiquarian interests provided Livy with information on religious and judicial procedures (as Ogilvie comments, Livy astonishingly ignores Varro); Claudius Quadrigarius, four times quoted in VI-X; L. Calpurnius Piso, who may have been quoted by Valerius Antias and not consulted directly (so Ogilvie); and Fabius Pictor, the father of Roman history, whom Livy may have read in the pages of Licinius Macer.

[36] See above, pp. 15-17.

[37] For details of treaties and other state-business, however, Livy regularly consults the annalists as well.

[38] Kahrstedt, *Die Annalistik*, 97.

[39] On whom see Badian's apposite comments above, pp. 18-20.

[40] Badian, *JRS* 50 (1962), 48 ff.

[41] See C. Questa, *Studi sulle fonti degli* Annales *di Tacito* (Rome, 1960).

[42] *praef.* 6.

[43] Claudius Quadrigarius, for example, began his history at 390.

[44] *praef.* 7.

[45] R. Bloch, *The Origins of Rome* (English edition 1960), 18. The recent survey of A. Momigliano, *JRS* 53 (1963), 95 ff, has very pertinent comments on the importance of the literary tradition.

[46] Especially important is Hellanicus of Mytilene, and perhaps Damastes of Sigeum. See in general De Sanctis, *Storia* I, 200.

[47] See E. Gjerstad, *Early Rome* III (Lund, 1960), 460.

[48] The problems relating to the historicity of these kings are well treated in Ogilvie's *Commentary*.

[49] In the literary account they are credited with the same achievements—the *cloacae,* the *circus*, the Capitoline temple.

[50] For Cicero's manipulation of the tradition in *De Republica* II, see R. Klein, *Königtum und Königszeit bei Cicero* (diss. Erlangen, 1962).

[51] See Ogilvie on Livy I, 5, 6, 7, 12-13, etc.

[52] E.g., his sensible comment on the Etruscan origin of the lictors, *sella curulis*, etc., at I, 8.3.

[53] II, 1.1.

[54] VI, 1.2.

[55] For more sceptical views, H. Stuart Jones, *CAH* VII, 320; R. M.Ogilvie *JRS* 48 (1958), 40.

[56] T. R. S. Broughton, *The Magistrates of the Roman Republic* (New York, 1951), xii.

[57] The theory is developed in Ogilvie's *Commentary*, *passim.*

[58] Livy VII, 9.5.

[59] So in the account of Lake Regillus, the encounter between Valerius and Tarquinius (2.20.1-3) may be modelled on that between Paris and Menelaus at *Iliad* III, 15 ff (Ogilvie, 286).

[60] *Nexum* is illustrated by the account of the old centurion (II, 23-4), the maid of Ardea is the exemplar of *conubium*, Verginia's tragic story of *vindiciae ad libertatem*, and so on.

[61] Some examples are given in *Livy*, 90.

[62] His name does not appear in the Fasti. His career seems to have been worked up from bare annalistic detail of importation of corn and from the foundation of the temple of Fortuna Muliebris, which is given a connexion with his mother's feat (Ogilvie, 316).

[63] See *Livy*, 157 ff.

[64] See, e.g., nn. 103, 108, 119 below. We may note, too, that Livy nowhere says that Saguntum is north of the Ebro; contrast Pol. 3.30.3 with Walbank's note.

[65] *Livy*, 145, 147, 149.

[66] See *AJP* 76 (1955), 369 ff.

[67] *Livy*, 144 ff, 151 ff.

[68] Especially as it affects M. Minucius Rufus, C. Flaminius, and C. Terentius Varro; see H. H. Scullard, *Roman Politics* (Oxford, 1951), 45 ff.

[69] *Livy*, 93 ff.

[70] Pol. XV, 18; Livy XXX, 37.

[71] As, for example, in citation of the treaty of Phoenice (XXIX, 12), or the settlement of Greece (XXXIII, 30; Pol. XVIII, 44).

[72] There are no fewer than 17 entries between XXXI, 4, and XLIII, 3.

[73] The figures are assembled in Frank's *Economic Survey* I.

[74] This by no means exhausts the types of information. H. Hill's *The Roman Middle Class* (Oxford, 1952) reflects the value of Livy as a source for such activities of the Equites as building and transport; and there are abundant citations of corn importations which enable economic historians to estimate approximate figures of corn-consumption at Rome and in the armies (see Frank, *Economic Survey* I, 160).

[75] XXVIII, 45.15 ff.

[76] Cicero, *De Or.* II, 62.

[77] Cic. *Or.* 37; Quint. X, 1.31. See, in general, J. F. D'Alton, *Roman Literary Theory and Criticism* (1931), 508 ff.

[78] E. Burck, *Die Erzählungskunst des T. Livius* (Berlin, 1934), 213 ff.

[79] Notes 106, 122 below.

[80] X, 1.101: 'adfectus quidem . . . nemo historicorum commendavit magis.'

[81] *loc. cit.*

[82] See, e.g., III, 31.1; XXVII, 11.2.

[83] K. Witte in *RhM* (1910), 270 ff, 359 ff, and E. Burck (n. 78) have demonstrated the technique in detail.

[84] Polybius often uses the same presentation: *Livy*, 169.

[85] V, 21.10 ff.

[86] *Livy*, 246-7.

[87] I, 29.2; XXI, 12.2, etc.

[88] X, 1.101: omnia cum rebus tum personis accommodata sunt.

[89] *Livy*, 208 ff (following Witte).

[90] See Badian's earlier chapter, p. 17.

[91] XXII, 51.

[92] See *RhM* (1954), 107.

[93] Especially effectively of the Aetolians, for example, at XXXIII, 31.

[94] See R. Ullmann, *La technique des discours dans Salluste, Tite-Live, et Tacite* (Oslo 1927).

[95] XXXIV, 2 ff.

[96] XXI, 15.3 ff.

[97] Klotz believes that this is Coelius; but it would be much more in character with what we know of Valerius Antias.

[98] See especially XXI, 19.

[99] 5.4.

[100] Livy 5.8 ff.; Pol. III, 14.

[101] 10.11.

[102] 22.9. See Ed. Meyer, *Kl. Schrift.* II, 368; H. Peter, *HRR*, I, 160.

[103] But note that Livy is more informative than Polybius on this point; see Walbank on P. III, 17.9 (Livy XXI, 7.5).

[104] XXI, 7.14.

[105] See XXXI 17.5.

[106] XXI, 16.

[107] The consuls were allotted Spain and Africa as provinces (17.1). Polybius (3.20.3) criticizes earlier historians for drawing lurid pictures of Roman dejection which is unlikely and untrue.

[108] E.g. XXI, 24.1-2 (Iliberris and Ruscino), 26.6 (Volcae).

[109] Sir G. de Beer, *Alps and Elephants* (1955), adopts this dissonant (? Valerian) version as the probable route.

[110] See, in general, Walbank, *JRS* 46 (1956) 37 ff.

[111] 28.1.

[112] 28.3.

[113] 28.11.

[114] Contrast 29-30 with Pol. III, 44.

[115] 32.7.

[116] 35.6.

[117] *Livy*, 232-3, 223.

[118] The Ticinus, 45.3, against Pol. III, 65.3 (see Walbank's note); Ticinus and Po, 47.2: the Trebia, 55 ff (see Dimsdale's note on 55.5 and Hallward, *CAH* VIII, 709); Victumulae, 57.9-14; Apennines 58 (Klotz, *Livius*, 136); Placentia 59.1 ff (already recounted, 57.7); Spain, 60-61 contrasted with Pol. III, 76.

[119] Sicily, L. 49-50 and P. III, 61.10, with Walbank's note; in the Italian campaign, only L. gives the winter-quarters of Scipio (Cremona) and Sempronius (Placentia).

[120] 53-5.

[121] 62-3.

[122] 57.1-2; Pol. III, 75.4.

[123] Martial XIV, 191; Quint. 2.5.19: etsi hic (sc. Sallustius) historiae maior est auctor (sc. quam Livius).

VI
Ammianus Marcellinus

E. A. THOMPSON

THE fifth and sixth centuries A.D. produced a splendid chapter in the history of Greek historiography. Shortly after the year 400 Eunapius published the second edition of his history of the Roman Empire in 14 books covering the years 270-404.[1] Olympiodorus of Thebes in Egypt wrote 22 books on the period 407-425, and seems to have provided his readers with a mass of unusually interesting and valuable facts.[2] Much of the work of these two men is summarized in the extant history of a certain Zosimus, whose dates are unknown; but fragments have survived independently of Zosimus. The middle of the fifth century was vividly dealt with by Priscus of Panium, the chief source of our knowledge of Attila and the Huns. Malchus of Philadelphia and Candidus of Isauria wrote the history of the later fifth century, and the surviving fragments of their work are written with great care and merit. The sixth century was covered in the incomparable narrative of Procopius and by his successors Agathias, Menander Protector and Theophylactus Simocatta. These brilliant writers, apart from Procopius and one or two others, have never received from students of Greek literature the attention and study that they deserve, principally no doubt because their works have survived only in fragments and paraphrases. But that is hardly the case with the great historian who stands at their head, a Greek of Antioch called Ammianus Marcellinus. Ammianus differs from the others, however, because like the Greek poet Claudian he wrote his work in Latin.

Most of these late Greek historians tell us far more about themselves and their personal experiences than had been customary among the classical Greek and Latin historians; and Ammianus is no exception. Neither he nor Olympiodorus nor Priscus nor Procopius believed that anonymity was a virtue or that their own personal adventures were of little consequence to the course of history. Hence, the events in which Ammianus himself took part receive a disproportionately extended treatment in his work, and we know far more about him than we do, for example, about Livy or Tacitus.

Apparently he was born *c.* 330 of a well-to-do pagan family of Antioch. As a young man he joined the army and was enrolled among the *protectores domestici*, a regiment of high social standing. In 353 he was on the staff of Ursicinus, Master of the Cavalry, at the important frontier town of Nisibis in the province of Mesopotamia. With Ursicinus he went from the East to Gaul to suppress the revolt of the Frankish usurper Silvanus at Cologne; and he stayed in Gaul long enough to take part in the Caesar Julian's first campaign on the German frontier in 356. In the following year he was sent back to the Eastern frontier where he fought the Persians in the severe struggles of 359. His account of the siege of Amida, which held out against the Persians for 72 days before being stormed and burnt, is one of the highlights of his history. He himself escaped from the blazing city after many adventures which he describes with great vividness. We next find him serving on Julian's fateful expedition into the Persian Empire in 363, and of this he gives a most detailed narrative, to which we shall return. In later years he visited Egypt, Greece, and the site of one of the lesser encounters which preceded the disastrous battle of Adrianople. Some time after 378 he settled in Rome; and it was in Rome and for Roman readers that he wrote his history, completing books I-XXV in 392 and books XXVI-XXXI about 395. It is important to notice that the last six books appeared some years after the rest of the work had been published: to this fact we shall revert. Although he corresponded with friends at Antioch, there is no evidence that he ever left the Western capital after he had once settled there. The date of his death is unknown.

It is clear, then, that Ammianus had seen more of the world about which he was to write than the majority of the extant historians of antiquity: only Herodotus can equal him as a traveller. Moreover, his many years of active service in the army left him admirably equipped to narrate the military history of this turbulent period.

The History is a continuation of the works of Tacitus. Beginning with A.D. 98, he narrated the history of the Roman Empire, with many excursuses on the peoples living beyond the Imperial frontiers and on other matters of interest, down to the battle of Adrianople in 378 and the immediate aftermath of that catastrophe. The complete work was in 31 books, but only Books XIV-XXXI have survived, covering the history of the Roman world from 353 (the year in which we find him on Ursicinus' staff at Nisibis) to 378. In other words, we have his account of the period of which he was an exact contemporary. It is clear that his history of the second and third centuries was written in much less detail than that of the age in which he lived. It was common, in fact, at this period to preface an historical work with an introductory book in which a summary was given of the period preceding that which the historian had set himself to describe at length. Examples will be found in Zosimus and the various works of Procopius; but these are not an exact parallel to the procedure of Ammianus. At all events, the extant portion of the History covers the second half of the reign of the grim and suspicious Constantius II (337-361), the entire reigns of Julian the Apostate (361-363), Jovian (363-364), Valentinian I (364-375) and his brother Valens (364-378), together with the earlier years of Gratian (367-383) and Valentinian II (375-392).

About these 25 years, then, Ammianus writes in great detail; he gives us a mass of facts, and that these facts are presented with a high degree of accuracy has never been denied. But whether the historian colours the facts and interprets them with some bias is another matter. Near the end of chapter XXVI of the *Decline and Fall* Gibbon remarks that the 'accurate and faithful guide', as he calls Ammianus, 'has composed the history of his own times without indulging the prejudices and passions which usually affect the mind of a contemporary'. This is to claim too much: the historian, like Gibbon himself, was not superhuman, and his work in some places is not wholly dispassionate. Moreover, it has not been left unaffected by certain outside influences which tended to rob him of such impartiality as he possessed.

It is a comparatively small matter that he reveals his partiality for his old chief Ursicinus, under whose command he had served for seven years in the East and in Gaul and then again on the Euphrates. In fact, Ursicinus appears to have been a solid though not a brilliant officer—only one other historian finds it necessary to mention him at all[3]—and the part which he played in overthrowing the unfortunate usurper Silvanus was a dishonourable one. It would be hard indeed to justify the prominence which Ammianus gives him in his early books. The historian believes him to have been wronged: his merits had never been recognized, his enemies had slandered him to the Emperor, the Emperor had plotted to take his life. But the historian's charges seem ill-founded. Ursicinus was disgruntled. Although Ammianus was his friend, he was a difficult man to work with: he felt deeply, but without adequate reason, that his merits and achievements had never been given the recognition which they deserved. And the historian, his subordinate, took his side and shared his dissatisfaction. He presents in his history Ursicinus' own view of his career rather than that of Constantius II. No great harm is done by this, though it undoubtedly results in distortion in two ways, first, by contributing to the historian's hostile picture of the ruthless and unattractive Emperor, and secondly, by throwing into excessively high relief the career of a not very remarkable army officer.

More serious perhaps is his attitude towards the Emperor Julian. The apostate Emperor was the hero of many pagans and not least of Ammianus. Again and again the historian turns aside from his factual narrative to draw attention, almost in poetical terms, to the extraordinary qualities of Julian. When praising him, no words are excessive. And yet Ammianus is no blind hero-worshipper. Although Julian dominates approximately eight books of the History and although he is so often the subject of panegyrical language, yet his faults are by no means passed over. On several occasions the historian criticizes his military judgment, particularly for taking risks which, though justified in the event, were not warranted by the military situation existing at the time when the risks were run.[4] Again, Julian's gay and impulsive character led him into many an action which, in the view of the historian, detracted from the dignity of the throne: he diminished the awe with which the masses of the people viewed the wealth and status of the Emperor (an opinion of Julian which was widely shared).[5] Moreover, being a comparatively well-off member of the middle classes at Antioch, Ammianus defends the interests of his class against Julian's interference with them, just as he had defended them against the interference of Julian's half-brother Gallus a few years before.[6] But what is most remarkable is that in spite of the great length at which he deals with Julian's career, he hurries quickly past the period of 18 months when Julian was sole Emperor. Here was the pagan hero at the height of his career: we should have expected more detail and more eulogy than ever in the narrative at this point. But that is not what we get. Apart from Ammianus' unexpected brevity here, it is precisely in this part of his narrative that we find practically all the historian's criticisms of his hero (other than the military criticisms). It is scarcely an exaggeration to say that Julian's whole career as Augustus in Constantinople and Antioch is criticized in every particular by his admirer. Few incidents are recounted of Julian as Emperor which redound wholly to his credit. Since the pagan Zosimus, too, has scarcely anything to say of Julian as Augustus before he set out on the expedition to Persia, and nothing at all to say about his religious policy, the question may be asked whether the times in which Ammianus and Zosimus wrote made it possible for them to praise so militant a pagan Emperor as Julian. Ammianus at least may have felt it expedient to moderate his praise of the Apostate at this point. And yet, so far as we can tell, the pagan Eunapius was under no such inhibition: in his militantly anti-Christian way he praised Julian fulsomely. There is a puzzle here which has not been resolved.

During the period of the late Roman Empire historians recognized that it was dangerous for them to write of contemporary, or nearly contemporary, events. Emperors did not welcome published criticisms of themselves or their policies, at any rate from comparatively humble figures like Ammianus. And apart from the Emperors, members of distinguished families resented criticisms of what their ancestors had done in the past.[7] The question arises, therefore, whether the far from liberal government of Theodosius I obliged Ammianus to distort any of his opinions or to omit any material from his history which he might well have wished to include. In my opinion, it did.

With the end of book XXV, having brought his narrative down to the death of the Emperor Jovian in 364, Ammianus decided to bring his work to a close. The events of the following years were so close to the time at which he was publishing that any further narrative would inevitably cause offence. People mentioned by him—or passed over by him—would make endless complaints. Secondly—and Ammianus makes this point with a solemn emphasis—to tell the truth would bring him into danger.[8] What was the nature of this danger? What trace, if any, has the historian's fear left on the narrative of his last six books? He was certainly not afraid of the great senatorial families: he criticizes openly and severely even the powerful house of the Anicii. But what of the Emperor?

At all events, in spite of the danger and unpopularity which he foresaw, Ammianus changed his mind for a reason which he does not tell us, and wrote on. Instead of ending at 364, he wrote six more books and finally stopped his narrative with the events of 378. Perhaps he was tempted to do so simply because of the success of his earlier books, which were read with enthusiasm at Antioch.[9] Now, no hero dominates books XXVI-XXXI as Julian and to a lesser extent Ursicinus dominate the earlier books. Indeed, scarcely anyone of whom Ammianus writes in the last six books is depicted in a favourable light: practically all of them are harshly condemned. But there is one exception—Theodosius the elder, the father of the Emperor under whom Ammianus published the completed History. This Theodosius is praised most fulsomely on every page on which he appears, more so than Ursicinus and even Julian. But the praises are stiff and formal. They contain none of the genuine enthusiasm which is evident in his eulogies of Julian. They are extravagant and yet cold and unconvincing. As a military commander Theodosius was excessively cruel and not particularly efficient. There is, in fact, a notable discrepancy between his qualities, as Ammianus reports them, and the language in which he applauds them. And since Ammianus was a sound and experienced judge of military matters, this discrepancy can hardly have been other than obvious to him.

The fact is, of course, that the historian was writing during the reign of Theodosius' son, and consequently in the conditions of the later fourth century he could not but give to the father's achievements a disproportionate prominence and approval, for Theodosius I was deeply attached to his family.[10] That is to say, Ammianus was obliged by the circumstances of his times to write these passages with considerably less than the deep sincerity which he shows clearly in all the rest of his work.

But to the present writer it seems probable that Ammianus has had to distort his narrative in a much more serious way owing to fear of possible reprisals by the Emperor. It was pointed out in the seventeenth century by Claude Chifflet[11] that, while Ammianus carries the history of the Eastern Empire down to the year 378, events in the West after 375 are for the most part omitted. And yet Ammianus had at one time intended to write a fuller account of Western affairs in the years 375-8 than he in fact gives us; for in XXVIII, 1.57 he promises to narrate in its proper place the execution of Maximinus and others, which occurred in 376, a few months after the execution of the elder Theodosius. When he changed his mind and omitted much of Western history in 375-8, he forgot to erase this promise and in fact says nothing of Maximinus' death. Yet he had collected his material for Western history in these years and has incorporated some of it, for he gives a detailed account of the elevation of Valentinian II and of Gratian's campaign against the Alamanni. Why then did he not give us a complete narrative? Why not continue and give us as full an account of Western events in these three years as he gives of Eastern events? No answer to this problem can in the nature of the case be proved to be true, and what follows is hypothetical. In my opinion, it is not likely to be a coincidence that the Western narrative comes down to the eve of the trial and execution of the elder Theodosius, and stops short without any discussion of that event or its aftermath. In fact, contemporary writers always steer clear of a description of the circumstances in which the father of Theodosius I met his end; and the result is that we do not know exactly why he was condemned and executed—we do not even know for certain whether it was Valentinian I or Gratian who had him killed. No wholly convincing explanation has been put forward to account for these phenomena. But, clearly, the facts could be explained if we supposed that the elder Theodosius met his death in circumstances which were discreditable to him, that in fact he was guilty of the charges (perhaps charges of treason) which were brought against him at Carthage. If we suppose that the Emperor Theodosius found it convenient to suppress, in so far as he could, the reason why his father was executed, Ammianus' procedure would be explicable. Most of what we know about the end of the elder Theodosius is provided by a variant in St Jerome's *Chronicle*, where we are told that his death was due to Maximinus, Praetorian Prefect of Gaul, and his supporters, who were themselves put to death shortly afterwards.[12] Now, apart from the broken promise mentioned above, there are two points to be noted in Ammianus' account of this Maximinus. The historian says that he will tell of some of the crimes which Maximinus perpetrated in Gaul, and adds: 'So whoever weighs what I have said will also ponder on the rest which I have not told, and like a prudent man will pardon me if I do not embrace all the ills which the wickedness of Maximinus' counsels brought about, by exaggerating accusations'.[13] Yet in fact he gives not a single example of Maximinus' criminal activities; but it is almost inconceivable that the historian had not the case of Theodosius in mind when he wrote this guarded sentence. Secondly, when he comes to describe Maximinus' activities in Rome Ammianus' narrative becomes most uncharacteristic. Instead of being factual and specific, it is confused and even misleading. Instead of being accurate and dispassionate, it is tendentious and designed to paint Maximinus in the darkest colours. We are left with the impression that, if Ammianus were to write about Maximinus at all, he had to depict him as being a great deal worse than he actually was: only a discreditable account of Maximinus was possible for an historian writing under Theodosius I whose father Maximinus had put to death. We may conclude, then, that in writing his last six books Ammianus had to be on his guard and make sure that no offence was given to the authorities.

It appears that somewhat similar considerations weighed with the historian when he had occasion to mention the Christians. (It will be remembered that he himself was a pagan.) In the years immediately preceding 392, when Ammianus published books I-XXV, Theodosius had been comparatively lenient towards paganism and had promoted eminent pagans to high offices of state. Accordingly, in books I-XXV Ammianus was at liberty to express himself with some freedom on the subject of Christianity and of his own religious beliefs. He even discusses at considerable length the matter of foretelling the future, a matter which was in some of its aspects of profound concern to the Christian Emperors.[14] He actually criticizes the policy of the Christian Emperors in this regard. He does not deny that all reasonable measures should be taken for the safeguarding of the Emperor's person. But he has no sympathy with the excessive use of such precautions. He writes that under Constantius II anyone found guilty of consulting a fortune-teller about the squeak of a mouse or a meeting with a weasel on the road was put to death and never even learned who it was that had accused him. In all, there is plenty of discussion in books XIV-XXV of pagan religion and religious practices and also, to a more limited extent, of the Christians.

But in 392 Theodosius changed his religious policies and became very much harsher towards the pagans. Distinguished pagans were dismissed from political office, and blow after blow was dealt to the practice of the pagan religions. The effect of this change of policy and atmosphere upon Ammianus' work is striking. It is scarcely an exaggeration to say that all discussion of religious matters has disappeared from books XXVI-XXXI. Indeed, if only the last six books had survived, it would not be easy to prove that Ammianus was a pagan. The plural of words like *deus*, *numen*, and the like, is not used. References to fortune-tellers are guarded and such as to dissociate the writer from the number of their admirers. There is no longer any eulogy or even discussion of the Neoplatonist philosophers. In the earlier books he sometimes praises Christianity while condemning individual Christians. In the later books he says nothing in praise of paganism and gives no hint that he was himself a pagan, although he sometimes has a word of praise for individual pagans.[15]

From what sources did Ammianus derive his knowledge of events in the years 353-378? He tells us that he was himself an eye-witness of some of the matters which he records and that he carefully cross-examined eyewitnesses of events at which he had not been present in person[16]: indeed, he sometimes tells us the names of those who supplied him with information.[17] He also consulted public records,[18] but he makes no mention in the extant part of his history of having drawn on earlier historical works. In fact, so far as his own words go, Ammianus' procedure will have resembled that of the sophist Libanius in writing his Eighteenth Oration. That speech is an Epitaphius on the Emperor Julian, composed in A.D. 365, a couple of years after the Emperor's death. In order to assemble his information Libanius questioned survivors of Julian's expedition of 363, on which the Emperor had met his death.[19] He wrote to one Philagrius asking permission to consult his diary of the campaign,[20] and wrote to urge another eye-witness to edit his account of the expedition.[21] But Libanius had no choice in the matter. He published only two years after Julian's death, when there were as yet few or no reputable and detailed histories to draw upon. Ammianus, on the other hand, did not complete his history until *c.* 395: are we to suppose that he wilfully ignored all the relevant historical works which had appeared before that date?

Discussion of the question has largely turned on his account of Julian's march into the Persian Empire in 363, for this is an event of which we have, in whole or in fragments, the histories of several other writers; and a comparison of these various narratives might be expected to be fruitful. The most detailed narrative of the campaign, apart from that of Ammianus himself, is the long account given by the historian Zosimus.[22] Zosimus is known to have drawn heavily on the history of Eunapius,[23] and some fragments of Eunapius' own work still survive.[24] But Eunapius himself was heavily indebted to a memoir written by the physician Oribasius of Pergamum, a friend of Julian, who took part in the expedition of 363 and wrote an account of it which is now wholly lost.[24] Zosimus' story, therefore, is told at third hand. Apart from these works and the Eighteenth Oration of Libanius, which we have already referred to, John Malalas preserves a considerable extract from a history of the expedition by Magnus of Carrhae, who also marched with Julian in 363, and a shorter one from the work of yet another participant in the campaign, Eutychianus of Cappadocia.[25]

Unhappily, the relationship between these various histories, and the use, if any, which Ammianus made of his predecessors, give rise to problems of great obscurity. There are numerous and striking similarities between the accounts of Ammianus and Zosimus, and yet there are also a legion of discrepancies between them. Early in the present century scholars believed that the similarities could be accounted for on the assumption that both writers alike drew heavily on the work of Magnus of Carrhae; and indeed this Magnus was identified with a certain Magnus mentioned by them both. But the identification, in fact, cannot stand, and in any case the theory will not account for the numerous differences and contradictions between the two narratives, and between both of them and the surviving extract of Magnus himself. So it is now generally abandoned.[26] The present writer put forward the view in 1947 that Eunapius not only used the memoir of Oribasius but also had direct or more probably indirect access to Ammianus' work: hence the similarities and differences between Ammianus and Zosimus (whose account of the expedition is a paraphrase of that of Eunapius).[27] But this theory, too, is hardly tenable, for the identification of what seems to be a hitherto unrecognized fragment of Eunapius' own history has suggested to one authority that Eunapius' information represents a distinct and different tradition from that of Ammianus.[28] And a more conclusive objection will be given below.

Although much study has been given to the question, the result until recently was negative so far as Ammianus is concerned.[29] His narrative seemed to be independent of our other sources of information. And yet anyone reading his account of the Persian expedition of 363 side by side with that of Eunapius as paraphrased by Zosimus will find it difficult to deny that there is *some* connection between the two narratives. Not only do they describe the same events in a somewhat similar way, but (though there are exceptional cases) the two writers to an extraordinary degree select the same events for description. Any two reliable accounts of any campaign will of necessity deal with the same incidents. But Ammianus and Zosimus to a most remarkable extent select the same details to illustrate and enliven their stories. The cases are too numerous and too striking to allow us to conclude that the similarities are due to coincidence; and yet no theory has, until recently, been able to show how the two descriptions of the campaign can be anything but independent of one another.

The way out of the *impasse* has been found as a result of a renewed study of the chronology of Eunapius' historical works. It has now been shown to be probable that what Eunapius published in or after 414 was a second and extended edition of his historical work, but that he had already published a first edition which contained biographies of Constantine and Julian followed by a general history of events after Julian's death in 363.[30] Since the work may well have been published in instalments, the instalment dealing with the events of 363 could have been published before 392, the latest year in which Ammianus can have published the relevant part of his work. The universally held opinion, therefore, that Ammianus could not have read Eunapius' description of Julian's last campaign is now shown to be without foundation.[31] And the only hypothesis which accounts for all the facts is that Ammianus accepted Eunapius' version of the Persian campaign as trustworthy and incorporated much of it in his own narrative, though he made numerous changes based on his own personal knowledge or on the enquiries which he made among other eye-witnesses.[32] Nor should such a conclusion surprise us. Eunapius was an esteemed writer in his day, at any rate among pagans, and Ammianus shared both his paganism and his admiration for Julian (though not his bitter hatred of the Christians). Moreover, there was at least one good reason why Ammianus should turn to an account based on Oribasius. Oribasius was a personal friend of Julian, and, marching as he did with Julian himself, he was better placed to obtain an over-all picture of the campaign than was Ammianus, who marched in the ranks. This indebtedness of Ammianus to Eunapius is the most important discovery about our historian's method of composition that has been made for many years: this alone can account for the curious relationship of the narratives of Julian's Persian campaign given by Ammianus and Zosimus.

As for Ammianus' procedure in the rest of his work, we must accept what he himself tells us without having any means of checking his veracity. The bulk of his information comes from his own notes and personal observation, supplemented by what he could learn from the eye-witnesses whom he met and questioned. He gives us no hint whatever that in writing the history of 353-378 he made use of works written by earlier historians, and he even seems to imply that he did not do so. In one of the very few cases where we can check him, this implication is confirmed, for he shows no knowledge of Julian's *Epistle to the Athenians*, although he might have derived some facts from it which would have been relevant to his work. On the other hand, there was an immense output of historical and other works, both in prose and in poetry, covering the period in question, especially the reign of Julian[33]; and, since Ammianus was nothing if not a diligent reader, it is hardly possible to believe that he put this enormous body of literature aside and made no use of it whatever. In fact, if it is true that he used Eunapius' version of the campaign of 363, it is almost inconceivable that he failed to use the works of other reputable historians for other events. What we may doubt is whether he had many such works upon which to draw. Some of the available sources of information will have been violently partial, or contradictory, or incomplete, or of a vague, cloudy and rhetorical character. Thus, the meagre narrative of Eutropius was at his disposal, and he did that sterile chronicler the honour of taking a couple of sentences from his work.[34] But that he derived the bulk of his information, not from his own notes and enquiries, but from one or two published histories, is unproved and improbable. It is agreed on all sides that he can have had few or no published sources for his last six books; for no sizeable history of the years 364-378 is known to have been published before his own. And yet Ammianus' merits as an historian show no falling off in books XXVI-XXXI.

Whatever his sources of information, no one can doubt the value of the vast mass of accurate and vivid facts which the History offers to us. The general accuracy of Ammianus' monumental work even in matters of the minutest detail has never seriously been called in question; and our knowledge of the political and military history of the important years 353-378 would be scanty indeed if books XIV-XXXI had met the same fate as books I-XIII. We should be reduced, as Gibbon says (in the passage to which we have already referred) when speaking of the reign of Theodosius I, 'to illustrate the partial narrative of Zosimus by the obscure hints of fragments and chronicles, by the figurative style of poetry or panegyric, and by the precarious assistance of the ecclesiastical writers who, in the heat of religious faction, are apt to despise the profane virtues of sincerity and moderation'. Whereas in fact we are better informed about the political, diplomatic and military history of these years than of any previous period of Imperial history save only those dealt with by Tacitus. The reliability of Ammianus' narrative, even in matters of small detail, is not shown only by that narrative's internal consistency and its agreement with the very sparse notices of other Greek and Roman historians. We have an Armenian translation of the Syriac history of Faustus of Buzanta (not Byzantium) in Cilicia. This work is our principal source for the history of Armenia in the fourth century,[35] and is completely independent of Ammianus. Now, Faustus, once we interpret him correctly, substantiates to an extraordinary degree Ammianus' account of the relations of the Roman Empire with Persia and Armenia. Faustus, it has been said, gives us 'a new confidence in the splendid accuracy and historical insight of Ammianus Marcellinus'.[36]

NOTES

[1] On the second edition of Eunapius see W. R. Chalmers, 'The *nea ekdosis* of Eunapius' *Histories*', *Classical Quarterly*, N.S. III (1953), 165-70.

[2] On him see E. A. Thompson, 'Olympiodorus of Thebes', *Classical Quarterly*, XXXVIII (1944), 43-52.

[3] Zonaras, XIII, 9.

[4] E. A. Thompson, *The Historical Work of Ammianus Marcellinus* (Cambridge, 1947), 79.

[5] Socrates, *Hist. Eccles.* III, 1.50.

[6] Thompson, *op. cit.*, 81 ff.

[7] Scriptores Historiae Augustae, *Gallieni Duo* XIX, 8 f; *Carus* XVIII, 5.

[8] XXVI, 1.1.

[9] Libanius, *Ep.* 1063.

[10] Victor, *Epit.* XLVIII, 18.9.

[11] See the edition of Wagner-Erfurdt (1808), cxi f.

[12] A. Schöne, *Die Weltchronik des Eusebius* (Berlin, 1900), 160 f; T. Mommsen, *Chronica Minora* I, 631.

[13] XXIX, 3.1.

[14] XXI, 1.6-14. There is a careful study of Ammianus' religion in W. Ensslin, 'Zur Geschichtschreibung und Weltanschauung des Ammianus Marcellinus', *Klio*, Beiheft XVI, 1923.

[15] Ammianus' references to Christianity and Christians are collected and discussed by Ensslin, *op. cit.*, 96 ff.

[16] XV, 1.1.

[17] Thompson, *op. cit.*, 20 f.

[18] XVI, 12.70; XXVIII, 1.30, etc.

[19] *Ep.* 1220, 8.

[20] *Ep.* 1434.

[21] *Ep.* 1508, 6.

[22] III, 12 ff.

[23] Photius, Cod. 98, p. 84.

[24] A new fragment has almost certainly been identified in Suidas by A. F. Norman, 'Magnus in Ammianus, Eunapius, and Zosimus: New Evidence', *Classical Quarterly*, N.S. VII (1957), 129-33.

[25] John Malalas, 328, 332, Bonn = Jacoby, 225 F 1, 226 F 1.

[26] Thompson, *op. cit.*, 28 ff, 134 ff.

[27] Photius, *loc. cit.*

[28] Norman, *art. cit.*, 131.

[29] The question of Zosimus' relation to Eunapius, for which see Norman, *art. cit.*, 132, does not concern us.

[30] Chalmers, cited in n. 1 above.

[31] Idem, 'Eunapius, Ammianus Marcellinus and Zosimus on Julian's Persian Expedition', *Classical Quarterly*, N.S. X (1960), 152-60.

[32] So Chalmers, *art. cit.*, 158.

[33] E.g. Zosimus III, 2.4.

[34] Eutropius IX, 26; IX, 24; Amm. Marc. XV, 5.18; XIV, 11.10.

[35] On it see E. Stein, *Histoire du Bas-empire* II (Paris, 1949), 713 n. 2, 835 f, with references.

[36] N. H. Baynes, 'Rome and Armenia in the Fourth Century', *English Historical Review*, XXV (1910), 625-43, at 643.

VII
Bede

J. CAMPBELL

BEDE was not only, or even primarily, a historian. He finished the *Historia Ecclesiastica Gentis Anglorum* only three or four years before his death in 735. He may have known that it would be the last of his major works, for he ended it with an almost elegiac sketch of his own life and a list of his writings. These were numerous. Bede devoted a fairly long life—he was born in 672 or 673—and formidable powers to become probably the most learned and certainly the most productive of the European scholars of his day. His works include treatises on grammar, metric and chronology, lives of saints, homilies and, above all, commentaries on the Bible. Much that he wrote was unoriginal, in so far as it consisted of the views—often the words—of his predecessors pieced together with some rearrangement, clarification and amendment. He set out to master and pass on a large part of the learning of the Christian Church; and succeeded in this. Many of his works became standard and remained so through the Middle Ages and sometimes beyond. His historical works comprise, if hagiography is excluded, only the *Ecclesiastical History*, the *Lives* of the abbots of his abbey of Monkwearmouth-Jarrow and the chronicles—lists of the principal events in the history of the world—appended to *Liber de Temporibus* (703) and *De Temporum Ratione* (725). They are merely a part, though an important one, of what Bede wrote and what he was valued for through many centuries. His history has to be interpreted in relation to the rest of his work, that of a man whose dominant intention was to expound, spread and defend the Christian faith by all the means in his power.[1]

The *Ecclesiastical History* shows how great these means were.

That which is first apparent to its readers is Bede's command of Latin. He writes grammatically and very clearly. Unlike some of his contemporaries, who wrote to impress by a florid style and an outré vocabulary, he intended to be understood by an audience the capacities of some of whom he did not value highly. He writes in his commentary on the Apocalypse, 'Anglorum gentis inertiae consulendum ratus . . . non solum dilucidare sensus verum sententias quoque stringere disposui'.[2] Bede knew very well how to be both simple and moving. The style in which he tells many of his stories recalls that of the gospels in its brevity, concentration on essentials, and use of direct speech. What he says is even more remarkable than the skill with which he says it. He sets out to give the history of the Church in his own land in about 85,000 words. Having begun with a short geographical and historical introduction, he gives some account of Christianity in Roman Britain, but devotes much of the first book and the whole of the remaining four to its progress in England from St Augustine's arrival in 597 until 731. The numerous sources which Bede collected and the skill with which he handled them make the *Ecclesiastical History* the masterpiece of Dark Age historiography. No history that can rival it appeared in Western Europe until the twelfth century.[3]

The *Ecclesiastical History* itself does much to explain how so remarkable a work could be undertaken. It shows the progress of Christianity in England to have been feeble and flickering until the generation following 635. But by 660 it was established in all the major kingdoms and began to flourish. Many monasteries were founded and many monks became learned. Theodore, archbishop of Canterbury 668-690, established a school at Canterbury where most subjects relevant to Christian learning, including Greek, could be studied. Benedict Biscop founded the twin monasteries of Monkwearmouth (674) and Jarrow (681-2) and collected abroad a library for them which must have been among the best in Europe. There were other important libraries and many monasteries owned books and contained more or less learned men, although only Aldhelm (?640-709) among Bede's English contemporaries approached him in eminence.[4] Although Bede lived on the edge of the civilized world he did not work in intellectual isolation. His reputation and his correspondence spread far beyond the borders of Northumbria. There were others in his own house who could write as well as he: perhaps the finest example of the Bedan style is the description of Bede's death by Cuthbert, his fellow-monk.[5] Bede's works were not only in great demand, but also occasionally criticized.[6] He was not alone in the production of hagiography and biography. We have biographical works by five of his English contemporaries and the fewness of the manuscripts of some of these makes it likely that there were other such works, now lost.[7] Bede would not have been able to accomplish what he did had he not been a member of a learned world with considerable intellectual resources. The achievements of his contemporaries hardly rivalled his, but we know them to have been considerable and may suspect them to have been more considerable than we know.

English learning was fed by that of other countries.[8] The chief debts were naturally to the sources of conversion, Italy and Ireland. Bede's scholarship depended largely on access to Italian manuscripts, the education of many of his contemporaries on access to Irish schools. Something was owed to Gaul, which gave England three bishops in the seventh century and with which some English ecclesiastics, especially Wilfred, had close connections. The cosmopolitan nature of the Church and the willingness of clerics to move to countries other than their own brought influences from further afield and created multiple opportunities for the diffusion of ideas. Archbishop Theodore came from Cilicia; his companion Hadrian was an African. The Irish founded monasteries in Gaul, Germany and Italy besides England; Ireland had access to the learning of contemporary Spain and indirect communication with the Near East. Between 690 and Bede's death Englishmen converted much of western Germany. Irish missionaries and perhaps a Spaniard were active there at the same time. One of Bede's English contemporaries went to Jerusalem and then settled at Monte Cassino. The Christian world stretched from Scotland and Ireland to Asia Minor and Spain. It was being reduced by the 'gravissima Sarracenorum lues', as Bede well knew, but it was still, if hardly united, much interconnected. The international connections of the Church were partly paralleled by those of the laity. The Anglo-Saxons had left kinsmen in Germany whom they recognized as such and sought to convert. Others had moved with the Lombards, to whom they were related, into Italy: this may have had something to do with the willingness of Englishmen to visit Italy and even to settle there.[9] Saxons had settled in Gaul as Franks may have settled in England. The coming and going of brides and exiles to and from Gaul accompanied and was connected with that of bishops and missionaries. The accumulation of instances may deceive. Many of the contacts between England and the Continent in the seventh century and the early eighth were episodic or tenuous. But there was enough communication to enable Bede to write as the heir to much of the learning of the Church and for an audience which was not entirely insular in its knowledge and interests.

In his historical works Bede was able to draw on many models and sources.[10] He made no use of the classical historians, though he could perhaps have done so—texts of some of their works which were available in Germany in the eighth century may have arrived there via England. His attitude towards most pagan authors was one of cautious reserve. The chief models and foundations for his work were, apart from the Bible, the works of Christian authors from the fourth century on. Perhaps the most important such author was Eusebius. His *Ecclesiastical History* set the standard for historians of the church.[11] It left secular affairs for the attention of the carnally minded. The wars it described were those against heresy and persecution; its heroes were the martyrs; the successions it recorded those not of emperors but of bishops. Distinguished from pagan historiography in technique as in content it included many documents and gave references to sources. Eusebius's *Chronicle* had a different function, to summarize universal history from a Christian point of view, correlating Biblical history with that of the rest of the world and showing the hand of God at work across millennia. Bede did not have either work in the original Greek; he used Rufinus's Latin translation and continuation of the *Ecclesiastical History* and Jerome's of the *Chronicle*. They provided models for his own work in either genre. He knew at least two other Christian histories, the *Adversus Paganos* of Orosius and Gregory of Tours's *Historia Francorum*. His view of history as the demonstration of the power of God, of orthodoxy and of sanctity, much resembles theirs and he owed a more direct debt to Orosius, whose geographical introduction he imitates and borrows from.[12] His aim seems to have been to do for the history of the Church in England what Eusebius had done for the whole and he follows him in choice of subject-matter and in technique. Nevertheless there are important differences between Bede's *Ecclesiastical History* and its predecessor, which make his work in some respects more like that of Gregory of Tours. Although, like Eusebius and unlike Gregory, Bede rarely recorded secular affairs for their own sake he had to devote considerable attention to them. Eusebius, writing under Constantine, had only one Christian emperor to deal with and so was concerned with the Church as opposed to the State. Bede had to describe a Church very much involved with the State and to show how Providence had affected the affairs of kings many of whom were Christian, some even saints. Secondly, while Eusebius had incorporated accounts of martyrs in his work much more of Bede's is devoted to the lives and particularly the miracles of saints. Belief in the miraculous had increased greatly between the fourth century and the eighth. The demand for it had been fed by hagiographies in the tradition which began with the life of Anthony by Athanasius (*c.* 296-373). Such lives were prominent among Bede's sources and he wrote some himself. Writing with a largely didactic purpose and for an audience which needed vivid and concrete demonstration of the power of God and of virtue Bede made his *Ecclesiastical History* a chronological hagiography as well as a record in the manner of Eusebius.[13] He is distinguished from most hagiographers of his time by his using miracle-stories only to reinforce religious teachings rather than to advertise the merits of a particular shrine.[14]

The works of earlier writers provided Bede not only with models, but with much of the information used in the first book of the *Ecclesiastical History*.[15] His account of the Romans in Britain came largely from Orosius and the pagan historian Eutropius. The interest taken by Gaulish historians in the Pelagian heresy enabled him to gain valuable information from the *Vita Sancti Germani* of Constantius. These, with an important British source—Gildas's *De Excidio*—a *Passio Sancti Albani*, some English tradition and a certain amount of misinformation from the *Liber Pontificalis* largely saw him through the twenty-two chapters devoted to the period before Augustine's mission.[16] His task in compiling his much fuller account of subsequent events was more difficult. Much is known of his sources for this since he describes some of them in his introduction and mentions others later. He obtained a considerable number of documents, especially papal letters, from Rome and Canterbury. Like a true successor to Eusebius he inserted many of them into his text; they comprise about a fifth of it and provide the backbone of his account of the conversion and of subsequent relations with Rome. His contacts with Rome were good enough to allow him access not only to such letters but also to the official history of the popes, the *Liber Pontificalis*; he used its account of Gregory II even while that pope was still alive. Otherwise his chief written sources were biographical—mainly hagiographical. He had *Vitae* of Fursey, Cuthbert, Wilfred, Ceolfrith, Aethelburh and perhaps of others. Some annals, regnal lists and genealogies were available to him but they seem to have afforded little information on events outside Kent and Northumbria or, for the earlier part of the seventh century, within them.[17] He was, for example, unable to record even the year in which Augustine died.

The written sources of which we know leave the origins of much of the *Ecclesiastical History* unaccounted for. Bede tells us that much of his information came from oral tradition, either directly or through correspondents.[18] To determine, or guess, the value of such information it is necessary to consider the forms in which it may have been preserved. Mrs Chadwick has recently suggested that many of Bede's sources were 'ecclesiastical sagas'. These were, she thinks, sometimes transmitted orally, sometimes at some stage written down, but retaining the characteristics of oral saga style—'leisurely, detailed, circumstantial and dramatic', often divided into three parts, recording proper names and retailing conversations verbatim.[19] In the extreme form in which she presents this theory—for example, maintaining that Bede's account of the Synod of Whitby is 'certainly an elaborate form of ecclesiastical saga'—it does not seem altogether helpful.[20] Her criteria appear to be capable of including very diverse works and hardly enable one to distinguish an 'ecclesiastical saga' from a *Vita* of a saint. Nevertheless, it is very likely that many of the traditions used by Bede had been transmitted in fairly defined and constant forms and this may have made them more reliable. How reliable is a matter for conjecture. Certainly even detail could be preserved from the fairly remote past. Bede was able to give a detailed description of the appearance of Paulinus from an oral tradition a century old.[21] Oral tradition can, however, be as false as it is circumstantial and if it is accurate in details may be so in nothing else. We cannot verify many of the traditions Bede records. He must himself have often lacked the means to do so, and sometimes, it may be, the inclination.

There is no doubt that Bede was exceptionally fitted to deal with such diverse and often bad sources. More learned in chronology and computation than any other scholar of his day he was well qualified to correlate chronological data which, although often scanty, were in diverse forms. His Biblical studies had involved the use of many of the techniques of the historian. He had taken particular care in the comparison of different texts of the scriptures. His preference of Jerome's more recent Latin translation of the Old Testament to the Greek of the Septuagint led him radically to revise Eusebius's chronology.[22] His Biblical work naturally involved chronological problems and the comparison of divergent texts describing the same events.[23] The compilation of commentaries required, *inter alia*, the exposition of the literal meaning of scripture and so enquiry into topographical and other facts; this may help to account for the interest in imparting topographical information apparent in parts of the *Ecclesiastical History*. Spurious texts required the attention of a Biblical scholar. Bede showed himself able to expose at least one such, the *De Transitu Beatae Virginis*, partly on historical grounds.[24] In writing the *Ecclesiastical History* at the end of such a scholarly career Bede might have been expected to produce a work of more than ordinary reliability and it is agreed that he did.

This is not to say that the *Ecclesiastical History* is technically flawless within the limits of Bede's intentions. The most conspicuous faults are chronological; the dates he gives are not always mutually consistent. Although Bede was the most expert chronologist of his day his task in dating events in England was very difficult. He had to correlate dates given according to the regnal years of the kings of different kingdoms with one another and with dates from ecclesiastical sources expressed in imperial or consular years or in terms of the position of the year in a nineteen-year cycle, the indiction. He gives dates according to several systems, frequently as years A.D.—it was largely through him that this system became current. The correlation of different dates which Bede gives according to different systems reveals discrepancies. Various attempts have been made to explain and correct these but many of the problems involved remain controversial. There is disagreement on when Bede began the year and on how he calculated regnal years. Thus cases have been put for the battle on the Winwaed's having taken place in 655, which is the year Bede gives, in 654 and in 656. All the theories advanced require the assumption that Bede made some mistakes. It is doubtful whether some of the problems will ever be completely solved. We have little evidence beyond what Bede himself provides. For many secular events he was dependent on dates expressed in regnal years. These may have often been inaccurate or expressed in complete years only. Different systems of calculation may have been used in different kingdoms at different times and Bede may not have been well informed about them. He may have made corrections or alterations on the basis of information unknown to us.[25]

Other errors can be detected in Bede's work which are due to slips, or to the difficulties of his material. Mr D. P. Kirby has shown recently that although Bede clearly implies that the marriage of Edwin of Northumbria to a Kentish princess took place in 625 he provides other evidence which makes it very likely that the marriage took place in or very near to 619. Either Bede made a false assumption—that Paulinus was consecrated before he left for Northumbria—or else he wrote the passage concerned rather carelessly.[26] Arch-Abbot Brechter in an elaborate study of Bede's account of St Augustine's mission to Kent has alleged that Bede knowingly falsified its chronology, ante-dating Ethelbert's baptism, post-dating Augustine's episcopal consecration, reversing their order and discarding a papal letter which showed him to be wrong.[27] This is too dramatic. Brechter's arguments for what the course of events really was are not conclusive, though neither are they implausible, especially on the date of Ethelbert's baptism. The evidence he offers for Bede's dishonesty is unconvincing. Bede may have erred through carelessness in saying that Ethelbert received the faith in 597, if he meant by this that he was baptized then.[28] He may have been wrong about the time at which Augustine was consecrated and certainly confused the archbishop of Lyons with the bishop of Arles and misdated a journey to Rome.[29] He had difficult sources to deal with, could slip, and did not write in an age in which it was thought necessary to distinguish between known facts and deductions or assumptions.[30] There is no need to assume more.

Some of the discrepancies and awkwardnesses in Bede's text may be attributable to the method and circumstances of his writing. He does not seem to have gathered all his evidence before he began to write, but rather to have made insertions in what he had already written as new material reached him. The type of text which Plummer calls C appears to preserve one recension slightly earlier than the last, differing from it chiefly in not including chapter XIV of the fourth book: traces of other insertions into an earlier version or versions appear in the text as we have it.[31] It may well be that Bede had to write under difficulties. He was fairly old by the time he wrote the *Ecclesiastical History*; the tone and nature of the last chapter suggest that he may have been ill. He may have been hindered by liturgical duties and shortages of writing materials and copyists. It was not perhaps easy for him to find his way about his own text or materials; indexes have been invented since his day. One may fancy the *Ecclesiastical History* as the last great work of an elderly and ailing scholar compelled to great labours by a sense of religious duty. It is surprising, not that there are inconsistencies, ambiguities, or loose ends in the *Ecclesiastical History*, but that they are so few. It is to Bede's credit rather than his discredit that it is possible to criticize him largely on a basis of evidence he himself provides. The quantity of the information he records and the care with which he uses it are such that he may be regarded almost as if he were a modern historian. Almost and sometimes, but it is wrong to judge his work, or to use it, as if he really were one.

It is not Bede's competence which marks him as the product of a distant age, but his purpose. His general aim is explicit and inevitable, to describe men and their deeds so that the *religiosus et pius auditor* may be excited to imitate good and to shun evil.[32] Much of the *Ecclesiastical History* is devoted to inculcating through stories about the past the virtues and the dogmas which Bede had spent most of his life expounding, probably to a narrower and more learned audience, in his commentaries. For example, in the commentaries Bede says that there are two kinds of compunction with the same outward manifestations. One came from the fear of hell and could develop into the other which came from the love of heaven. The story of Adamnan of Coldingham in the *Ecclesiastical History* gives an instance of this. Adamnan, thanks to an accident and his own scrupulousness, continued throughout his life a regime of mortification which had been intended to last for a shorter time and

> quod causa divini timoris semel ob reatum compunctus coeperat, iam causa divini amoris delectatus praemiis indefessus agebat.[33]

Most of the doctrines which Bede dramatizes and makes memorable in the *Ecclesiastical History* are naturally of more general application than this. Thus his accounts of visions of the other world, which are perhaps the most obvious demonstrations of his homilectic intentions, drive home such points as the folly of depending on the chance of being able to make a death-bed repentance, the certainty that even the least thought or action will be taken into account after death, the purpose and frightfulness of purgatory and the much greater frightfulness and eternity of hell.[34] The value of such instruction remains, no doubt, *semper, ubique et pro omnibus*. But much of what Bede seeks to teach by giving examples in the *Ecclesiastical History* is directed towards the particular circumstances of England in his own day and the nature of his work can be fully understood only in relation to these.

The *Ecclesiastical History* was intended to reach a lay as well as a clerical audience. It is the only one of Bede's works to be dedicated to a layman, Ceolwulf, king of Northumbria 729-37 or 38; he had been sent a draft to comment upon. It is not known whether he or other laymen were capable of reading it.[35] A few may have been, but in any case Bede's references to those who were either to read or to hear it suggest that he did not expect knowledge of it to be confined to the literate but rather that it would be read out and, presumably, translated.[36] Offa, king of Mercia 756-97, had a copy of the *Ecclesiastical History* and it was the only one of Bede's works which Alfred had translated.[37] No doubt Bede knew and intended that its main audience would be clerical. But the English Church contained too many nobles and was too dependent upon kings to be indifferent to the needs and interests of secular rulers. Much of the *Ecclesiastical History* was intended to show how the needs of kings could best be fulfilled and where their true interests lay.

England in Bede's day was divided into a number of kingdoms whose relative power fluctuated and whose rulers lacked security. In the course of the seventh century the dynasties of Kent, East Anglia, Mercia, Northumbria and Wessex had in turn been the most powerful in England. All at some stage fell from greatness, some to recover it later, others not. All kings had enemies inside as well as outside their kingdoms. Aethelbald of Mercia, whose superiority south of the Humber was recognized at the time when Bede completed the *Ecclesiastical History*, was to die at the hands of his own bodyguard. A major theme of the probably near-contemporary poem *Beowulf* is that the wages of greatness and heroism is death. The poet constantly reminds his audience that the great kings and kingdoms with which he is concerned all came to disaster.[38] English kings had to struggle hard to stay successful, and alive, in a very dangerous world. It is a question what part the Church and Christianity played in this struggle and it was a question then what part they could and should play. The acceptance of Christianity in the seventh century was part of the process by which England grew more civilized under the influence of those parts of the Continent where the wreck of Roman civilization had been less complete than it had been in Britain. The Church was successful in England partly because it suited the needs and aspirations of kings. It made some contribution to royal government, which may have had to face new problems in the seventh century as some dynasties built up kingdoms of a size unprecedented since the Anglo-Saxon conquest of England. It must in some degree have changed kings' views of themselves and of their functions. But if kings owed something to the Church, the Church was very dependent upon kings and by the time that Bede wrote some kings were seeing their interest in exploiting rather than in protecting it. Although the English Church had a unity which transcended the boundaries of individual kingdoms and although it always in some degree acted in accordance with its own principles rather than with royal demands it was, nevertheless, very much subject to royal power. Bishops were often or usually appointed in accordance with the will of a king. A monastery which lacked royal favour could hardly hope to prosper.[39] Kings were becoming covetous of the wealth of the Church and demanding a share of it. According to St Boniface, Ceolred of Mercia (709-716) and Osred of Northumbria (705-716) were the first kings to violate the 'privilegia ecclesiarum in regno Anglorum'.[40]

The *Ecclesiastical History* is in part an attempt to demonstrate the role of a Christian king, what the Church did for him and what he ought to do for the Church. Bede repeatedly emphasizes the connection between Christianity and success. His account of the career of Cenwalh, king of Wessex 643-674, is a good example. When Cenwalh succeeded his Christian father he rejected the 'fidem et sacramenta regni caelestis' and not long after 'etiam regni terrestris potentiam perdidit'. While in exile he became converted and then regained his kingdom. But when he expelled his bishop his kingdom became subjected to severe and frequent attacks by his enemies.

> tandem ad memoriam reduxit, quod eum pridem perfidia regno pulerit, fides agnita Christi in regnum revocaverit; intellexitque, quod etiam tunc destituta pontifice provincia recte pariter divino fuerit destituta praesidio.[41]

When Oswy of Northumbria was hard-pressed by his enemy Penda and was unable to buy him off he turned to God. ' "Si paganus", inquit; "nescit accipere nostra donaria, offeramus ei qui novit, Domino Deo nostro . . .".'[42] And so he won a great battle. This campaign is one of the rare events described by Bede of which we have an account in another source. The *Historia Brittonum* attributed to Nennius, a compilation made in Wales probably in the early ninth century, tells a rather different story. It too mentions an offer of treasure to Penda, but one which was accepted. Nennius is later than Bede and the value of his work a matter for speculation. But in this instance he seems to have had information which Bede did not have or use and his employment of the apparently archaic Welsh phrase *atbret Iudeu*, 'the restitution of Iudeu' (? Stirling), to describe the incident suggests that it did take place and was well known in Welsh tradition.[43] The whole truth of the matter will never be known. It is conceivable that there were two offers of treasure, one accepted and one rejected. The suspicion remains, however, that Nennius and Bede were describing the same incident and that Bede was retailing an inaccurate version which suited his didactic purpose. Here and constantly he is insistent that the benefits which the Church can confer come in this world as well as in the next.

The king to whom Bede gives most attention is St Oswald and his account of him is an excellent instance of how Christianity could be presented to suit the needs and feelings of the rulers of England. If the Church deprived the kings of Northumbria of the gods whom they had regarded as their ancestors it soon provided their dynasty with a royal saint, a hero of exactly the kind most appreciated by the Anglo-Saxons, a great and famous man who met disaster nobly. It has been said that the greatest of heroic German themes was that of the inevitable death of the great, the theme of *Beowulf* itself in which 'as in a little circle of light about their halls men with courage as their stay went forward to that battle with the hostile world and the offspring of the dark which ends for all, even the kings and champions, in defeat'.[44] Oswald was an improved version of this type of hero. He came to greatness through being a Christian:

> non solum incognita progenitoribus suis regna caelorum sperare didicit; sed et regna terrarum plus quam ulli maiorum suorum, ab eodem uno Deo, qui fecit caelum et terram consecutus est.[45]

Although he met his inevitable fate and died fighting bravely far from home he lived elsewhere and retained power, which was demonstrated in a concrete way by miracles. As a Christian saint he is a somewhat curious figure. No miracles performed during his lifetime were attributed to him (unless his victory at Heavenfield be counted such); he died fighting an army which, though Bede does not tell us so, may well have included Christians; as he died he was popularly thought to have prayed, not for his enemies, but for the souls of his own men.[46] As the product of the interaction between Christianity and the needs of a dynasty in a certain climate of thought and belief his cult is perfectly intelligible. Oswald was not the only type of Christian king. A surprising number of others in the seventh and eighth centuries abandoned their kingdoms in order to enter a monastery or to go to Rome. Christianity was by no means always to a king's earthly advantage. Aidan's remark when Oswine of Deira humbled himself before him was a pregnant one. ' "Scio", inquit, "quia non multo tempore victurus est rex; nunquam enim ante haec vidi humilem regem".'[47] Bede recognized that there was more than one way in which a king could be virtuous. But he makes the duty of a king while reigning clear. It is to protect the Church, to observe its teaching and to defend his people in battle. The happiest times since the English came to Britain were, he says, those 'dum et fortissimos Christianosque habentes reges cunctis barbaris nationibus essent terrori'.[48] In the period of which he is writing here, the last generation of the seventh century, the 'barbari nationes'—

he was probably thinking chiefly of the Picts—were all more or less Christian. There is a point where his admiration for the leader and defender of a Christian people meets a less specifically devout delight in the *strenuitas* of a warrior king.[49] It was not that Bede was committed in a simple way to the interests of the kings of Northumbria: he approved of a Mercian rebellion against Oswy and disapproved of a raid made by Ecgfrith on Ireland. It was rather that he was writing for an audience which saw Christianity in heroic terms and which may have believed in a more than rational connection between the virtue of a king and the prosperity of his people.

Bede's account of secular affairs is nearly always intended to show how virtue and vice were rewarded in this world as well as hereafter, or to present models of Christian kingship, or is simply incidental. For example, we learn from him of one of Penda's attacks on Northumbria only because it was involved with a miracle of Aidan's. He does not even tell us the names of the British kingdoms against which the kings of Northumbria fought. He says very little indeed about the political events of the early eighth century, which were those about which he must have known most. Indeed, he gives less space to his own times than he does to any other period after 597; of the four books and twelve chapters devoted to the period 596-731 the years from 687 to 731 receive one book only.[50] The contrast with Gregory of Tours is striking. Gregory devotes six of the ten books of his history to the period of his own greatness, *c.* 573-591. The more he knew the more he wrote. It seems with Bede the more he knew the less he wrote. A clue to the reason for this may be given by his remark on the reign of Ceolwulf—that it was so troubled that 'quid de his scribi debeat quemve habitura sint finem singula, necdum sciri valeat'.[51] This is partly, no doubt, an expression of his usual discretion, but also an intimation that he was waiting for the pattern of God's judgments on the past to emerge. Until it had done so he would not write.

If much of the *Ecclesiastical History* is directed towards the laity, more is directed towards the clergy. The English Church in Bede's day enjoyed a status within the universal Church which it was never to reach again. Bede's own work indicates its learning. During his lifetime Englishmen converted much of Germany and they were soon to reform the Church in Gaul. Bede was proud of English achievements and devoted much of his fifth book to describing the work of English missionaries on the Continent, though he strangely says nothing of St Boniface, who was becoming the greatest of them.[52] But it is not for nothing that much of the rest of the book consists of accounts of visions of hell. Bede felt that much was amiss with the Church and in particular in his own kingdom of Northumbria. We have the letter which he wrote at very nearly the end of his life to Bishop Egbert, of York, lamenting the ills which plagued the church.[53] His criticisms were, briefly, these. There were not enough bishops to ensure that pastoral duties (which then fell largely on the bishop in person) were properly discharged. Large dioceses were maintained because bishops were anxious to exact all the dues they could. Some bishops were surrounded by men given to laughter, jokes, tales, feasting and drink. Many priests were ignorant, many monks ill-conducted. Monasteries were often such in name only, being in fact the property of laymen who sought chiefly the rights and exemptions associated with the monastic tenure of land. The kingdom had become so demented with this 'mad error' since the death of Aldfrith that its security was threatened since there was not enough land left to support the young men who should have defended it.

It is not, of course, unusual in any period for the clergy to be wicked and neglectful or for the laity to seek to batten on the Church. These evils then took particular forms reflecting the nature of the Church and of society in the seventh century and the relations between them. Christianity had, after a slow start, spread very quickly in England. In 630 there was only one kingdom in which it was established at all firmly. By 660 it was established for good in all but one. The Church had become a native one just as quickly. Until 644 there was no English bishop. By 678 there was only one who was not English, Theodore himself. As the Church grew, and grew acclimatized, much of its way of life seems to have become assimilated to that of lay society and the *mores* of its rulers to those of the aristocracy from which so many of them came. The career of Wilfred affords the best illustration of many of the circumstances and difficulties.[54] Born in about 634 he entered the monastery of Lindisfarne, thereafter going to Canterbury, Rome and Gaul and returning to England in time to play a leading part at the synod of Whitby in 664. He then became bishop in Northumbria, exercising his functions there from 669 or somewhat earlier until 678 when king Ecgfrith expelled him. He remained a wanderer in England and abroad for most of the rest of his life, with intervals during which he was restored to some power in Northumbria from 686-7 to 691-2 and from 705-6 to his death in 709. He was certainly one of the greatest ecclesiastics of his day. Ascetic, deemed a saint by some, the founder of several monasteries according to the rule of St Benedict, he established Christianity in Sussex and attempted to do so in Frisia. At the same time his life and conduct were in some respects like those of a great Anglo-Saxon nobleman. As he grew powerful he surrounded himself with a great household, not only of clerks, but also of young men who did not proceed to enter the Church.[55] Like many of the great of his day he had to go into exile more than once and he went surrounded by his followers. He served more kings than one and so became very rich.[56] He gained much for the Church, but what he gained was organized as a personal ecclesiastical empire. He owned many monasteries in several kingdoms. To some he may not even have appointed subordinate abbots; they were his and his alone.[57] Some abbots put themselves under his protection in almost the way that a nobleman might enter the service of a king.[58] He behaved towards those beneath him with the generosity expected of a ruler. When he went to visit all his abbots in the south he either increased their livelihood with grants of land or rejoiced their hearts with money.[59] He is difficult for us to judge, as Bede seems to have found him difficult to judge. Active, munificent and it may be holy he was nevertheless very much part of a noble society which cared greatly for power and show, the possession of a loyal *comitatus* and the opportunity to exchange rich gifts. His career was in some respects unparalleled and may have owed something to Merovingian example. But in its reflection of the relations between the Church and the world it is typical of much that went on in Bede's day. *Beowulf* was almost certainly written in a monastery, probably at some time in the eighth century. Its learned author was a Christian; the feeling which inspires it is only intermittently so and is very much that of a warrior nobility. Even Cuthbert, one of the most ascetic of saints, had as his pectoral cross a jewel worthy of a king, or else it was thought appropriate that he should be buried with one.[60] The Church in Bede's day was not one in which it is, or was always, easy to draw the distinction between the lay and the clerical or even between good and evil.

Bede offered it models. Of the many lives of saints included in his history three seem to be particularly intended to give guidance to monks and bishops in their relations with the secular world, those of John of Hexham, Cuthbert and above all Aidan. If the high ecclesiastics of Bede's day 'immensum rerum secularium pondus et vectigal exigunt' Aidan and his immediate successors at Lindisfarne had 'nil pecuniarum absque pecoribus'.[61] When he died Wilfred had thought it necessary for his abbeys to have treasures with which to buy the favour of kings and bishops.[62] Aidan gave 'potentes' nothing but food when they came to see him. The money they gave him he gave to the poor or used to ransom captives. There was, Bede thought, all too much ecclesiastical drinking and entertaining in his own time, but in those days 'tota cura cordis excolendi, non ventris'. If the king and his followers came to a monastery 'simplici tantum et cotidiano fratrum cibo contenti, nil ultra quaerebant'.[63] In the letter to Egbert Bede complained that there were many villages and hamlets 'in montibus . . . inaccessis ac saltibus dumosis positi' which had not so much as seen a bishop for years 'quorum tamen ne unus quidem a tributis antistiti reddendis esse possit immunis'.[64] But Aidan and Cuthbert had taken pains to tour the country to preach and teach and it was to just such places that Cuthbert had particularly gone.

> Solebat autem ea maxima loca peragrare illis praedicare in viculis qui in arduis asperisque montibus procul positi.[65]

Bede describes the lives of these saints and in particular that of Aidan not simply as good examples but as good examples in strong contrast to the conduct of the Church in his own day—'vita illius a nostri temporibus segnitia distabat'.[66] It is noticeable how much he stresses those aspects of Aidan's conduct which defied the customs of Anglo-Saxon society which had so powerful and inevitable an effect upon the Church, in particular entertainment and gift exchange. Hospitality was of the greatest importance to the Anglo-Saxons. It was of the essence of kingship for the king to dine with his nobles in his great hall. In their turn nobles frequently entertained kings. At all levels of society public or communal entertainment was a most important part of life.

Similarly with the exchange of gifts. Even Cuthbert thought of it in his last hours when he asked to have the priest with him who had been accustomed to serve him

> ideoque donationum acceptationumque eius omnium conscius erat indubius. Quem ob id maxime secum manere voluit, ut si cuiuslibet acceptis muneribus digna recompensatione non respondisset, illius admonitione recoleret et priusquam obiret, sua cuique restitueret.[67]

Thus much of the *Ecclesiastical History* is by implication a criticism of the Church in Bede's own day and expresses his longing for a return to a primitive simplicity which he thought had existed only a short time before. He may well have realized that if the Church was to survive it had to involve itself more with the world than he would wish. He remarks of Putta, Bishop of Rochester, who after his church and its possessions had been ravaged by Aethelred of Mercia, retired elsewhere,

> nihil omnino de restaurando episcopatu suo agens; quia, sicut et supra diximus, magis in ecclesiasticis quam in mundanis rebus erat industrius.[68]

It is a slightly curious but a revealing way of putting it. His sympathies clearly lay with Putta; he thought the world was bad and the Church too much part of it. He wanted a poverty, simplicity and devotion which, if they had ever characterized the English Church, were never to do so again.

Bede's account of the Church in the *Ecclesiastical History* is distinguished by great discretion. While his commentaries contain numerous references to the shortcomings of the Church and in his letter to Egbert he is open and violent in denunciation he has very little to say directly about the sins of the clergy in his history. A few sinful clerics are mentioned, but, Britons apart, almost always incidentally. His account even of Ceolred and Osred, kings who, so we learn elsewhere, oppressed the Church, is limited to the dates of their respective accessions and deaths. The nearest he comes in the *Ecclesiastical History* to the long account and denunciation of fictitious monasteries in the letter to Egbert is the cryptic statement that so peaceful are the times that many Northumbrians have preferred to enter monasteries rather than to exercise the arts of war. 'Quae res quem sit habitura finem, posterior aetas videbit.'[69] Similarly in his *Lives* of the abbots of

Monkwearmouth-Jarrow Bede makes no reference to the incident described in the anonymous biography of Ceolfrid—which he used—of Ceolfrid's leaving the abbey partly because of the behaviour of certain nobles, who could not endure his regular discipline.[70] Had we to rely on the *Ecclesiastical History* for our knowledge of the Church in the first generation of the eighth century we should know little of it, and still less of Bede's severe judgment on it. There can be little doubt that Bede's failure to describe the conduct of those of his contemporaries of whom he disapproved was deliberate. In his commentary on the Book of Samuel he is explicit that it is wrong publicly to denounce even evil priests:

> nos quoque in exemplum beati Samuhelis erga tales modeste agere neque eos traducere oportet quos incorrigibiles et divino iam iudicio non dubitamus esse damnandos, maxime si hos aliquo gradu ecclesiastico

and

> docet quanta reverentia sit divinis adhibenda sacramentis quamvis per malorum manum dispensatis, quantus personis sacri altaris officio mancipatis honor impendendus, quantum ab harum laesione quamlibet male viventium propter insigne gradus sit cuiuslibet temperanda praesumptio . . . Cavendum ergo ne episcoporum, presbiterorum, diaconorum famam passim lacerare et attaminare praesumamus.[71]

He clearly did not think it appropriate to enlarge on the deficiencies of the clergy in a work such as the *Ecclesiastical History* which was intended for a fairly wide audience. A letter to another cleric such as that to Egbert was another matter, though even there he mentions no names. Others of his day were not so backward, like the monk who wrote to a friend describing a vision of hell where many named sinners had appeared in torment, among them 'your abbot'.[72]

Bede's discretion is most apparent in his treatment of Wilfred.[73] He had access to some and probably the whole of the biography of Wilfred attributed to Wilfred's clerk, Eddius Stephanus. His account differs, however, from that of Eddius. While he adds to Eddius's descriptions of Wilfred's defence of Roman orthodoxy and of his conversion of Sussex he says nothing of the important part which Wilfred played in Merovingian politics after 658 and his account of the struggle for ecclesiastical power in Northumbria is shorter and differs in emphasis. Eddius maintains that Wilfred was wronged not only by kings Ecgfrith and Aldfrith but by bishops, and, in particular by archbishops Theodore and Berhtwald. Bede does say briefly that several bishops were involved in Wilfred's expulsion in 691 but otherwise presents the disputes as between Wilfred and the kings of Northumbria alone, saying nothing of the parts played by the archbishops of Canterbury. He omits any mention of the synod of Austerfield (?703) at which, according to Eddius, the bishops led by the archbishop behaved aggressively and disingenuously towards Wilfred. He does not mention, as Eddius does, that Wilfred was imprisoned for nine months by Ecgfrith, *c.* 680 and he gives a different account of the circumstances of Wilfred's appointment to a Northumbrian see in 664.

These differences have for long attracted the attention of historians. R. L. Poole, in what remains the standard account of them, came to the conclusion that in the matters at issue Bede was almost always right and Eddius almost always wrong.[74] But, while it is true that Eddius was committed to Wilfred's cause and capable of misrepresentation to support it, Poole assumes rather than demonstrates Bede's greater veracity; and Bede's veracity is what is at issue, since Eddius is almost the only contemporary source of any length with whom we are able to compare him.[75] There is a consistency in the ways in which Bede's account of Wilfred differs from that of Eddius which suggests, not that Bede was more truthful, but that he was more discreet and that his view of the function of a historian was different.[76] Wilfred's career must have presented Bede with great difficulties. He always speaks of Wilfred with great respect, and had reason to respect him, not least as the great protagonist of Roman orthodoxy. But he probably disapproved of some aspects of Wilfred's career, which diverged considerably from his ideal. It was in Wilfred's presence that Bede had been accused of heresy and his accusers—whom he describes, with the approach to venom which characterizes him when his own orthodoxy is questioned, as wanton, drunken bumpkins—were probably members of Wilfred's household.[77] In any case Wilfred's contentious life presented incidents which it was difficult to make edifying, disputes between bishops, two worthy kings, Ecgfrith, 'venerabilis et piissimus', and Aldfrith, 'vir . . . doctissimus', flouting papal decisions, perhaps even two archbishops doing so.[78] Part of Wilfred's misfortunes probably sprang from his resistance to Theodore's policy of dividing up large sees. Bede thought such division was necessary, but Wilfred appears to have gained some degree of papal support.[79] It was a matter which was difficult to describe so as either to encourage the good or deter the bad for it is likely that in Bede's view these disputes were between good men who were all in some degree in the wrong. We do not have enough evidence to be sure to what extent he or Eddius conceals or distorts the truth. The likelihood is that Eddius gives a better, though partizan, account of what really happened while Bede steers a careful course, giving additional information on the most edifying aspects of Wilfred's career while omitting or playing down those which were to the discredit of the virtuous; sometimes, perhaps, he 'through necessity concealed the truth by the use of very cautious words'.[80] It is worth observing that almost none of the passages in Eddius which enable us to see how closely Wilfred's life in some aspects resembled that of the secular nobility were used by Bede. He very probably did not approve of them and, fond though he was of facts, his tendency was so to describe men and events that they appear timeless. If the names were changed it would often be difficult to tell of which century or of what kind of society he is writing.

A theme which stands out above all others in Bede's attempt to instruct and edify through the *Ecclesiastical History* is that of the struggle for the unity and orthodoxy of the Church. To record the nature and fate of heresy was one of the most important functions of an ecclesiastical historian. Eusebius had given much attention to so doing. As a theologian Bede was concerned to refute many heretics and heresies—Plummer collected references to twenty-nine.[81] As a historian he was concerned with one heresy, Pelagianism, and one group of errors, those of the Celtic Churches which departed from orthodox custom, especially in the calculation of the date of Easter. Pelagius's heresy of the denial of the necessity of grace for salvation may have originated in the British Isles. Bede thought that it had been imported in the fifth century, and in his first book describes at some length two visits made by St Germanus to extirpate it. Pelagian views seem to have continued to be held in Ireland in the seventh and eighth centuries and it may well have been from Ireland that there came the two works of the Pelagian Julian of Eclana and the one of Pelagius himself to which Bede had access.[82] The first book of his commentary on the Song of Songs was devoted to the refutation of Julian. His account of Pelagianism and its defeat in the fifth century was then of more than historical significance; the evidence he gives of God's condemnation of it in the past was a useful lesson for his own day.

The errors which received most attention from Bede were those of the Celtic Churches which diverged from Roman customs. The most important difference was that on the calculation of the date of Easter.[83] It was regarded not as a minor point of discipline, but as a rift in the unity of the Church with serious doctrinal implications. For such a theologian as Bede, always seeking mystical interpretations, the movement of Easter and its proper calculation —and no one knew the proper calculation better than he—was loaded with the weightiest significance. Consider, for example, the words Bede attributes to the dying Cuthbert who warns his companions to have no communion with those who depart from the unity of Catholic peace 'vel pascha non suo tempore celebrando, vel perverse vivendo'.[84] A considerable part of the *Ecclesiastical History* is devoted to the subject. In the second book we are told how Augustine attempted to induce the Britons to accept the Roman usages or to assist the evangelization of the English. He failed and prophesied that the recalcitrant Britons would perish at the hands of the English. Bede records with some relish the fulfilment of this prophesy when Aethelfrith massacred the monks of Bangor. Here, as in his use of Gildas's account of the Anglo-Saxon invasions in the fifth century, Bede is able to reconcile two loyalties by showing his pagan ancestors to have been the instrument of God's revenge. He goes on to describe later attempts to persuade the Britons to accept the Roman Easter. The climax of the third book is his famous account of the synod of Whitby at which Oswy agreed that Roman usages should prevail in Northumbria, while those who did not accept them left. In the fifth book Bede now explains how Iona, northern Ireland and the king of the Picts were converted to a proper view—southern Ireland had become orthodox long since. The emphasis given to the Easter controversy throughout the *Ecclesiastical History* is clear. It receives the longest chapter in the third book and the longest in the fifth. The chapter which describes the conversion of Iona is the last in the whole except for that which gives a final survey of the general state of Britain. It must have given particular satisfaction to Bede to record the acceptance of Catholic unity by the house whence had come Aidan and the Irish missionaries whom he so much admired, but whose adherence to unorthodox usages he so much deplored. The battle for Roman uniformity was still not completely won at the time when he wrote. The Britons remained 'inveterati et claudicantes'.[85] As with Pelagianism, so with the Easter controversy, Bede was writing not only an account of the past, but a tract for his own times.

Bede's preoccupation with the defence of orthodoxy and his distrust of the Britons who had erred, and in his own day still and alone continued to err, may have influenced his selection of subject-matter and coloured his account of what he selected. As always the lack of other sources prevents reasonable certainty as to how far this was so. Thus Nennius gives an account of the conversion of Northumbria quite at variance with that of Bede; it was accomplished, he says, by the British Church, Edwin being baptized by Rhun, son of Urien, a member of the royal dynasty of the northern British kingdom of Rheged. Until recently most scholars have rejected this story. Nennius is later than Bede, less scholarly, and recounts much that is fabulous. A considerable part of Bede's account of the conversion of Northumbria must be broadly true; he can hardly have fabricated the letters of Pope Honorius to Edwin and his queen which help to confirm his account. But Professor Jackson and Mrs Chadwick have recently argued that Nennius's tale should be taken more seriously.[86] It is consistent with the fragments of knowledge which we have about the rulers of Rheged and about Edwin's relations with the Britons. Much of this information inspires more interest than confidence, but it is not negligible. In particular Nennius gives another piece of information about the relations between the royal houses of Rheged and Northumbria, namely that King Oswy had two wives, *Riemmelth*, whose descent is given and who seems to have been a member of the royal house of Rheged, and Eanfled, daughter of Edwin. Bede mentions the second, but not the first. That Nennius's information on this was accurate is suggested by the occurrence of what seems to be an Anglo-Saxon version of the first wife's name at about the right place in the 'list of the names of the queens and abbesses of Northumbria' in the, presumably independent, *Liber Vitae* of Durham.[87] This fragment of evidence by no means proves Nennius's account of the conversion of Northumbria to have been true. But it does suggest relationships between Northumbria and its British neighbours of which Bede tells us, through ignorance or design, nothing; and it raises the suspicion that the British Church did play a more important part in the conversion of Northumbria than his account, which allows it none, indicates.

The problems involved in assessing Bede's account of the conversion of Northumbria are characteristic of those which arise in connection with the *Ecclesiastical History*. Bede was very learned and very intelligent. His aim was partly simply to describe the history of the Church in England and his care in collecting evidence and the methods, derived from those of Eusebius, with which he handled it enabled him to perform this task in a manner which makes this work more scholarly, in the modern sense, than that of any other Dark Age historian. This aspect of his work has always and rightly attracted attention and praise. But his principal intention was not just to record the past, but to use it to teach lessons to the present, mainly by treating seventh-century England as a gallery of good examples. Excellent instances of the reaction he sought are to be found in the work of Victorian historians, for example W. Bright—'We think not only of the noble earnestness of Ethelbert, of the heroic sanctity of Oswald, of the sweet humility of Oswin but of the genuine conversions of Eadbald and Kenwalch . . .', etc.[88] The differences in the historiographical fortunes of seventh-century England and seventh-century Gaul, the one often being regarded as moving and edifying, the other as repellent and vicious, are attributable not so much to one society's being nobler, or nicer, than the other as to Bede's aims and tastes being different from those of Frankish historians.[89]

Bede wrote then not only in the Eusebian tradition but also in that of hagiography. The principles of hagiographers were largely contrary to those of scholarship, though they sometimes adopted a misleadingly scholarly air, setting store by citing evidence for things which did not happen or which did not happen at the time or to the persons they alleged. They wrote in the attitude of mind with which the Bible is now often interpreted. Moral truth, not literal truth, was what mattered.[90] Emphasis was placed on the need for belief, not on the advantages of doubt. 'Vera lex historiae' is, says Bede, 'simpliciter ea quae fama vulgante collegimus ad instructionem posteritatis litteris mandare.' He prides himself that he has used an earlier life of Cuthbert 'simpliciter fidem historiae quam legebam accomodans'.[91] Hagiographers tended to turn the men and events they described into types. 'Vous lui demandez un portrait', says Fr. Delehaye of the hagiographer, 'il vous répond par un programme'.[92] Bede's account in the *Ecclesiastical History* of such saints as Aidan and Cuthbert is almost purely hagiographical and contrasts with the more factual and sober treatment of other biographies in his *Lives of the Abbots*.[93] It is a question how far what appear to be the more purely historical parts of the *Ecclesiastical History* are affected by his didactic purposes. These purposes certainly determined his selection of subject-matter; it can hardly be doubted that he was very discreet and sometimes suppressed that which could not edify. But one must wonder how far his account of the course of events is affected by his believing that he ought to give the version which best demonstrated the truth of his faith rather than that which best corresponded with the truth, and how far his judgment of what was likely was affected by his conviction of what was appropriate. He is so far our only source for so much of what he describes that no firm judgment on these matters is possible. But a comparison of Bede with such other sources as Eddius and Nennius, questionable though they are, suggests that the veneration which he has so long and so rightly been accorded ought to be tempered by some mistrust. Historians have sometimes been too ready to assume Bede's reliability as axiomatic when it is the point at issue. It is not even safe to assume that the attitudes and emphases of the *Ecclesiastical History* fully reflect Bede's personal views. He thought it the duty of a teacher to suit his teaching to his audience.[94] Some of the apparent crudities in his approach to Christianity, for example the repeated emphasis on its connection with worldly success and on the importance of miracles, may indicate not so much his own view of his faith as his judgment of the limitations of his audience.[95]

Clear, almost simple, though the *Ecclesiastical History* is it is the product of a complex mind working under difficult circumstances. On the one hand Bede was concerned for the truth, interested in hard facts, excellently equipped technically and writing with the good model of Eusebius before him. On the other hand he was using history to teach lessons which he felt to be badly needed;

he was writing partly not as a historian but as a hagiographer; he had to suit his work to his audience and present it in such a way that it moved men less learned and less subtle than he. He was a barbarian, one of the first handful of his people to have become literate, yet very learned in a tradition which sprang from the remote world of the Roman empire. He was very devoutly, indeed sternly, Christian and writing in and for a Church which had accommodated itself to the ways of its world. He sought to recall it to what he thought to have been its primitive simplicity while treating it with the respect and discretion which any Church deserved. Many of the difficulties in assessing the *Ecclesiastical History* derive from those inherent in Bede's intellectual position and in the nature of his task.

Whatever the difficulties, few of those who read his book and even fewer of those who work on it fail to come to admire it. Bede had and has the power to seize the imagination of his reader and to transport him to a strange world; strange because it is so distant in time and circumstances, even stranger because it is a world so directly dominated by God, where ordinary historical causality hardly applies. Most Dark Age historians provoke a sense, usually an overwhelming sense, of superiority. We know better, we are cleverer than they. Bede defies patronage. Remote, almost bizarre, though his view of history is he expounds it in the manner, and it is more than just the manner, of an educated, rational and moderate man. The *Ecclesiastical History* is not only the record of most of what we shall ever know of a century or more of English history, but a monument to the extraordinary skill and power of Bede.[96]

NOTES

[1] The chronicles are best edited by T. Mommsen, *M.G.H. Scriptores Antiquissimi,* XIII (1898), 223-354, and the other historical works by C. Plummer, *Baedae Opera Historica* (2 vols., Oxford, 1896); references below are to Plummer's edition unless otherwise stated. For editions of Bede's other works see M. L. W. Laistner and H. H. King, *Handlist of Bede Manuscripts* (Ithaca, N.Y., 1943) and M. T. A. Carroll, *The Venerable Bede: his Spiritual Teachings* (Catholic University of America, Studies in Mediaeval History, new ser., IX (Washington, 1946)). The poems, homilies and some of the commentaries have been re-edited in *Corpus Christianorum Series Latine,* CXIX and CXX, ed. D. Hurst, and CXXII, ed. D. Hurst and J. Fraipont (Turnhout,

1962, 1960 and 1955 respectively). For general accounts of Bede see *Bede, his Li e, Times and Writings*, ed. A. Hamilton Thompson (Oxford, 1935), E. S. Duckett, *Anglo-Saxon Saints and Scholars* (New York, 1947), pp. 217-338, W. F. Bolton, 'A Bede Bibliography: 1935-60' *Traditio*, xviii (1962), 436-45.

[2] *Venerabilis Bedae Opera*, ed. J. A. Giles, XII (1844), 341.

[3] For Bede as a historian see e.g. W. Levison, 'Bede as Historian', in *Bede, his Life, Times and Writings, op. cit.*, pp. 111-51; C. W. Jones, *Saints' Lives and Chronicles in Early England* (Ithaca, N.Y., 1947) and 'Bede as Early Medieval Historian', *Medievalia et Humanistica*, fasc. IV (1946), 26-36; P. Hunter Blair, *Bede's Ecclesiastical History . . . and its Importance Today* (Jarrow Lecture 1959, Jarrow-on-Tyne, n.d.).

[4] For the history of the church see e.g. M. Deanesly, *The Pre-Conquest Church in England* (1961).

[5] Ed. Plummer, *Baedae Opera Historica* I, clx-clxiv.

[6] Carroll, *The Venerable Bede . . ., op. cit.*, pp. 43-6; M. L. W. Laistner, 'Bede as a Classical and Patristic Scholar', *Transactions of the Royal Historical Society*, 4th ser., XVI (1933), 83.

[7] The anonymous life of Ceolfrith and Eddius Stephanus's life of Wilfred survive in only two manuscripts each, the Whitby life of Gregory the Great in only one (*Baedae Opera Historica*, ed. Plummer, I, cxl-cxli; *The Life of Bishop Wilfred by Eddius Stephanus*, ed. and trans. B. Colgrave (Cambridge, 1927), pp. xiii-xvi; B. Colgrave, 'The Earliest Life of Gregory the Great', in K. Jackson, N. K. Chadwick and others, *Celt and Saxon: Studies in the Early British Border* (Cambridge, 1963), pp. 119-21). So much damage seems to have been done by the Scandinavian invasions to English libraries that works which were not popular, and in particular not popular on the Continent, must have had only a limited chance of survival.

[8] For this paragraph, W. Levison, *England and the Continent in the Eighth Century* (Oxford, 1946); K. C. King, *The Earliest German Monasteries* (Nottingham, 1961); J. M. Wallace-Hadrill, 'Rome and the Early English Church', *Settimane di studio del centro italiano di studi sull'alto medioevo*, VII (Spoleto, 1960), 519-48; *Bede's Europe* (Jarrow Lecture 1962, Jarrow-on-Tyne, n.d.); K. Hughes, 'Irish Monks and Learning', *Los monjes y los estudios* (Abadia de Poblet, 1963), pp. 61-86, and H. Farmer, 'The Studies of Anglo-Saxon Monks A.D. 600-800', *ibid.*, pp. 87-103; J. N. Hillgarth, 'Visigothic Spain and Early Christian Ireland', *Proceedings of the Royal Irish Academy* LXII, C (1961-3), 167-94.

[9] Levison, *England and the Continent*, p. 40; C. E. Blunt, 'Four Italian Coins Imitating Anglo-Saxon Types', *British Numismatic Journal*, 3rd ser., V (1945-8), 285.

[10] M. L. W. Laistner, 'Bede as a Classical and Patristic Scholar', *op. cit.*; 'The Library of the Venerable Bede', *Bede, his Life, Times and Writings, op. cit.*, pp. 237-266; both articles are reprinted in *The Intellectual Heritage of the Early Middle Ages* (Ithaca, N.Y., 1957).

[11] A. Momigliano, 'Pagan and Christian Historiography in the Fourth Century A.D.', *The Conflict between Paganism and Christianity in the Fourth Century*, ed. A. Momigliano (Oxford, 1963), pp. 79-99.

[12] J. M. Wallace-Hadrill, 'The Work of Gregory of Tours in the Light of Modern Research', *The Long-Haired Kings* (1962), pp. 49-70.

[13] Jones, *Saints' Lives and Chronicles, op. cit.*, pp. 82-5.

[14] Bede thought wonder-working shrines could diminish rather than increase faith when the unworthy were not healed (Carroll, p. 197) and he attributes to Cuthbert the view that when such a shrine became a sanctuary for evildoers it also became a nuisance to its keepers, *Two Lives of St. Cuthbert*, ed. and trans. B. Colgrave (Cambridge, 1940), p. 278.

[15] The best accounts of Bede's sources are those of Plummer, Levison and Laistner in the works cited in notes 1, 3 and 10 above.

[16] For the *Passio Sancti Albani*, W. Levison, 'St. Alban and St. Alban's', *Antiquity*, XV (1941), 337-59. Discussion of the possibility of at least part of the *De Excidio* being of a date later than the mid-sixth century one usually accepted has recently been revived: P. Grosjean, 'Remarques sur le *De Excidio* attribué a Gildas', *Archivum Latinitatis Medii Aevi*, XXV (1955), 155-87; 'Notes de hagiographie celtique', *Analecta Bol andia*, LXXV (1957), 185-226.

[17] English sources of an annalistic nature possibly used by Bede are discussed by Jones, *Saints' Lives and Chronicles, op. cit.*; P. Hunter Blair, 'The *Moore Memoranda* on Northumbrian History', *The Early Cultures of North-West Europe*, ed. C. Fox and B. Dickins (Cambridge, 1950), pp. 245-57; 'The Northumbrians and their Southern Frontier', *Archaeologia Aeliana*, 4th ser., XXVI (1948), 98-126; and P. Grosjean 'La date du Colloque de Whitby', *Analecta Bollandia*, LXXVIII (1960), 255-60. Some information may have come to him from inscriptions, C. Peers and C. A. Ralegh Radford, 'The Saxon Monastery at Whitby', *Archaeologia*, LXXXIX (1943), 40-6.

[18] *H.E.* pp. 6-7.

[19] N. K. Chadwick, in *Celt and Saxon, op. cit.*, pp. 138-85, esp. pp. 169, 177.

[20] Jones is equally confident that Bede's account of the synod is in a different genre, modelled on *Acta Synodi Caesareae, Saints' Lives and Chronicles, op. cit.*, 181.

[21] *H.E.* II, 16, 117.

[22] Levison, 'Bede as Historian', *op. cit.*, p. 117.

[23] C. Jenkins, 'Bede as Exegete and Theologian', *Bede, his Life, Times and Writings, op. cit.*, pp. 196-9.

[24] Laistner, 'Bede as a Classical and Patristic Scholar', *op. cit.*, pp. 84-5; cf. Jenkins, *op. cit.*, pp. 160-1.

[25] For the literature on Bede's chronology, D. P. Kirby, 'Bede and Northumbrian Chronology', *English Historical Review*, LXXVIII (1963), 514-27.

[26] Kirby, 518, 522-3.

[27] (H.) S. Brechter, *Die Quellen zur Angelsachsenmission Gregors des Grossen* (Beitr. zur Gesch. d. Alten Mönchtums u.d. Benediktinerordens, Heft 22), Münster i. W., 1941), pp. 228-52, critically discussed by F. A. Markus, 'The Chronology of the Gregorian Mission: Bede's Narrative and Gregory's Correspondence', *Journal of Ecclesiastical History*, XIV (1963), 16-30.

[28] It is likely that Bede did not know when Ethelbert was baptised.

The use of *interea* with the perfect tense to introduce his account of Augustine's journey to be consecrated abroad suggests that when he wrote I, 26 and 27, he was uncertain of the relationship of this event to the baptism of Ethelbert (cf. III, 20, 169; III, 28, 194; IV, 4, 213). The absence of a date for the baptism from the chronological summary in V, 24, strongly suggests that his sources did not give him one. The phrase 'post XX et unum annos acceptae fidei' in II, 5 (p. 90), is not entirely unambiguous. It probably refers to the baptism or conversion of Ethelbert which Bede would therefore here place in 597. If so this may well be a slip on his part. There is other evidence that II, 5, was carelessly written (Kirby, *op. cit.*, p. 521).

[29] The dating of this journey is connected with the vexed question of the authenticity of the *Responsiones* to Augustine attributed to Gregory, for which see M. Deanesly and P. Grosjean 'The Canterbury Edition of the Answers of Pope Gregory I to St. Augustine', *Journal of Ecclesiastical History*, X (1959), 1-49; P. Meyvaert, 'Les "responsiones" de S. Grégoire le Grand a S. Augustin de Cantorbery', *Revue d'Histoire Ecclesiastique*, LIV (1959), 879-94; 'Bede and the *Libellus Synodicus* of Gregory the Great', *Journal of Theological Studies*, new ser., XII (1961), 298 n.; M. Deanesly, 'The Capitular Text of the *Responsiones* of Pope Gregory I to St. Augustine', *Journal of Ecclesiastical History*, XLI (1961), 231-4.

[30] It is not altogether clear that Bede's well-known account of the co-operation of Oswy of Northumbria and Egbert of Kent in choosing an archbishop of Canterbury is not a mere deduction based on the conflation of a letter from Pope Vitalian to Oswy and some account of Egbert's sending a candidate for the see to Rome, *H.E.* III, 29, 196-9; IV, 1, 201; *Hist. Abb.*, ed. Plummer, *Baedae Opera Historica*, I, 366; cf. Plummer's note, II, 200-1.

[31] For textual questions see Plummer, pp. lxxx-cxliv, *The Leningrad Bede*, ed. O. Arngart (Copenhagen, 1952), pp. 13-35; *The Moore Bede*, ed. P. Hunter Blair and R. A. B. Mynors (Copenhagen, 1959), pp. 11-37.

[32] *H.E.*, p. 5.

[33] *H.E.* IV, 23 (25), 264; Carroll, *The Venerable Bede . . .*, *op. cit.*, pp. 162-3, 234.

[34] *Ibid.*, chapter IV; *H.E.* V, 12-14.

[35] Aldfrith, Ceolwulf's predecessor, was literate; laymen brought up in such a household as Wilfred's might have become so, *Eddius*, ed. Colgrave, *op. cit.*, p. 44. Wilfred himself was literate well before he was ordained priest and could have gone on to a secular career, as others perhaps did after a similar beginning, *Eddius*, pp. 8, 10, 18.

[36] E.g. *H.E.*, p. 6; V, 13, 313.

[37] D. Whitelock, *After Bede* (Jarrow Lecture 1960, n.p., n.d.), p. 11.

[38] A. G. Brodeur, *The Art of Beowulf* (Berkeley, 1959), pp. 76-85, 103, 116, 119.

[39] *S. Bonifatii et Lulli Epistolae* (*M.G.H. Epistolae Selectae* I), ed. M. Tangl (Berlin, 1916), no. 14.

[40] *Ibid.*, nos. 73, 78, 115; cf. E. John, *Land Tenure in Early England* (Leicester, 1960), pp. 70-3.

[41] *H.E.* III, 7.

[42] *H.E.* III, 24, 177.

[43] K. Jackson, 'On the Northern British Section in Nennius', *Celt and Saxon, op. cit.*, pp. 35-9. Jackson argues convincingly that the *Historia* is partly derived from written sources embodying annals recorded during the seventh century.

[44] J. R. R. Tolkien, 'Beowulf, the Monsters and the Critics', *Proceedings of the British Academy*, XXII (1936), p. 18 of the offprint.

[45] *H.E.* III, 6, 137-8.

[46] *H.E.* III, 12, 151.

[47] *H.E.* III, 14, 157; cf. Sigbert, king of Essex, said to have been murdered because he would forgive his enemies, III, 22, 173.

[48] *H.E.* IV, 2, 205.

[49] Wallace-Hadrill, 'The Work of Gregory of Tours in the Light of Modern Research', *op. cit.*, pp. 60-2.

[50] The period 596-687 occupies 239 pages of Plummer's edition, that after 687, 71.

[51] *H.E.* V, 23, 349.

[52] Wallace-Hadrill, *Bede's Europe, op. cit.*, pp. 11-12.

[53] Ed. Plummer, *Baedae Opera Historica* I, 405-23.

[54] The most recent extended account of Wilfred is that of Duckett, *Anglo-Saxon Saints and Scholars, op. cit.*, pp. 101-216.

[55] *Eddius*, ed. Colgrave, *op. cit.*, pp. 44, 48, 50, 94.

[56] *Ibid.*, pp. 16, 36, 48, 82-4, 136, 140.

[57] *Ibid.*, p. 134.

[58] *Ibid.*, p. 44.

[59] *Ibid.*, p. 140.

[60] *The Relics of St. Cuthbert,* ed. C. F. Battiscombe (Oxford, 1956), pp. 308-25.

[61] *In Esdram et Nehemiam . . . Expositio*, ed. Giles, *Bedae Opera Omnia* IX, 21 (qu. Carroll, *op. cit.*, p. 149n), *H.E.* III, 27, 190.

[62] *Eddius*, p. 136.

[63] *H.E.* III, 27, 190-1.

[64] Ed. Plummer, p. 410.

[65] *H.E.* IV, 25 (27), 270.

[66] *H.E.* III, 5, 136.

[67] *Two Lives of St. Cuthbert, op. cit.*, p. 276.

[68] *H.E.* IV, 12, 228.

[69] *H.E.* V, 23, 351.

[70] *Baedae Opera Historica*, ed. Plummer, I, 390.

[71] Ed. Hurst, *Corpus Christianorum Series Latine* CXIX, *op. cit.*, pp. 135, 244-5; Carroll, p. 150.

[72] *S. Bonifatii et Lulli Epistolae, op. cit.*, no. 115.

[73] For Wilfred, see pp. 173-4, above.

[74] 'St. Wilfred and the See of Ripon', *English Historical Review*, XXXIV (1919), 1-24.

[75] Thus it is extremely likely that Aethelwalh, king of Sussex, was already a Christian before Wilfred arrived, although Eddius implies that Wilfred converted him (Poole, pp. 6-7). But most of Poole's arguments for Eddius's unreliability are no more than demonstrations that his account differs from

that of Bede. His attempt to show that Eddius's account of Wilfred's role in Merovingian politics gives independent evidence of his untrustworthiness is unconvincing. Eddius may well exaggerate the importance of his hero. The sources for the events in question are, however, so poor and Eddius so important among them that it is not possible to demonstrate this. Modern historians of the Merovingians have accepted Eddius's account in general, *faute de mieux* it may be (e.g. W. Levison in his edition of Eddius, *M.G.H.*, SS. Rer. Mer., VI, 163-263, L. Dupraz, *Le Royaume des Francs* (Fribourg-en-Suisse, 1948, chapter 4). Poole's allegation that Eddius states Ebroin to have been alive when he was in fact dead (p. 5) is not sufficient to discredit Eddius's general reliability on Merovingian affairs even if it is justified and Eddius's account of Wilfred's movements is in any case just compatible with Ebroin's having been alive when he says he was (Dupraz, p. 352 n. 1).

[76] Bede may have omitted any account of the synod of Austerfield because, as Poole suggests, he knew Eddius's account to be wrong, but did not know enough to correct it; but this is a strange argument to justify complete silence. It seems likely that he similarly omitted Eddius's story of Wilfred's imprisonment by Ecgfrith, not because he knew it to have been wrong, but because it was unedifying. Poole's argument that the incident is chronologically unacceptable is not strong. It depends on taking Bede's statement that Wilfred was in Sussex 'usque ad mortem Ecgfridi' quite literally, while it need be no more than a general indication (cf. Plummer, ii, 319) and if taken otherwise leaves an unnecessary gap in Wilfred's career between 685 and 686-7, when the sources agree that he was restored in Northumbria. The most famous crux is in connection with the events of 664. Eddius says Wilfred was made Bishop of all Northumbria but that Chad was intruded in his place while he was abroad to be consecrated. Bede clearly implies, though he is nowhere perfectly explicit, that Northumbria was divided between them. The considerations which might lead one to incline to one side or the other are very evenly balanced; for the extensive literature see Duckett, *op. cit.*, p. 143 n. That Eddius was not alone in his view of Chad's position is suggested by a (? mid-eighth century) verse martyrology mentioning all the bishops of York up to Wilfred II (718-732) except Chad, H. Quentin in *Dictionnaire d'archéologie chrétienne et de liturgie* II, 642-4.

[77] *Bedae Opera de Temporibus*, ed. C. W. Jones (Cambridge, Mass., 1943), p. 307, 'Sed haec tristi mox admixtione confudit, addendo videlicet quod me audires a lascivientibus rusticis inter hereticos per pocula decantari'.

[78] Plummer, ii, 316.

[79] This policy probably led to disputes of which Bede only hints, see c. ix of the decrees made at Hertford (*H.E.* IV, 5, 216) and Bede's reticent account of the deposition of Bishop Wynfrid, which may have been connected with the division of his see (IV, 3, 212; IV, 6, 218; ii, p. 216).

[80] As he thought King David might have done, Carroll, p. 152.

[81] Plummer, pp. lxii-lxiii n.

[82] Hughes, 'Irish Monks and Learning', *op. cit.*, pp. 62, 72; *H.E.* II, 19, 122-4; Laistner, 'The Library of the Venerable Bede', *op. cit.*, pp. 252, 265.

[83] For what was at issue see e.g. J. K. Kenney, *Sources for the Early History of Ireland* I (New York, 1929), pp. 210-17.

[84] *Two Lives of St. Cuthbert, op. cit.*, p. 284.

[85] *H.E.* V, 22, 347.

[86] K. Jackson, 'On the Northern British Section of Nennius', N. K. Chadwick, 'The Conversion of Northumbria: a Comparison of Sources' in *Celt and Saxon, op. cit.*, pp. 20-62, 138-66.

[87] Jackson, pp. 41-2.

[88] *Chapters of Early English Church History* (Oxford, 1878), p. 435.

[89] If Grosjean is right in identifying Agilbert, bishop of Dorchester 650-60, with the Agilbert who helped to lure an enemy of Ebroin's to his death by swearing an oath on an empty reliquary ('La date du Colloque de Whitby,' *op. cit.*, p. 251) a Frankish historian could reveal other qualities in this man than the *eruditio* and the *industria* to which Bede refers (*H.E.* III, 7, 140).

[90] E.g. Jones, *Saints' Lives and Chronicles, op. cit.*, chapter 4; B. Colgrave, 'The Earliest Saints' Lives Written in England', *Proceedings of the British Academy* XLIV (1958), 35-60; and in general H. Delehaye, *Les légendes hagiographiques*, 4th ed. (Brussels, 1955).

[91] *H.E.*, pp. 7-8; Jones, *Saints' Lives and Chronicles*, pp. 82-3.

[92] Delehaye, p. 24.

[93] Jones, *Saints' Lives and Chronicles*, pp. 29, 54.

[94] Carroll, p. 245; *H.E.* III, 5, 137.

[95] The attitude towards physical miracles of some of the Fathers, including even Gregory the Great, who records so many of them, was one of some reserve, e.g. Jones, *Saints' Lives and Chronicles*, pp. 76-7, Carroll, pp. 196 ff.

[96] I am very grateful to Mr M. W. Frederiksen, Mrs B. M. Mitchell and Mr J. M. Wallace-Hadrill for reading a draft of this paper and for their helpful comments.

Index

INDEX

INDEX

Printed in the United States
by Baker & Taylor Publisher Services